THE BRAHMANS, THEISTS AND MUSLIMS OF INDIA

THE BRAHMANS, THEISTS AND MUSLIMS OF INDIA

Studies of Goddess-worship in Bengal, Caste, Brahmaism and Social Reform, with descriptive Sketches of curious Festivals, Ceremonies, and Faquirs

By

John Campbell Oman
FORMERLY PROFESSOR OF NATURAL SCIENCE IN THE GOVERNMENT COLLEGE, LAHORE AUTHOR OF
"The Mystics, Ascetics, and Saints of India" "Indian Life, Religious and Social." "The Great Indian Epics" "Where Three Creeds Meet" Etc. Etc.

WITH ILLUSTRATIONS FROM PHOTOGRAPHS AND FROM DRAWINGS BY WILLIAM CAMPBELL OMAN, A.R.I.B.A.

GYAN

Published by

Gyan Publishing House
5, Ansari Road
Daryaganj, New Delhi-110002
Phone: 011-47034999, 9811692060
E-mail: books@gyanbooks.com

Distribution Network
gyanbooks.com
India, USA, Canada, UK, Australia, France

ISBN : 978-81-212-2484-0 (HB)
First Published, 1907

2nd Impression 2021

Printed at: Gyan Press, Delhi.

The Brahmans, Theists and Muslims of India
Author: John Campbell Oman

THE BRAHMANS, THEISTS AND MUSLIMS OF INDIA

Studies of Goddess-worship in Bengal, Caste, Brahmaism and Social Reform, with descriptive Sketches of curious Festivals, Ceremonies, and Faquirs

BY

JOHN CAMPBELL OMAN

FORMERLY PROFESSOR OF NATURAL SCIENCE IN THE GOVERNMENT COLLEGE, LAHORE

AUTHOR OF
"THE MYSTICS, ASCETICS, AND SAINTS OF INDIA" "INDIAN LIFE, RELIGIOUS AND SOCIAL" "THE GREAT INDIAN EPICS" "WHERE THREE CREEDS MEET"
ETC. ETC.

WITH ILLUSTRATIONS FROM PHOTOGRAPHS AND FROM DRAWINGS BY WILLIAM CAMPBELL OMAN, A.R.I.B.A.

PHILADELPHIA

GEORGE W. JACOBS & CO.

PUBLISHERS

My object in writing this book being to interpret, however imperfectly, the present-day Indians to the English public, I have done my best to bring my readers into actual touch, as it were, with contemporary India at various points, using my somewhat exceptional personal experiences, as much as possible, in illustrating and elucidating the subjects dealt with, which, although by no means esoteric, have yet to be sought for, and do not, in ordinary course, come within the ken of Europeans in India whether official or non-official. Following the plan adopted in my previous books, I have included in this volume such legends and stories as seemed to me to throw light upon the habits or the mental peculiarities of the Indian people.

The figures recorded in the recently published Report on the Census of the Empire show that more than a half of the entire number of men and women under British rule follow the *Hindu* religion; that Islam claims another quarter of the inhabitants of the Empire, and that the remainder is made up of Christians (*including those of the United Kingdom, Ireland, the Colonies, and India*), and of Buddhists, Jains, Jews, etc.

Very striking and significant figures indeed are these, and may well awaken many trains of thought and speculation.

PREFACE

Confining our attention to India (with Burmah), we find that when the last census was taken (1901) there were in those vast territories less than three millions of Christians (Europeans and Natives all told) against two hundred and seven millions of Hindus, and over sixty-two millions of Muhammadans, *each of these divisions being composed of a great variety of races and nationalities speaking diverse tongues.*

The Buddhists, Jains, Sikhs, Animists, etc., inhabiting India and Burmah made up a further total of about twenty-two millions.

These notable statistics are enough to make it clear that out of the vast and profound ocean of Indian social and religious life, it was only possible for me to take just a few examples of what may be gathered in that obscure yet seductive region of investigation.

Hinduism, with its enormous and varied following, its heterogeneous structure and its fascinating remoteness from European feeling and sentiment, afforded the largest choice of subjects and occupies the major portion of this volume. But *Islam,* which, as regards numbers, ranks next amongst the religions of India, has also a place in the book; being represented—no doubt very inadequately—by two papers ("Muharram" and "Faquirs") intended to bring into view some of the more salient features of that great Semitic cult so nearly allied to Judaism.

In describing and commenting upon such examples of Indian beliefs and practices as I have selected to lay before my readers, my own limitations have been ever present to my mind, yet I claim that my constant endeavour has been towards accuracy of statement and fairness of interpretation.

To my son, Mr. W. Campbell Oman, I am indebted for the illustrations which appear in this volume; also for reading the entire MS. of the book very carefully, and helping me with many suggestions.

J. C. O.

MUSWELL HILL, LONDON, N.

CONTENTS

CONTENTS

CHAPTER II

CASTE IN INDIA

CONTENTS

CONTENTS

CONTENTS

CONTENTS

CONTENTS

PART III

CHAPTER I

THE MUHARRAM IN INDIA

CHAPTER II

FAQUIRS

LIST OF ILLUSTRATIONS

PART I

KALI-GHAT AND HINDUISM (GODDESS-WORSHIP) IN BENGAL

CASTE IN INDIA

THEISM IN BENGAL (BRAHMAISM)

HINDU SOCIAL REFORMERS

KALI-GHAT AND HINDUISM IN BENGAL

CHAPTER I

KALI-GHAT AND HINDUISM IN BENGAL

SECTION I.—Visit to the temple—The Kali cultus—Bloody sacrifices—Legends of the goddess and her temple—Subordinate temples.

CALCUTTA, with its showy palaces and its mean huts, its fleets of stately ships from Europe, and its lumbering country boats for traffic on the Hugli; Calcutta with its bazaars and marts had, for years, been well known to me. Fort William, reminiscent of the early days of British ascendancy in Bengal, was indelibly associated in my recollections with the incidents of "Panic Sunday" in the trying days of '57. The Cathedral on the spacious *maidan*, and other churches of the great city, were connected in my mind with many pleasant memories. Near the little mosque, surmounted by a dozen minarets with gilded finials, situated at the corner of the Esplanade, I had often paused to watch the devout Muslim prostrate himself in worship of Allah. But Kali-Ghat, the world-famous temple near Calcutta, I had not seen until, after years of absence from the Indian Metropolis, a brief sojourn there was turned to account in a visit to the shrine.

By the tramway was for me the most convenient way to Kali-Ghat. A ride of over three miles with a number of perspiring and somnolent Bengali companions brought me to the limit of the tramway line, where I alighted in a crowded suburb of thatched cottages embosomed in the exuberant foliage of Lower Bengal, made up of graceful palm trees, broad-leaved plantains, slender bamboos, and close-foliaged tamarinds. By tropical sunlight such greenery affords pictures of rare beauty, and after dark is often simply gorgeous with the living lamps of myriads of fireflies, fluttering hither and thither in a sort of fairy revel.

The small huts amidst the verdure, the homes of so many millions of people in Bengal, have some peculiarities which can hardly fail to attract the attention of the European observer, and may detain us a moment because of their connection with the style of the temple architecture of Bengal, and as an interesting instance of the way in which physical conditions influence national types of architecture. Of these huts the more rigid portions of the roofs, the roof-frames in fact, are made of the exceedingly strong, but very pliable, bamboo, of which an abundant supply is always available in Eastern India. To give this material sufficient strength to bear a transverse strain, it must be arched, hence the ridge pole, the hips and also the eaves of the cottages are all curved outwards. The effect of this mode of construction is, in the case of neatly thatched dwellings of modest dimensions undoubtedly pleasing; but when the style is copied in brick or stone, it is by no means agreeable, though the favour it has gained in Hindustan may be inferred from the fact that it has found its way from Bengal as far west as Delhi and Lahore, and even Kashmir.[1]

From the tramway terminus to the temple I had to walk. My mere inquiry about the way to Kali-Ghat collected round me a crowd of men and women, who accompanied me with evident curiosity to the shrine of their favourite and highly honoured goddess *Kali-Ma* (Mother Kali).

In a few minutes I found my way into a paved courtyard surrounded by a high brick wall, and stood before an unimportant-looking building, said to be three hundred years old, which was nothing but a reproduction in brickwork and lime-plaster of the huts I have just described. There were in the temple before me the same characteristic curved ridges and eaves-lines already alluded to. In fact it resembled in form a rather tall Bengali hut with another much smaller one of the same kind surmounting it; this addition being designed to give a decent elevation to the structure. Such was the famous temple of Kali-Ghat which I had gone out to see. Its interest for Hindus centres in the ill-lighted chamber, the cella, wherein the presiding divinity, housed in mysterious twilight, receives the adoration of her awed votaries. No provision is made here for congregational worship, which is quite unknown and unthought of amongst Hindus; though recently it has come into fashion with the small theistic sects called into existence by Western influences.

Close by the temple on the south side stands an open pavilion or detached portico of moderate dimensions, for the convenience of the Brahmans and for visitors to the place; and there are some small buildings for the accommodation of the temple priests and attendants. Near the pavilion, on the side farthest from the shrine, is *the place of sacrifices*, with its repulsive stakes all crimsoned with the blood of many victims. On the eastern side of the temple is a sacred pond known as *Kundoo*, and at a short distance towards the west flows Tolly's nullah, a small tidal river connected with the Hugli. To this stream, held sacred as being one of the original channels of the Ganges, there is a

[1] Dr. Fergusson, *History of Indian and Eastern Architecture*, p. 548.

direct road, between rows of little shops, leading from the temple gate to the bathing *ghat* on the river.

An interesting and highly characteristic feature of Kali's temple is the number of shrines of other deities clustered about it, in architectural subordination it is true, but still challenging recognition, adoration, and offerings. To this point I shall revert later.

Observing with critical eyes Kali's famous temple, which enjoys an immense reputation in India, I could not help asking myself how far one could reasonably draw inferences regarding the spirituality, the piety, the liberality, and largeness of conception of peoples and nations from the dimensions, arrangements, and architectural styles of their temples. A comparison of the *Mandir* of Kali-Ma near Calcutta with the shapely Parthenon adorned with the highest efforts of Greek plastic art, or the noble Pantheon of pagan Rome with its majestic dome ever open to the sky, or the stately mediæval cathedral with "its long drawn aisles and fretted vaults," or the grand Musjids of the Muslims with their graceful minarets, would no doubt sadly discredit Bengali ideals and artistic conceptions. Nor would Kali-Ghat bear comparison with Hindu temples elsewhere in India, and especially those impressive monuments characteristic of the Southern Peninsula. Yet religion, the whole-hearted desire to reach towards God and live in the divine presence, is not necessarily associated with the stately products of artistic genius which have been rendered possible only through the lavish munificence of opulent States or rich individuals. Possibly the reverse might be true, and superb ecclesiastical edifices be characteristic more of cultured wealth than of earnest religion. Any way physical conditions and environments are very dominant factors in such cases, for, all things considered, it is hardly conceivable that a York Minster or a St. Mark's could be raised by men born and nurtured generation after generation on the low alluvial plains and amidst the rank vegetation of moist and enervating Bengal. Moreover, the absence of stone in the Gangetic delta is undoubtedly a very real drawback to the development of a stately and imposing style of architecture, though what can be done without stone is

Photo by Bourne & Sheppard, Calcutta

BATHING IN THE RIVER AT KALIGHAT

apparent in many European cities, — the Westminster Cathedral being the latest and perhaps best example. Even in India the architectural features of Calcutta developed upon European lines, and the huge, not ungraceful *pucca* buildings, which adorn the Muhammadan city of Lucknow show, clearly enough, the potentialities of brick construction. Not Bengali architecture alone, however, owes its peculiarities to the climatic and geological conditions of the land, for the sensitive and sensual character of the people, who are not Aryans but of Mongolo-Dravidian race, also bears an unmistakable relation to the warm, damp climate and prolific soil of their country.

To return to the temple after this digression. The door of the shrine itself was not open when I arrived before it, and several officious men, clothed merely in the usual *dhoty* or loin-cloth, with nothing but the sacred cotton thread of six strands as a garment for the person above the waist, offered to conduct me over the courtyard. They were hereditary priests, each entitled to, and eager for, his share of the profits of the establishment. There was really very little for these worthies to show the visitor, and when they had drawn attention to the places in the enclosure set apart for animal sacrifices, indicated too obviously by the forked stakes, to which the victims are secured, their duty as guides seemed over. At these sacrificial spots on the great annual festival of the goddess, and on certain other and not infrequent occasions when rich worshippers visit the temple, goats, sheep, and buffaloes are sacrificed in hecatombs, their blood flowing like water before the shrine of the goddess, for she delights in animal sacrifices, and, as certain Hindu scriptures affirm, "constantly drinks blood."[1] Neither the bull nor the cow are of course ever offered here, these animals being considered sacred by all Hindus throughout India. Although my visit was not on a feast or festival day, there was ample gory evidence of the sacrificial activity of the priests of Kali, whose predecessors, only a few generations back, immolated human victims, the traditions of these sacrifices being still religiously preserved in many old

[1] *Tantras.* See Sir Monier Williams, *Religious Thoughts and Life in India*, p. 189.

Bengali families in which, on the occasions of the Kali and Durga festivals, effigies are offered up in lieu of living men.[1] "But for us," writes Sir John Strachey, "even in the province where education has made its greatest progress, Kali would still claim her human victims. Not many years ago, in a time of drought, near a railway station twenty-five miles from Calcutta, a human head was found before her idol decked with flowers, and in another temple in Bengal, a boy was savagely murdered and offered to the goddess."[2] So recently as June 1901 an attempt was made by one Gajadhur to sacrifice a man at Akhra, near Calcutta, before a newly made idol of Kali.[3]

Hinduism is associated, in the minds of so many in Europe, and even in India, with the idea of the most scrupulous tenderness towards all animated things—"the mild Hindu" is so proverbial a figure of speech—that it somewhat staggers one to walk about the shambles of a temple like this, and hear the boastful Brahman slaughter-man regret that you had not the good fortune of seeing the place on a gala day, adorned with its holiday carpets of red. So many centuries separate us from the sacrificial system of the Hebrews whose spiritual descendants we are, and we have become so oblivious of the bloody sacrifices of our Norse ancestors, that we almost fail to realise the aims and effects of such a system until we are thus confronted with pools of the warm blood of animals killed to propitiate the arbiters of man's destiny.

The flesh of a number of the victims slain daily at Kali-Ghat is sold for the ordinary consumption of the orthodox Hindu, and as the business is a profitable one, a regular charge being levied by the priests for each animal killed within the sacred courts of the temple, rival shrines have been set up in several parts of Calcutta to meet the

[1] Dr. Rajendra Lalla Mitra, *Indo-Aryans*, vol. ii. p. 109.

[2] Sir John Strachey, *India*, p. 354.

The *Kalika Purana* says: "The flesh of the antelope and the rhinoceros give my beloved (Kali) delights for five hundred years. By a human sacrifice, attended by the forms laid down, Devi is pleased for a thousand years, and by the sacrifice of three men, a hundred thousand years."—Rev. J. W. Wilkins, *Hindu Mythology*, p. 262.

[3] *Civil and Military Gazette* (Lahore), 3rd July 1901.

demand, apparently an increasing one, for *sanctified butchers' meat.*[1]

Before the closed door of the temple I waited a long time to have a glance of the interior and of the dread occupant, who, I recalled to mind, was the patron goddess of that nefarious sect of assassins, the well-known *Thugs* of India, and of thieves and robbers of all kinds, some of whom might, for all I knew to the contrary, have been present there that morning, paying their respects to their grim protectress.

A partial opening of the door induced me to press forward, and a hint, not difficult to understand, made me throw some small silver coins towards the officiating janitor, who could, if so minded, afford me a better view of the image of the goddess. Hardly had the little shining pieces of British money rung out their true tones on the floor outside the temple door, when, to my great surprise, the space near the entrance, in view of the great goddess herself, became the scene of an animated and most unseemly struggle. Some girls were amongst the first to get possession of the bright pieces as they clinked upon the floor, but in the strife with the angry covetous Brahmans, they soon lost them, although they fought and struggled on the ground like little furies. One rather pretty girl of about eleven or twelve years of age, of slight and graceful figure, dressed in the national *saree* of thin muslin, had had her delicate wrist cut with her bangles in the indecorous battle I had unintentionally raised. Showing me the bleeding wound, she insisted upon *baksheesh.* Not a moment's peace would she give me. Her blood was evidently upon my head, and nothing but *baksheesh* could wash the stains away. The little martyr's persistence, aided perhaps by her good looks, secured for her what she wanted, but immediately gave rise to a chorus of petitions from many bystanders, which, needless to say, received the attention it deserved.

After the struggle was over, I got a glimpse of the goddess from a short distance through the doorway; but as a large crowd had been gathered by the expectation of more largesse, I was not encouraged to make a nearer scrutiny of the idol. However, I had not lost much in getting only an

[1] Shib Chunder Bose, *The Hindoos as they are*, p. 148.

imperfect view of Kali in her gloomy temple, for the horrific figure of the goddess is a familiar one to every resident in Bengal, and I knew it well, having seen it on a hundred occasions. Moreover, it is a form to be remembered for its grotesque and startling ugliness,—a hideous black woman enjoying the possession of no less than four well-developed arms, and with a huge pointed blood-red tongue hanging out of her mouth. In one hand she holds a drawn sword, in another the severed head of a mighty giant, while the other two hands are supposed to be engaged in welcoming and blessing her votaries. Thus in her visible manifestation does the goddess unite her attributes of avenger and protector of her people.

Such then, in outward semblance, is the Goddess Kali of the Bengalis. Sometimes she is represented standing with one foot planted on the breast and the other upon the thigh of her prostrate husband, the great God Siva. When so depicted, her girdle (she has no other covering for her person) consists of the severed hands of her defeated foes. For ornament the terrible being wears a necklace of the heads of giants whom she had slain, and whose warm blood she had actually quaffed in savage delight. Her ear-rings are the dead bodies of her slaughtered enemies. Such is this terrible object of adoration! who in this form appears to her worshippers as the very embodiment of power, and to whom her trustful, if timid votaries, appeal for brave hearts and martial ardour. In the Mahabharata, Arjuna, acting on the advice of Krishna, offers a special prayer for success to Kali, the "giver of victory,"[1] and similar invocations are still addressed to her, though by less formidable persons than that famous son of Kunti. Only a few years ago, a Hindu vernacular paper made the following sad and significant appeal to the goddess:—

> "O, Mother, behold, we are fallen. We have been deprived of our old martial spirit. Thy sons are now a pack of arrant cowards, trampled under the shoes of the *Mlechchas*,[2] and so dispirited as to lose all sense when angrily stared at by them. Thou art power

[1] Mahabharata—Bhisma Parva, Section xxiii.

[2] A contemptuous term applied to Europeans and other barbarians.

perfected. How canst thou tolerate such emasculation of thy dear sons? O, Mother, take pity on India, and infuse the timid souls of thy children with the force of thy invincible power."[1]

No one can tell in what age it was that divinity revealed itself to the spiritual vision of some aboriginal or Dravidian seer in the grotesque form of Mother Kali, nor does any record exist regarding the audacious hand that first modelled, in the plastic clay of Bengal, those awful features which have so strange a fascination for the children of the soil, crudely embodying in visible form the very real dread of femininity always working in the minds of a most sensuous people, too prone to fall before the subtle powers of the weaker sex. This, however, we may boldly affirm, that the events we refer to occurred long ages ago. And it is only reasonable to believe that the strange shapes of Kali, and some other gods and goddesses of the Hindus, must have an immense antiquity, must, in fact, date back to primeval times, and may be regarded as only the fantastic shadows of divinity, seen by the untutored savage in the dim twilight of the world's morning.

For those who delight in *explanations* of religious mythological fancies, the following will have interest: "In India, however, as in the Western world, there was a constant tendency to convert names into persons, and then to frame for them a mythical history in accordance with their meaning. Thus two of the ever-flickering tongues of the black-pathed Agni were called Kali the black, and Karali the terrific; and these became names of Durga, the wife of Siva, who was developed out of Agni! and a bloody sacrificial worship was the result."[2]

How simple all this appears. But is it really true?

That, as in Kali's case, one of the highest and most respected deities of the Hindu Pantheon should have a monstrous form, is at least noteworthy. The Teutonic gods, though sometimes maimed, as the one-eyed Odin, or the limping Loki, are by no means monstrous. Amongst the

[1] Reproduced in the *Civil and Military Gazette* (Lahore), 25th December 1890.

[2] Cox, *Mythology of the Aryan Nations*, p. 421.

Greeks the shapeless wooden *xoana* which were amongst the earliest objects of worship, made way, at a comparatively early period, for higher artistic conceptions. It is true that terrible forms like that of the Artemis of Pellene were not unknown, but curiously enough some mythologists find the same Artemis to be no other than Kali herself, and believe, or imagine, they can trace the dread goddess of Bengal through Asia Minor and Greece to Imperial Rome.[1]

After the description I have given of the personal appearance of Kali, it is time to record what is taught regarding this embodiment of female prepotency, who commands the homage of so many millions of men. With respect to her recognition as a Hindu divinity, I think it may be assumed without rashness that the shrewd and politic Brahmanical priesthood, finding in their progress eastwards the ever mysterious Kali, a predominant power in the archaic religion of the aborigines of Eastern India, made a place for her in their great pantheon, and, as a consequence, the Hindu *shastras* under the deft hands of wily Brahmans soon contained ample evidence that the great goddess of Bengal was of the very first rank, being indeed the wife of the great God Siva. This process of adopting local gods and naturalising them as it were in the existing Pantheon, has been, and still is, a process familiar to Hinduism, and goes far to explain the heterogeneous character of the divinities who are revered by the Hindus.

In the repulsive form in which Kali is worshipped, she is said to have successfully rid the universe of a dangerous giant, whom she overthrew in a terrific conflict, wherein the victorious goddess, carried away by the excitement of battle, indulged in an excess of reckless and ungovernable fury. After her victory she danced in such a frantic way that the earth itself was in danger from her. Siva tried to calm her frenzy, but failing in his object threw himself down on the ground amongst her slain enemies. Presently Kali found him under her feet. Recognising her lord, she protruded her long tongue in astonishment, after the manner of Indian women, and immediately desisted from her mad dance of triumph, which had threatened to shake the world to its

[1] C. W. King, *The Gnostics and their Remains*, pp. 165–172.

foundations. This is the commonly accepted legend explaining the attitude of Kali standing upon the prostrate body of her husband; but a learned Brahman writer, Dr. J. N. Bhattacharjee, says[1] that the true esoteric explanation, to be found in the scriptures known as the *Tantras*, is something very different and too obscene for possible explanation. Well did Edgar Quinet write: "Ne croyez pas, en effet, connaître un peuple si vous n'êtes remonté jusqu'à ses dieux."[2]

It is a significant and noteworthy circumstance that Kali's gigantic and audacious opponent, like a host of others figuring in Indian mythology, was, according to the Brahmans, an *ascetic* who had acquired by the practice of severe austerities and the performance of suitable ceremonies, a degree of power which made him an object of terror to the gods of the very highest rank in the Olympus of the Hindus.

Some reason must needs exist or be invented to account for the special claims to sanctity of the temple at Kali-Ghat. A suitable legend is, indeed, indispensable in such a case. One such, which, weird and grotesque in the extreme, amply fulfils all requirements, is narrated by Dr. Alexander Duff, the famous Free Kirk missionary of Bengal. The legend in question, derived no doubt from satisfactory local sources, is as follows:—

> "Brahma, it would appear, in his earthly form or incarnation of Daksha, had a daughter named *Sati*, who was given in marriage to Shiva. On one occasion a quarrel arose between Daksha and Shiva. The former then refused to invite his son-in-law to a splendid banquet which he resolved to give in honour of the immortals. To this insulting slight he also added the foulest reproach—stigmatising Shiva as a wandering mendicant, a delighter in cemeteries, and a bearer of skulls. On hearing her husband thus reviled, Sati, overwhelmed with grief and sorrow, hastily returned to the banks of the Ganges, and there determined to yield up her life 'on the altar of domestic affliction.' This, we may remark in passing, is the *divine example* constantly held forth for imitation to poor widows, who are greatly stimulated thereby to become *Satis* or

[1] *Hindu Castes and Sects*, p. 408.

[2] *Le génie des Religions*, p. 12.

Suttees, by sacrificing themselves on the funeral piles of their husbands. Shiva, on observing the lifeless form of his spouse, became quite distracted. In the bitterness of his anguish, he thrust his trident through the dead body, and lifting it in the air, commenced dancing about in the most frantic manner. By the violence of his aerial motions, the three worlds were shaken to the foundations. Gods and men were filled with alarm. Vishnu, the Preserver, hastened to arrest the threatened catastrophe. Shedding tears of sympathy, he endeavoured to console the frenzied husband, by reminding him that 'nothing was real' in this world, but that everything was altogether *maya,* or illusion. But Shiva's grief was too poignant to yield to any consolation based on a cold metaphysical abstraction. As he continued to reel in agony, he burst into a flood of tears; and these uniting with the sympathetic tears of Vishnu, formed a capacious lake, which afterwards became a celebrated place of pilgrimage. Still he was utterly inconsolable. At length the Preserver shrewdly conjectured that were the object of his grief removed out of view, calmness would be restored to his agitated soul. Accordingly, armed with a scimitar, he continued as the body was whirling round to cut off one limb after the other. The different members, as they were successively severed—from the projectile force impressed on them by Shiva's violent movement—were scattered to different and distant parts of the earth. In the excess of his distraction, the bereaved husband discovered not his loss till the whole body had disappeared. His grief was then assuaged, and the universe delivered from impending destruction. Soon after his beloved *Sati* reappeared, but in a new form, announcing that she had happily been born again, as the daughter of Himavan or Himalaya, the ruler of mountains. In this form she became known as *Parvati* (from Parva, the ordinary term for mountain)—inseparable companion of Shiva.

"In the meantime, the scattered fragments of *Sati's* body—amounting together with the ornaments to the exact number of fifty-one—conferred peculiar sanctity on the places where they happened to fall. All of these were consecrated as repositories of the divine remains, and adoration there became an act of extraordinary merit. At each, a temple was reared and dedicated to the goddess, and in it was placed an image representing one or other of her thousand forms; along with an image of her husband Shiva, under the designation of Bhairob, or fear-inspirer, in which capacity he acts as guardian or protector of the place; and is always worshipped at the same time as his spouse.

"The toes of the right foot of the goddess are said to have fallen a little to the south of Calcutta, on the banks of one of the cross branches of the Ganges—supposed to have been once the channel of the main stream itself. There they were buried in the earth, unsubjected to corruption or decay. The sacred spot, though illumined with beams of resplendent light, remained for ages undiscovered in the deepest recess of the forest. At length, in the vision of a dream, the site was made known by the goddess herself to a holy Brahman. Moved and directed by the heavenly oracle, he lost no time in raising a temple over the divine deposit. The temple, by express revelation, was dedicated to the goddess under her form of Kali; and has ever since been famed under the designation of Kali-Ghat."[1]

In one of those eloquent sermons for which he was so famous, and which Sunday after Sunday some years ago filled St. Paul's Cathedral to overflowing, the late Canon Liddon said, "The idea of God kindles in the soul the sense of beauty, and beauty that meets the eye suggests the immaterial beauty of the invisible King. No religion can afford, in the long-run, to neglect this instinct in the soul of men." With this in mind let any one go to Kali-Ghat, visit the pagoda there, study its surroundings, behold the grim goddess in her sunless shrine, and *realise* how great is the difference of the climate of religious opinions in which the eloquent Canon lived and breathed, and that which envelops the terrible four-handed goddess before whom millions of worshippers cower in abject terror.[2]

[1] Rev. Alexander Duff, D.D., *India and Indian Missions, including Sketches of the Gigantic System of Hinduism* (Edinburgh, 1839), pp. 248–250.

[2] "Her black features, the dark night in which she is worshipped, the bloody deeds with which her name is associated, the countless sacrifices relentlessly offered at her altar, the terrific form in which she is represented, the unfeminine and warlike posture in which she stands, and last, but not least, the desperate character of some of her votaries, invest her name with

The total absence of beauty, either sentimental or artistic, from the legends and the ritual of Kali-ism, is not compensated by anything ennobling in the religion of the dread goddess in whom robbers and cut-throats recognise a congenial patroness. Not many years ago, quite within my own personal recollection, men used to honour Kali by having themselves swung round a lofty pole suspended from the extremity of a cross piece pivoted at the top of it. They were supported by iron hooks passed through the muscles of the back. This barbarous mode of worship has been prohibited by the British Government, but I witnessed one exhibition of the kind before its suppression. In the case I saw, the man who undertook to be swung in honour of Kali, had the muscles of his back terribly stretched by the hooks; but he was also supported by a cloth tied firmly under his arms, which somewhat relieved the tension and would have prevented his falling to the ground had the flesh given way under the severe strain to which it was exposed. As the man was whirled aloft high above the heads of the excited onlookers, he threw down amongst them small pieces of cocoa-nut and sweetmeats resembling comfits, while the drums made a deafening noise, and the multitude shouted "Victory to Mother Kali." Votaries, less bold than he, passed skewers or canes through the muscles of their sides and hands, and even through their tongues; all for Kali, to whom no offering could be made more acceptable than blood, and in whose honour they danced about in wild enthusiasm.

Blood being what Kali thirsts for and delights in, her worshippers gratify her to the utmost of their ability. "There is," says Dr. Rajendra Lalla Mitra, "scarcely a respectable house in all Bengal the mistress of which has not, at one time or other, shed her blood (a few drops) under the notion of satisfying the goddess by the operation, and rescuing some beloved object (perhaps a husband or son) from the jaws of death."[1]

A simple touching statement of fact is this, beneath which

a terror which is without a parallel in the mythological legends of the Hindoos."—Shib Chunder Bose, *The Hindoos as they are*, p. 137.

[1] *Indo-Aryans*, vol. ii. p. 111.

we may find the reason why women in general, everywhere and in nearly all stages of civilisation, are more religious than men. Elaborate if not entirely satisfactory attempts have been made to account for women's superior religiosity; but, in my opinion, it is attributable mainly to certain physiological and domestic experiences essentially peculiar to women. Amongst these causes gestation and maternity, involving as they do a sense of dependence, stand first, for while intimately personal and always mysterious, they call into being special emotions and anxieties unknown to the stronger sex—emotions and anxieties which find natural expression in almost unreasoning affection and blind desire for help in the interests of the loved ones. Except perhaps in the "highest" modern civilisation, where women avoid maternity altogether, or else gladly delegate to trained or untrained hirelings the *business* of rearing their offspring, it falls to the lot of most mothers at some time or other to have to struggle, as it were, for the lives of their children or that of the bread-winner, and it is these, often prolonged and intense strivings with the Unseen Powers, lurking behind disease and death, which keep the light of religion burning, generation after generation, in the sensitive souls of mothers and wives, and will continue to do so till good mothers and good wives of the old type are in the process of time eliminated by the ultimate triumph of a soulless civilisation, built upon lucre and corroded with luxury.

At the temple of Kali, the promised victim is despatched by the priest on receiving a certain fixed fee. He retains the head for himself, and places a little of the blood before the idol, to which the worshipper makes his obeisance and passes on, having fulfilled his vow and performed his duty.

An interesting incident connected with Kali-worship in Northern India came to my notice in the early part of 1893. It was given out during the heat of certain religious controversies in Lahore, between the orthodox and certain unorthodox sects of Hindus, that a worshipper of Kali had offered a slice of his tongue to the goddess as a sacrifice, and that the gratified divinity had miraculously restored the mutilated organ to its original state. Five days after this incident, a procession in honour of the event paraded the city on the 31st March 1893. This procession, as I saw it wend its way through the narrow streets of the native quarters of the town, was of the usual kind. Preceded by drummers and cymbal players who led the way, came a litter well filled with long necklaces of white strongly scented flowers. Almost smothered beneath this floral tribute was a picture of the goddess, about six or seven inches long and three or four inches wide. Beside the litter walked the hero of the hour, but he declined to show the tongue which had been miraculously restored by the goddess.

Behind the litter came a cart drawn by one strong well-fed bull. It carried a *tukta-posh*, or low wooden table, whereon were seated gods and goddesses. Mahadeva (Siva), Durga, Kali, and Ganesa were there, personated by men or boys, necessarily masked, as in the case of the elephant-headed Ganesa.

A second cart of the same kind followed, one of the occupants indulging in disgusting buffoonery. Then came a third cart, so contrived as to be doubled-storeyed. This was filled with boys and men.

The procession was poor and tawdry, yet the crowd that came out to take part in it, and the numbers who rushed out to see it as it passed along the streets, made a very considerable gathering. Women formed only a small proportion of the following; but they were in force on the sides of the road, at the windows, on the balconies, and on the house-tops.

A native who had, at my request, visited the temple where the miraculous event occurred, told me that he found a vast crowd—mostly women—assembled there. On a tray he saw a piece of something very red indeed, and was assured by the attendants that it was the tongue of a man who had cut it off, and made an offering of it to the goddess. The man whose severed tongue was being exhibited was lying—wrapped up head and all—motionless on the floor of the temple, and the Pujaris (officiating priests) assured the visitors that before many hours would elapse the faithful devotee would have his tongue restored to a perfect condition.

A friend of mine heard a somwehat different story in the city. Her informants were girls of the Mission School. According to them, the self-mutilated person was a *girl*, well known to them, who had made an offering of her tongue to Devi as atonement for some sin or other. The goddess, they said, had forgiven the penitent sinner, and had graciously restored the tongue, all but one little piece, which left a cicatrice in evidence of her act of devoted self-sacrifice. One of the young persons who told the European lady about the miracle, added characteristically, "Oh, Madam, it is not true what you say about Devi that she cannot hear and answer prayer! She can hear, and does answer prayers, and what *you* tell us is not true."

And so the worship of the goddess flourishes, the hearts of her votaries being stirred to their depths by such irrefutable manifestations of her compassion and power.

In the early part of this chapter (p. 6) I mentioned incidentally that many shrines cluster about the famous temple at Kali-Ghat, and I now revert to this interesting circumstance, which reveals to the most casual visitor the polytheistic character of Hinduism.

I have before me a sketch-plan of the temple at Kali-Ghat and its environs, which a friend in Calcutta had prepared for me. This shows no less than fifteen minor temples standing in the neighbourhood of the principal edifice; some near the sacred pond Kundoo, others on the side of the road leading to the river, and two alongside the bathing ghats. Of these smaller temples the greater number are dedicated to Siva, Kali's divine consort, worshipped under that well-known phallic symbol the lingam. One temple has been built in honour of Siva's son Ganesa, the God of Wisdom. Two or three of the shrines are, I fancy, erected to Siva under one or other of the *thousand* names which he is said to possess. But the most interesting of the minor temples we are considering is, in my opinion, an insignificant one within the main enclosure dedicated to Krishna (Vishnu) and his mistress Radha. Now the presence of this shrine was to me a by no means unwelcome discovery, for it at least proved that the more recent and far gentler cult of the Chaitanite sect of Bengal, which dates from the beginning of the sixteenth century, had been able to obtain a recognised footing even in the gory stronghold of the much older religion of Kali. And I accepted the fact as indicating a tendency amongst Bengalis towards less inhuman ideals than those which are embodied in Kali-ism, for Chaitanya, the apostle of the Krishna-cum-Radha cult, was strongly opposed to all animal sacrifices. Moreover, when we call to mind that Hinduism is divided off into two marked divisions, namely, the cult of Siva, his consorts, etc., on the one hand, and the cult of Vishnu and his consorts, etc., on the other, the amicable contiguity of shrines devoted to the principal gods of these two main sections of Hinduism is not without significance.

All who know the people of India will admit that they are on the whole extremely and genuinely religious, being, in fact, living examples of the belief that "the fear of God is the beginning of wisdom."[1] But though men and women everywhere turn appealingly to God in times of danger or trouble, it is rarely that they come to record publicly, in the divine presence, oaths in respect of their political engagements. Therefore I was struck by the fact, lately reported in the Indian newspapers, that at the height of the excitement aroused by the partition of Bengal, thousands of irate Bengalis had pledged themselves by solemn oaths taken before the dread goddess Kali, that they would refrain from using all goods of European manufacture. When analysed, the facts referred to reveal the hysterical nature and strong religious bias of the Bengalis, as also their eagerness to secure divine countenance and assistance, and at the same time disclose only too clearly their want of self-confidence and their mutual distrust.

[1] Even Dr. Alexander Duff, the great Scotch missionary to India, while lamenting the dark superstitions of the Hindus, often contrasts their religious earnestness and sincerity with the lukewarmness of his own money-making and pleasure-seeking countrymen, *e.g.*, *India and Indian Missions*, pp. 202, 203.

KALI-GHAT AND HINDUISM IN BENGAL
—*continued*

SECTION II.—The Goddess Durga—Hindu idea of the acquisition of supernatural power by means of austerities—The *Durga pujah*—Its excesses.

GREAT as is the prestige of *Mother Kali* in Eastern India, the favourite deity of the Bengalis is nevertheless *Durga*, represented usually as a golden coloured, ten-armed goddess with a gentle expression of countenance, even when engaged in slaying the giant Mahisha. She also is the consort of Siva, and assumed various forms for the express purpose of destroying dreadful giants and monsters, who, by the practice of austerities, had become a cause of great apprehension to the gods.

In the composite Pantheon of the Hindus, it is often a difficult or even impossible task to assign a correct position to any particular divinity, as it often happens that one and the same god or goddess is worshipped under different names and forms associated with particular appearances and actions. Siva's consort, as *Durga*, is a special manifestation of martial power for the destruction of certain beings obnoxious to gods and men, and the various shapes in which, under special names, she makes her different appearances are commonly regarded as distinct divinities. Hence it comes about that of these manifestations of power, which are many in number, the goddess Kali already sufficiently described is one, and, next to the original Durga, the recipient of the highest honour and worship.

There are many different accounts of the origin of Durga and Kali, but I pass them over, having no intention of involving myself in mythological details. As for the battles these warrior-goddesses fought with their giant opponents, they are such as only the wildest imagination could possibly have conceived. In Hindu legends one looks in vain for ordinary men and women. Only gods, superhuman monsters, and perhaps ascetic saints as fierce, unscrupulous, and powerful as the others, figure in the troubled pictures and dark creations of the myth-makers of India.

Dreadful monsters and divine deliverers loom dimly in the early dawn of many religions; but in the cases we are now considering, the old gorgons and chimæras dire, together with their destroyers, appear to have somehow blundered into the daylight of the twentieth century, in their crude primitive forms, unmodified by time and unsoftened by culture.

The belief that the dangerous monsters of the primeval world of India acquired their supernatural power by means of sacrifices, austerities, spells, and ceremonies, is a noteworthy feature of Hinduism, well known to the most superficial student of Indian religions, and seems indeed to be the most important part of the stock-in-trade of the Indian mythologists. But more extraordinary than this strange idea itself is the fact that it has lost none of its freshness in the minds of the Indian people, and, as I have pointed out elsewhere,[1] the Yogi of our own day is still a man who acquires superhuman power in the old way.

In connection with the worship of the goddess Durga, vividly do I recall to mind the annual *Durga pujah* processions, as I have seen them times and often in the streets of Calcutta. On these occasions the excitement is intense, and the spectacle at night truly remarkable. The enthusiastic crowds of dusky worshippers, wrought up almost to frenzy; the flaring torches throwing their yellow glare upon the gaudy idol carried aloft on the willing shoulders of men; the discordant and deafening

[1] *The Mystics, Ascetics, and Saints of India.*

din of the drums and other instruments mingled with the tumultuous shouts of the thronging multitude, make up a spectacle and produce an impression not easily effaced from the memory.

Of all the Bengali religious festivals the *Durga pujah* is by far the most popular. It is the season of annual family reunions, to which old and young travel long distances. It is the recognised occasion for the interchange of presents, a time especially suitable for the exercise of benevolent feelings, and is often marked by extensive, sometimes large-handed liberality, both within and without the family circle. Religious ceremonies and the making of offerings and animal sacrifices occupy a large part of the three days of the *pujah*; but the last of these usually presents a scene of orgiastic boisterousness, in which men intoxicated with fanaticism, smear themselves with the gory mire of the sacrificial slaughter-places, and then dance in delirious ecstasy before the idol, abandoning themselves, with the sensuality of their race, to immundicities of song and gesture which seem to be inseparable from the worship of the goddesses they adore.[1] However, such scenes of religious excitement cannot last, and in the grey morning, at the conclusion of the *pujah*, the worshippers consign their painted clay idol to the water of the most convenient stream or pond. No doubt the festival being over, the presence of the goddess in the consecrated image ceases, and it loses its special sanctity; yet, having even for a brief period harboured the celestial power, the effigy is too sacred to be exposed to profane handling, and is consequently dismantled, and committed to the purifying element.[2]

[1] Shib Chunder Bose, *The Hindoos as they are*, chap. viii.

[2] A short article by Mr. B. C. Mazumdar, M.R.A.S., on the origin and history of Durga, purporting to show that the goddess was of non-Aryan origin, and that her worship was introduced into Bengal from the Vindhya mountains, appeared in the *Journal of the Royal Asiatic Society* for April 1906.

KALI-GHAT AND HINDUISM IN BENGAL
—continued

SECTION III.—Three-fourths of the Hindus of Bengal worship Durga and Kali—These cults have extended beyond the limits of India proper.

THE worship of Durga and Kali, attended in both cases with animal sacrifices on an extravagant scale, and with licentious songs and lewd dances of a highly unseemly character, is practically the religion of probably three-fourths of the 46,740,661 persons who, at the date of the last census (1901), constituted the Hindu population of Bengal, the remaining one-fourth being Vaishnavas or worshippers of Vishnu. Amongst the latter the Chaitanites, devoted to the Krishna-cum-Radha cult, form no unimportant section, and include in their body sub-sects addicted to decidedly immoral practices.

Bearing in mind that amongst the Durga, Kali, and Krishna worshippers are to be found men of every caste, every degree of intelligence and education, and every grade of society in a Province commonly considered to be the most advanced in India, the above facts and figures cannot fail to arrest the attention of the most casual reader, especially if he learn at the same time that the *native* Christian population of Bengal according to the already cited census was *below a quarter of a million.*

To the immense number of Durga and Kali worshippers,

many millions of so-called Muhammadans in the eastern portions of the country might be added, for they, too, dread and propitiate these terrible female divinities, who have, moreover, a not inconsiderable following in other Provinces of India, outside the limits of Bengal, and even in the valleys of the Himalayas, the mountains of Nepal, and the great tableland of Tibet.[1] Kali-worship has even penetrated into that exclusive stronghold of Buddhism, the no longer mysterious Lhassa.[2]

[1] Throughout Northern India and the Punjab, Durga is worshipped in every Hindu family at the time of the Dosahra festival, which is in honour of Rama, but coincides in point of time with the *Durga pujah* of Bengal.

The Tantric worship has even extended to Tibet, and the Hindu Tantras have been translated into the language of that country.

Dr. Rajendra Lalla Mitra, *Indo-Aryans*, vol. ii. p. 105.

[2] Rai Sarat Chunder Dass Bahadur in a lecture on Tibet, delivered in April 1904 at Calcutta, mentioned that the goddess Kali was worshipped by the Tibetans, and that there is a temple at Lhassa dedicated to that goddess under the name of Shridevi.

It is a rather curious and not uninteresting fact that Durga has even invaded the domain of modern science, a contemporary entomologist having named one of the Cicadidæ of Eastern India *Cosmopsaltria durga*, after the famous goddess. (*A Monograph of the Oriental Cicadidæ*, by W. L Distant, p. 56.)

KALI-GHAT AND HINDUISM IN BENGAL
—continued

SECTION IV.—Indian worship of the Female Energy in Nature and its obscene rites—Position of women in Bengali society.

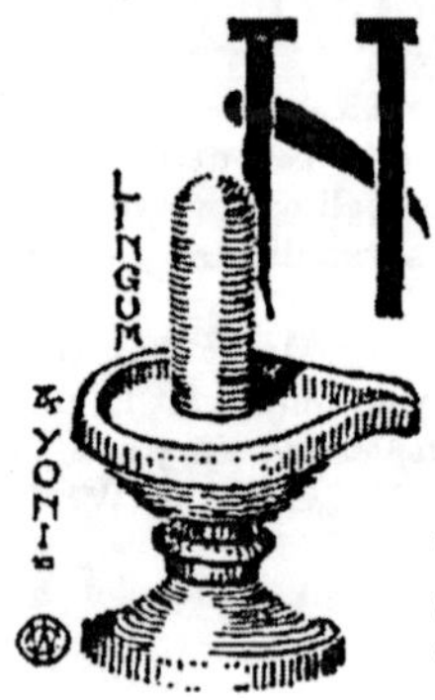

NOTWITHSTANDING what has been said regarding the drunken orgies connected with the worship of female divinities in Bengal, it may startle many readers to learn that rites such as were practised of old in Assyria, Babylon, and Phœnicia in honour of Ishtar, Nana, and Astarte, have their analogues in ceremonies and customs in vogue in India at the present time; but such is the undeniable fact, and it is probable that the worship of the great nature goddess of Asia has never died out, but in some form or other has kept its hold upon the sensuous races of the East, justifying to some extent the belief that sexual morality is, after all, *purement géographique.*

In Bengal, and outside Bengal too, is to be found a sect known as Saktas, devoted to the worship of Sakti, the female energy in Nature, having as their Scriptures the *Tantras.* This form of worship evidently finds favour with the Brahmans, for Dr. Bhattacharjee, himself a Bengali Brahman, states that "the majority of the Brahmans of Bengal, Mithila, and Punjab are Saktas of a moderate type." He also says that the Karhadeh Bramans of the Mahratta country are Saktas, and adds that the members of the influential Kayastha caste are also mostly Saktas.

The Sakta sect is divided into three sub-sects—

1. Dakshinachari, or the right-handed Saktas,

2. Bamachari, or the left-handed Saktas,
3. Kowls, or the extreme Saktas;

and it must in justice be stated that the extreme forms of this worship are not held in general esteem by the bulk of the Hindus of Bengal, and consequently members of these sub-sects usually, though by no means always, conceal from the world the fact of their belonging to the brotherhood; but that the rites referred to are secretly practised by great numbers of people, particularly Brahmans, both in and out of Bengal, there is no gainsaying.

Of these secret rites, unseemly and unsavoury though they be, it is necessary that I should now state something more definite if my reader is to be in a position to understand the real inwardness of the Hindu religion, as it exists in Bengal, and therefore I reluctantly venture to record the following particulars.

For the purpose of Tantric worship, eight, nine, or eleven couples of men and women meet by appointment at midnight. All distinctions of caste, rank, and kindred being temporarily suspended, they go through prescribed religious ceremonies, set up a nude woman, adorned only with jewels, as representative of Sakti (the female energy), worship her with strange rites, feast themselves on flesh and fish, indulge in wine, and give themselves over to every imaginable excess. During these orgiastic *religious rites*, every man present is, according to their pantheistic notions, Siva himself, and every woman there none other than Siva's consort.[1]

[1] These facts I have ascertained directly from the people themselves; but the reader desiring fuller information may consult on this subject:

(1) Rev. W. Ward, *A View of the History, Literature, and Religions of the Hindus*, pp. 152, 153, and 232–234. (2) Professor H. H. Wilson, *Essays on the Religion of the Hindus*, vol. i. pp. 254–263. (3) Professor Sir Monier Williams, *Religious Thought and Life in India*, pp. 190–192. (4) Rev. W. J. Wilkins, *Modern Hinduism*, pp. 94, 95. (5) Dr. J. N. Bhattacharjee, *Hindu Castes and Sects*, pp. 407–413. The Muhammadan author of the *Dabistan* (A.D. 1615–1670) was aware of these practices, and refers to them in his work.—Shea and Troyer's translation, vol. ii. pp. 152–154.

Some sixty years ago, according to a Bengali writer, "The Tantric worship flourished in Bengal with all its midnight horrors and corruptions" (Jogindra Chandra Bose's preface to the works of Raja Ram Mohun Roy), and there is no special reason to conclude that it has undergone any marked discouragement of late.

Now, coexisting with the obvious polytheism of the Hindus is a subtle pantheism which embraces all that is best in Hindu speculation. Of this pantheism in its highest development, the essential religious spirit is, as I shall presently explain, a desire, a yearning for direct communion with the world-soul, and for ultimate absorption into the Infinite. This aspiration may be traced throughout all the vagaries of the strange cults which Hinduism has accepted and appropriated or itself developed under the influence of its environment and local antecedents. And even in the Sakti worship, where all seems impure and degraded, the same desire is, strange to say, distinctly recognisable.[1]

As, amongst the peoples of India, the Bengalis are, *par excellence*, the Saktas, or worshippers of the female energy, we may profitably pause for a moment to consider how their notions in regard to the position and treatment of the female sex have been affected by their religious conceptions. If general opinion is to be trusted, a Bengali mother is respected by her children in an almost extravagant degree, and the wife's position in most households is an honourable and honoured one, although both custom and religion require that girls in Bengal should begin married life at quite a tender age.

In connection with the point we are considering, there is one feature of social life in Bengal which, though peculiar to only a small section of the community, should not be overlooked. I mean the practice of *Kulinism* or extensive polygamy by a certain class of Brahmans known as Kulins. This is confined to Bengal, and annually condemns to inevitable misery thousands of women, consigned—sometimes a whole family of sisters, cousins, and aunts together—to the embraces of these Kulin Brahmans, whose object in such wholesale alliances is often merely pecuniary

[1] It is a curious fact that the vague "Religion of Humanity," the latest philosophical creed of the West, which we owe to the Positivists, encourages the *worship of women*, as the representative of humanity, and as suggestive of universal love.—Rev. Professor T. R. Thomson, *Non-Biblical Systems of Religion*, p. 186.

I wonder what this worship, if it does not die out very soon, will eventually lead to!

benefit; for the parents of the brides have to continue to support them, while paying handsomely the high-caste husbands for the honour of their attentions.

So objectionable and barbarous is *Kulinism* that if it did not actually exist, it might well be thought impossible in any community regulated upon rational principles. As often as not the Kulin husband selected for a girl, or a family of girls, is a decrepit libertine, tottering on the verge of the grave, and already united to scores of unwilling wives. What such a system must lead to is obvious, and need not be discussed.

KALI-GHAT AND HINDUISM IN BENGAL
—continued

SECTION V.—The Higher Hinduism explained—Inoperative as regards the masses—Religion a sacred disease.

MY brief sketch will have made it clear that Hinduism in Bengal is practically the worship of *goddesses*, attended with the shedding of much blood, and these are peculiarities of the faith in Eastern India, including Assam.

In the north-western parts of Aryavarta, the great gods, Siva and Vishnu, the latter in his Krishna and Rama incarnations, are the favourite deities, and their cults do not countenance animal sacrifices.

Turning from bloody sacrifices, objectionable customs, and midnight orgies, it is a relief to be able to affirm that there is a brighter side to Hinduism (whether ancient or modern), a side which has of late become known, and even been much appreciated in Europe through the labours of Sanskrit scholars, and the preaching and writings of contemporary Hindu reformers.

Let me explain this important matter briefly.

In the pantheism which pervades and colours all Hinduism, we find the following generally accepted doctrines.

That the human soul is an emanation from the All-Spirit which is immanent in the universe, from which indeed *all* things proceed, and to which all things return :

That the embodied soul has a natural longing for reunion with the First Cause, but is debarred from such reunion by the taint of its earthly desires, due, of course, to the corporeal frame in which it is imprisoned:

That while such earthly desires remain unextinguished, and while earthly passions or longings continue to exist, the human soul is subject, on the dissolution of its corporeal frame, to be *reincarnated* again and again, perhaps through æons of time, until finally emancipated from all mundane hopes and affections it is fit to be reunited to the pure source from which it sprang:

That the circumstances of each embodied existence are the result of the works done in previous existences:

That souls, according to their actions, may enjoy periods of happiness in this world, or the heavens of the gods, or, on the other hand, suffer periods of punishment on this earth, or in the hells reserved for evil-doers; but the blissful *ending* is hastened or postponed by the actions of the soul in its successive incarnations, and will only arrive when the soul has emancipated itself from all hopes and fears:

That consequently in every embodied existence, it is the soul's interest and duty to strive against worldliness, and to free itself from all carnal desires, so as to ensure its early release from the deadly trammels of matter, and to effect its own blissful reunion with the All-Spirit, a reunion assured in every case.

Now, in these subtle doctrines, which are not of Aryan origin, and not traceable in the Vedic hymns, the cultured Hindu finds a satisfying explanation of the inequalities and apparent injustices of which he has experience and knowledge. He also finds sufficient reason for the worship of the gods who can bestow many blessings; but he also learns that his final salvation must be *worked out* by his own soul, and depends entirely upon its *Karma* or actions.

The doctrine of metempsychosis found its way to Europe during the Crusades. In the thirteenth century we find the heretical troubadours publicly accused of believing in the transmigration of souls and repeated reincarnations;[1] while to-day the same tenets coupled with *Karma* have been accepted by and received vigorous support amongst

[1] J. E. Rowbotham, M.A, *Troubadours and Courts of Love*, p. 304.

the active Theosophists of the United States of America.[1] And the transmigration of souls as a recognised tenet finds acceptance in other new religious movements of our time.[2]

Although the truth of the doctrines stated above, like the verity of the corresponding dogmas of other creeds, *can never be proved*, still they are undoubtedly competent to afford hope, to teach resignation in existing troubles, to discourage worldliness and promote virtuous living.

Thus we find that floating above the shoreless sea of chaotic superstition and gross licence, which is practically the religion of the Hindu masses, there are discernible bright clouds of purer doctrine and nobler sentiment. Unfortunately, however, they are very far overhead, casting only an uncertain reflection of their beautiful forms upon the dark waters below; for truth demands the acknowledgment that although much that is elevating may be found in some sacred literature of the Hindus, and in the philosophico-religious teachings of Indian sages, these influences for good have but a limited effect upon the conduct of life amongst the masses of the Hindu population to-day, and truth equally demands the admission that the incongruity between doctrine and practice, in the case of Hinduism to which I have just drawn attention, is by no means confined to that faith, but is very conspicuous also in the other religions of the world, whether professed by Orientals or Occidentals.

"But what," it may be asked, "is the attitude towards religion of the more intellectual classes in Bengal? Surely *they* do not countenance the obscenities of popular Hinduism in their native country?"

English education has made considerable progress in Bengal, and some of its results are strikingly apparent in the persons of many Bengalis who hold and adorn some of the highest legal and other appointments under the British Government. I have had the pleasure of being fairly well acquainted with some highly educated Bengalis, and whatever their private opinions might be, I know that, out-

[1] C. M. Leadbeater, *The Other Side of Death* (Theosophical Publishing Company).

[2] *Hibbert Journal*, October 1906, pp. 174, 175.

wardly at least, they generally conform to the religious customs, and respect the social prejudices of their people. And more than that I should not like to affirm. The fact that Bengal produces many clever lawyers, successful physicians, capable professors, good orators, smart journalists, persistent political agitators, and valuable public servants, is not sufficient ground for concluding that even in the case of these more advanced members of the community, the racial characteristics have undergone very much, if any, change.

Old religious ideas, sentiments, rites, and customs derived from a remote past, enshrined in the national literature and folk-lore, woven indeed into the very fabric of a people's life, cannot be easily set aside, especially when the women cling to them tenaciously, with all the conservative instinct of the sex. Hence it is highly probable that even at the present day, as in times past, the more thoughtful and cultured Bengalis are able, from the serener summits of what has been called the "Higher Hinduism," the philosophico-religious Pantheism of their sages, to regard with indulgent, and even sympathetic tolerance, the peculiar religious sentiments, customs, and practices in which they have themselves been reared.

No one who knows the people of India will doubt for a moment that *they are essentially a religious people*, but when the actual outcome of their religious aspirations in the most populous and advanced province of the Indian Empire is such as I have briefly outlined in the preceding pages, one may be excused for giving a qualified adhesion to the doctrine of Heraclitus that religion is a disease, though a sacred disease. In Bengal, assuredly, religion would seem to be a morbid emotional affection, whether sacred or not, to which, in some form or other, every man and woman is subject; and to-day, as in past generations, this morbid emotional affection tends to sap the manhood of the people and effeminate the race.

CASTE

BRAHMAN AT PRAYER

CHAPTER II

CASTE IN INDIA

SECTION I.—The more obvious features of the present-day caste system.

EVEN the casual tourist in India, if he keep his eyes and ears about him, when his train stops on a hot day at any of the larger railway stations, will not fail to discover, as he watches the bustle and movement on the platform, and hears the shouts of the thirsty native passengers, that there are two watermen to supply the needs of the Hindus and Muhammadans respectively, the former carrying his store in a metal vessel, the latter in a leathern bag known as a *mashk*, and he may further note that the Muhammadan water-carrier will, if required, minister to the wants of the white soldiers in the second-class car, but the Hindu will pass them by, notwithstanding their importunities.

These simple but significant facts will at once reveal the great gulfs of social exclusiveness which irreconcilable beliefs have produced in India, and serve to accentuate the hyper-sensitiveness of the Hindus in respect to intercourse with either Muslim or Christian.

With the wider experience which is gained by residence in India, the European learns that the Hindus are themselves divided into a multiplicity of well-recognised *groups of families*, the members of which may not marry persons outside their own group; that little social intercourse takes place or is permitted between individuals belonging to these distinct groups which constitute the Hindu *castes*; and that amongst Indian Muslims also caste divisions in a modified form exist to some extent. It will not be long before the foreign resident learns that *jat* or *zat* and *jat-bhai*, meaning caste and caste-mates respectively, are words for ever on the lips of the people; that at the top of the caste scale stand the Brahmans who are the hereditary priesthood, and below them a variety of castes with pretensions, customs, and sometimes occupations which differentiate one from the other. Theoretically there were originally only three *superior* castes, the Brahmans, Kshatriyas, and Vaisyas, and at the bottom of the social scale one great servile caste known as Sudras. Though these names, except in the case of the Brahmans, have lost their old significance, they are still frequently used and have to be borne in mind.

According to the census of India, taken in 1901, the Hindu population excluding the Sikhs numbered 207,147,026 souls, while the tables appended to the Report include no less than 2378 main castes and tribes and 43 races or nationalities.

Under the caste system, as it prevails amongst the Hindus, the social and religious life of the members of each caste is governed by rules peculiar to itself, but precise in their requirements, while all infringements of such rules expose the delinquent to various penalties, including ostracism of divers degrees of stringency.

Some of the rules are extremely inconvenient in their operation, especially such as require the higher castes to avoid the touch of men of inferior caste-status, and sometimes lead to situations which border on the ludicrous. For example, one might notice a customer standing respectfully outside a draper's shop in the bazaar, desirous of buying a bit of cloth. After the usual chaffering, he deposits the price on the edge of the boarded floor which projects on the street at about two feet above the ground, and having done this, stands patiently outside the shop while the draper measures out the quantity paid for. Presently the required number of yards of the selected material are thrown unceremoniously towards the purchaser, who makes a low obeisance and retires. This is a case of business conducted between a low-caste man and one several degrees above him in the caste scale; the latter being painfully anxious to avoid the slightest contact with the low-caste fellow, because it would entail ceremonial defilement requiring at the very least religious ablution before any food could be eaten by the person thus contaminated.

A close scrutiny of the two men, draper and customer, would probably make it clear that their racial characteristics were by no means identical; that the man who claimed superiority had finer features, and perhaps a somewhat lighter complexion, suggesting that ethnic differences had, very likely, something to do with caste distinctions.

As examples more or less typical of the working of the Hindu caste system, as seen by the outsider, I may here narrate the following incidents.

In a notebook of mine, now many years old, I find recorded an event which occurred during a visit I paid to the town of Coconada, near the mouth of the Godavery River. A serious disturbance had taken place there because some wealthy natives of the caste of fishermen had presumed to ride in palanquins, a privilege from which they were debarred by immemorial custom. While discussing this riot and the peculiar ideas underlying it, a European official who knew that part of the country well, assured me that *pariahs* had often to stand for hours at a ferry before they could get the opportunity of crossing, since one of these inferior beings dare not enter the same boat with a Brahman; and he supported his statement by the following anecdote:—

Watching the passengers disembark from a ferry-boat, my friend observed a Brahman run in an excited manner up to a woman who, shrinking timidly from observation, was evidently trying to conceal herself behind the throng of people who had just left the boat. Off went the Brahman's slipper as he reached the woman, and he struck her repeatedly with it; nor was it till the European had interfered personally, and forcibly, that he desisted from this unmanly assault. The victim of the attack was a pariah woman, who had presumed to enter the same boat with a man of the sacerdotal caste. That was the serious crime for which she received public chastisement, with the approval, no doubt, of all Hindu onlookers.

Temporary contamination from the mere touch of a European may be experienced by a high-caste Brahman, although such tainture may under existing political conditions be lightly faced for personal ends. Professor Sir Monier Williams recording his experiences of travel in India says: "I may mention, in illustration, that I often wondered, when in India, why certain great Pandits proposed calling on me very early in the morning, till I found out accidentally that by coming before bathing they were able afterwards to purify themselves by religious ablutions from the contamination incurred in shaking hands and talking with me."[1]

On this point a Bengali Brahman writes: "The orthodox Hindu's prejudices are such, that after sitting on the same carpet with a Mahomedan or a Christian friend, or shaking hands with such a person, he has to put off his clothes, and to bathe, or sprinkle his person with the holy water of the Ganges."[2]

One feature of the Hindu caste system which early

[1] *Modern India* (1878), p. 182.

[2] Dr. J. N. Bhattacharjee *Hindu Castes and Sects*, p. 121.

attracts the attention of the European in India, is the hereditary character of many handicrafts and occupations, and much too hastily it is often concluded that all blacksmiths, for example, are of the same caste, that all potters are of the same caste, and so on. But that this is very far from the truth cannot be too emphatically affirmed. All who follow a particular industrial calling do not necessarily belong to the same caste. However, it is true that a common occupation or trade is not infrequently the most evident bond of union in a local Hindu caste or sub-caste, and that the status in the caste scale of such an occupational group is largely dependent upon the nature of its calling, that is whether highly skilled or not, whether clean or otherwise.

Voyaging along the eastern coast of the Indian Peninsula in 1863, I noticed a considerable number of natives embarking in a ship lying in the roadstead off Coconada. They were mostly of the hereditary weaver caste, emigrating to the West Indies. I ascertained that these men had been thrown out of employment because all the cotton in their own country was being bought up at high prices and exported to feed the Lancashire power-looms, which had been deprived by the prolonged civil war in the United States of their usual supply of the raw material.

It was to me a very interesting fact that a conflict in distant North America should drive Indian weavers to find employment beyond the sea, and occasion their emigration to the Western world itself, where the cause of their trouble lay.

All the comments about this emigration which I heard at the time pointed to the irrationality of the narrow caste system, which alone seemed to be held responsible for the abandonment of their own country by the Indian weavers. But it did not strike me then, any more than it does now, that a body of men deprived by an accident or a calamity of their usual employment, whether a hereditary one or not, can quite easily take up some other vocation near home. Were this the case we should not at any time hear of labour troubles, distress, or increase of pauperism in Western countries, or of emigration from those favoured lands.

Amongst Hindus commensalism is confined to the members of the same or closely allied castes, and this hard-and-fast rule restricting commensation has given rise to many others affecting the preparation, handling, and consumption of food. For example: A Hindu's meals must as a rule be prepared by one of his own caste or by a Brahman, while his cooked food, and water for his drinking or his culinary purposes, if touched by a man of an inferior caste, become unfit for consumption. Fortunately for all concerned, water in bulk, as in rivers and tanks, does not get contaminated by the contact of the inferior castes.

The regulations about receiving food and water from the hands of persons of alien castes are not precisely the same everywhere; in fact they are peculiar to each endogamous group. They seem complicated if we take them in the aggregate, but they are simple enough when considered with reference to any one particular caste. In the case of persons who live such a simple life as the Hindus do, the regulations in question may ordinarily be observed without inconvenience. But when they are disregarded, trouble ensues.

About ten or twelve years ago it came to my knowledge that intense excitement prevailed amongst the Kashmiri Brahmans, usually called Pandits, scattered over Northern India from Lucknow to Lahore, and had extended to their homeland, the Happy Valley itself. The trouble was due to the infringement of certain *caste* regulations, and had separated the whole community into opposing camps. One Vishnu Pant, a Kashmiri Pandit, had visited England, and by so doing had become unclean, and had consequently been cut off from communion with his own people. On his return to Lucknow, however, he made amends for his serious breach of caste requirements by the prescribed purificatory ceremony, and was thereupon admitted by certain of his caste mates into communion with themselves, that is to say, they ate and drank with him. But it was held by competent persons that the lustration had not been performed in the proper manner, irregularly perhaps, or too hastily, I cannot say; and those Pandits who had broken bread with the sinner were at once *outcasted*, and not only they but also all others who had at any time after this event eaten with *them.* The contamination spread like the "French disease" in the Middle Ages, and the whole community of Pandits was convulsed with alarm and horror. Families got cut off from one another, and even in the same household the fission was so pronounced that the father perhaps would not receive food from his own son's hand.

The *purohits* (family priests), fearing to be involved in the general social *débâcle*, made it a rule not to receive food from either the Vishnu Pantis, or from their opponents the orthodox party. This resolution was, of course, adopted in order that they might be able to keep in with *both* parties. I am not aware whether the embers of the fire kindled years ago have now grown cold; but this I know, that Kashmiri Pandits have visited England since the great split in their community, and by so doing have probably added to the former social confusion, and aggravated the domestic troubles in no small degree.

It would be by no means surprising if these dissensions gave rise to new sub-castes as has occurred in many similar cases of differences within a caste.

No doubt it is not too flattering to Western conceit to find that by intercourse with Europeans of whatever rank in life, the high-caste Hindu becomes *impure*, at least for a time. Speaking on this point, an urbane Brahman, probably more polite than truthful, once said to me, that members of his caste looking upon Europeans as a superior race, as indeed one of the same rank as themselves, would not have objected to admit them to their own privileges had the Europeans not contaminated themselves by eating beef, by the employment of cooks of all castes, and by allowing themselves to be touched by men and women of even the lowest castes.

The exigencies of political conditions, and the dictates of self-interest tend, as time goes by, to make the offence of social intercourse with Europeans less heinous in the eyes of the Hindus than formerly, and the lapse from a state of purity caused thereby is, at any rate amongst the higher classes, readily condoned now. The purificatory ceremonies necessary in such cases for the complete rehabilitation of a man of rank would seem to be of a rather perfunctory character, if we may judge from the following casual entry by the Maharajah of Bobbili in his diary after his visit to Europe in 1902:—

"At Bezwada I had to wait the whole day till 9.30 p.m. for the mail train from Madras. As I had to stay so long there I had previously summoned the necessary Brahmans from Bobbili to meet me there to perform the usual *Prayaschittam* ceremony, simply to satisfy my friends and relations as I did after my previous tour."[1]

I am not unaware, indeed I have personal knowledge of the fact, that there are many educated Hindus who deliberately, though secretly, break through the rules of caste when it suits them to do so, and that many apparently orthodox Babus enjoy, in convenient European hotels in Calcutta and elsewhere, a hearty meal of forbidden food, cooked and served up by Muhammadans. There is nothing surprising in this. European education and influence has to an appreciable extent undermined respect for such caste rules as interfere with social intercourse between the ruling and subject races.

The advanced Babu, especially if he belong to a low caste, is rather proud of his emancipation from old-world restrictions, and likes to think that if he cannot eat with the Brahman, he can do so with the *Sahibs* who rule India. Besides, Hindu culinary preparations are not too tasty, and cannot be compared with Muslim or European dishes. However, the time for *open* revolt has not yet come, and only covert infringements of time-honoured customs can be safely attempted even by those whom the Native Press love to refer to as "men of light and leading." That in earlier times, too, a Hindu, or even a Brahman *bon-vivant*, was by no means averse to dine with non-Hindus if he could do so without prejudice to himself, may be illustrated by the following quaint story taken from *The Dabistan*:—

> "Azadah (this was his adopted title) is a Brahman. One day he ate at table with some Muselmans and drank wine. They said to him: 'Thou art a Hindu, and thou takest thy meal in common with Muselmans?

[1] The Maharajah of Bobbili, *Diary in Europe*, 1902, p. 101. (Madras: printed at the Addison Press, 1903.)

> Your people never eat but with persons of their own religion.' Azadah replied: 'I did not suppose that you were Muselmans; hereafter I will at eating and drinking keep myself separate from you.' Another day he found himself again drinking wine in company with them, and did not turn his head from the meal; during the repast they said to Azadah: 'Yesterday we made ourselves known to thee as Muselmans.' He answered: 'I knew that you were joking with me. God forbid that you should be Muselmans.'"[1]

How the origin of a new sub-caste may be *accounted* for by those interested in putting as favourable a construction upon the matter as possible, is instructively illustrated by the story of the origin of the well-known *Pirali Brahmans* of Bengal. According to the traditions of the family, it would appear that during the period of Muhammadan rule in Bengal, certain Brahmans had been invited to the house of a Muslim official named Pir Ali, and while there became polluted by *unavoidably smelling forbidden food.* These now degraded Brahmans were henceforth known as *Piralis,* and their descendants, although often in possession of great wealth and influence, have somehow never been able to recover the original caste status of the family.[2] I should add that although the legend I have referred to may be acceptable to the *Piralis* themselves, and may satisfy a credulous public, it is, as Dr. Bhattacharjee has pointed out, by no means deserving of credence, as even the *voluntary eating* of forbidden food is not, according to the Shastras, an inexpiable offence.[3]

As we have seen, the caste regulations for the avoidance of personal contact with inferiors and non-Hindus, as well as the rules limiting the families and persons with whom it is lawful to partake of food, or from whom it may be received, are strict enough. Yet the preservation of caste and the caste system depends more upon the strict observance of certain prescribed nuptial laws than upon adherence to the rules regulating ordinary social intercourse with outsiders. Amongst Hindus the *jus connubii*

[1] *The Dabistan,* translated by Shea and Troyer, vol. ii. p. 114.

[2] S. C. Bose, *The Hindoos as they are,* pp. 171–174.

[3] *Hindu Castes and Sects,* p. 120.

of each caste is very rigid, and any breach of it is a most serious offence. Two rules which hold good generally throughout the caste system are that marriages may be contracted only between members of the same caste; but that such alliances may not be made within one family, or, as M. Senart puts it: "*La loi de la caste . . . est une loi d'endogamie par rapport à la caste, d'exogamie par rapport à la famille. Dans ces termes vagues, elle est absolue.*"[1]

The field of selection for a bride or a bridegroom being within the caste, or even sub-caste, it has been prudently left entirely to the parents to conclude the necessary nuptial contracts, while the parties primarily concerned are still mere children without any personal preferences. Marriage being imperative in the case of every Hindu, and the field of selection being restricted by the caste regulations, the choice of a bride or a bridegroom is often a real and pressing difficulty which has produced the marriage-broker, whose knowledge of the genealogy of Hindu families, their means, and their eligible unwedded offspring, is at the service of anxious parents whose interests are his own.

But even under the most careful management and most comprehensive safeguards, irregularities will occur, and may lead to far-reaching consequences. In this connection, the following extract from an Indian newspaper[2] may be both interesting and informing:—

> "FISSIPAROUS HINDUISM.—Writing of the excommunication of three hundred Bombay Bhattias who had married wives from among the Bhattias of Hardwar, the *Indian Social Reformer* says: 'The incident is interesting as an instance before our very eyes of how new sub-castes have been formed in such large numbers in India. It is absurd to speak of excommunicating three hundred families. What has happened is that a number of Bhattias with Bombay wives have refused to have social intercourse with a number of Bhattias with Hardwar spouses. It is not alleged that the Hardwar marriages are invalid according to the Hindu law, so that what the conservative Bhattias

[1] *Les Castes dans l'Inde*, p. 27.

[2] *Pioneer Mail* (Allahabad), 5th June 1903.

resent is practically the loss of custom. The three hundred heroes of this matrimonial Thermopylæ will, of course, form a new caste, which in the course of the next twenty years would trace its origin to immemorial antiquity.'"

Amongst Hindus mixed marriages entail serious disadvantages on the offspring of such unions. In the case of a Brahman woman stooping to marry a Sudra, her children become *Chandalas*, mere outcasts. This is, of course, consonant with universal practice; for in all countries men visit with the greatest social penalties the women of their own class who prefer to mate with men of inferior degree. In Hindu society, the Brahmans having been the lawmakers, did their utmost to keep their women to themselves. They did not restrict their own choice quite so stringently, permitting themselves originally one wife from *each* of the *four* primitive castes already referred to; though this privilege is no longer admitted.

How Europeans stand with respect to the Indian caste system and its marital privileges, will be apparent from the following extract from a paper conducted by Indians:—

> "The Hindu or Mahommedan father is not yet born who would consent to bestow his daughter upon even the son of an English peer, who, in spite of an uninterrupted descent from Norman brigands, is only a *mlechha* or a *kaffir* carrying pollution in his very touch."[1]

Any one long resident in India may, occasionally, come upon a picturesque group of persons of the lower classes seriously discussing some question of seemingly great interest to themselves, and learn that it was a sort of caste tribunal assembled for the trial of one or more of the members for some breach of the prescribed or customary caste laws. The elders under the guidance of a president would take evidence, examine witnesses, hear what the accusers and accused had to say, and decide accordingly.

[1] Rais and Rayyet, quoted in *Civil and Military Gazette* (Lahore), 26th September 1884.

The court might be assembled on the side of a quiet road under a few shady trees, or in the open *maidan*. As likely as not the case under consideration might be one touching the infidelity of a wife, and the culpability of her husband, for surely the man who cannot rule his own house deserves punishment. If found guilty, the sentence of the assembly (*panchayat*) of his caste-mates would probably be that the culprit be debarred from all social intercourse with his brethren, not to eat, drink, or smoke with them, until he shall have confessed his fault, promised to do better in future, humiliated himself before the elders, and presented them with certain gifts. When these conditions had been duly fulfilled, the delinquent would probably be required to provide a feast for his caste-mates, who, by partaking of such feast in his company, *i.e.* eating and drinking with him, would testify publicly that he was readmitted to the privileges of the community. Occasionally, though not so much amongst the lowest classes, charity to the Brahmans would not be forgotten.

It is hardly necessary to add that in all cases, whether serious or trifling, the penalties imposed would be proportioned to the enormity of the offence committed, as measured by caste standards, and might range from a mere reprimand to final expulsion from the community.

The system of *panchayats* which has flourished for ages has no doubt helped very considerably to keep alive an interest in the affairs of the *brādri* (caste-brotherhood) on the part of every one of its members, and has thus aided in the perpetuation of caste as an institution of almost vital importance to the Hindus. That the system of *panchayats* must encourage espionage and intermeddling is obvious, but its value as a force for the maintenance of a better moral standard and for the strict observance of caste customs, is undeniable. Nor are the functions of the *panchayat* always those of a police: it is sometimes appealed to for advice or approval in cases of adoption and marriage contracts.

Having stated most of the salient features of the caste system as they come under the observation of the European in India, I now sum up more specifically what constitutes a serious breach of caste rules, and what is involved in the penalty of absolute exclusion from caste.

On both these points, I cannot do better than quote a learned Hindu writer, a Brahman by caste, and a specialist in regard to the subject in question.

"*Exclusion* from caste," he says, "would result from any of the following acts:

"1. Embracing Christianity or Mahomedanism.

"2. Going to Europe or America.

"3. Marrying a widow.

"4. Publicly throwing away the sacred thread.

"5. Publicly eating *Kachi* food cooked by a Mahomedan, Christian, or low-caste Hindu.

"6. Publicly eating beef, pork, or fowl.

"7. Officiating as a priest in the house of a very low-class Sudra.

"8. By a female going away from home for an immoral purpose.

"9. By a widow becoming pregnant."

"In the villages," adds the same writer, "the friendless and the poor people are sometimes excluded from caste for other offences, as, for instance, adultery, incest, eating forbidden food and drinking forbidden liquors. But when the offender is an influential personage, or is influentially connected, no one thinks of visiting him with such punishment."[1]

The ceremony of expulsion from caste, as prescribed in the laws of Manu, is a solemn and imposing proceeding, meant to symbolise the living death of the outcast. According to the lawgiver, the condemned man's relatives and connections should assemble on the evening of an "unlucky day" and offer, as if to his manes, a libation of water, a priest and the culprit's *guru* (spiritual guide) being present. As at a Hindu funeral, a pot of water should be solemnly broken, not, however, by the nearest of kin, but by a slave girl. After this act the assembly should disperse, each individual present at the ceremony being regarded as impure for one day.

[1] J. N. Bhattacharjee, M.A., D.L., *Hindu Castes and Sects*, p. 17.

Little imagination is needed to realise how painfully affecting and impressive such a rite would appear to the kith and kin of the man thus ostracised.

The nature of the penalty of exclusion from caste is thus explained:

"When a Hindu is excluded from caste—

"1. His friends, relatives, and fellow-townsmen refuse to partake of his hospitality.

"2. He is not invited to entertainments in their houses.

"3. He cannot obtain brides or bridegrooms for his children.

"4. Even his own married daughters cannot visit him without running the risk of being excluded from caste.

"5. His priest, and even his barber and washerman, refuse to serve him.

"6. His fellow-castemen sever their connection with him so completely that they refuse to assist him even at the funeral of a member of his household.

"7. In some cases the man excluded from caste is debarred access to the public temples."[1]

Where the rules are so explicit it follows, of course, that means are duly provided, as indeed we have already seen, by which the offender against caste rules may expiate his errors or misfortunes and so recover his caste-status. These means are the performance of prescribed religious rites, and purificatory ceremonies, the feasting of Brahmans and bestowing suitable presents on them, and last, but not least, banqueting the members of his own caste.

Necessarily readmission to the privileges of caste under such conditions means the expenditure of money, often a very considerable amount of money, and makes it comparatively easy only for the rich man to brave the risks of breaking caste rules. Of one well-known and not over-scrupulous Bengali millionaire it is related that, "when the subject of caste was discussed, he emphatically said that

[1] According to the *Smritis*, "Outcasted persons have no share in inheritance." (Dr. J. Wilson, *Caste*, vol. i. p. 403.) But this law is not recognised by the British Government.

'caste was in his iron chest,' the meaning of which was that money has the power of restoring caste."[1]

On the other hand, infringements of caste rules by the poor bring upon the delinquents terrible hardships, driving many men and women to crime and even to suicide.

Amongst the minor penances prescribed for breaches of caste rules, the following (taken from Dr. Wilson's *Caste in India*) may be mentioned as examples:—

The *Sántapana*—Fasting for a night and a day and swallowing the *panchagavya,* the five products of the cow—milk, butter, curd, etc.

The *Piajapatya*—Fasting for three days, eating for three days; abstaining from asking anything for three days, and fasting for three days.

The *Krichchhra*—Abstaining from water for twenty-one days.

The *Paraka*—Fasting for twelve days.

The *Tapta-Krichchhra*—Drinking hot water, milk, and *ghee* for three days each.

The *Yavamadhya Chandrayana*—Eating the first day of the moon one mouthful of food; the second day, two; the third, three; and so on till full moon, when the supply is to be lessened by a mouthful daily till a new moon occurs.

The *Pipilika Chandrayana.* In this the procedure prescribed in the last case is *reversed.*

[1] S. C. Bose, *The Hindoos as they are,* p. 177.

CASTE IN INDIA—*continued*

Section II.—The origin and development of the caste system as explained by the Pandits.

ACCORDING to ancient Hindu Scriptures, there are but four *varnas*, colours or castes, ranged in descending scale as follows:—

1. *Brahmans*—Priests and legislators.
2. *Kshatriyas*—Rulers and warriors.
3. *Vaisyas*—Merchants, herdsmen, and agriculturists.
4. *Sudras*—Handicraftsmen, servitors, domestics, and the rest.

In respect to the duties of these four castes, Manu, the famous Hindu lawgiver, says:

> "To Brahmans the Supreme Being assigned the duties of reading the Veda and teaching it, of sacrificing, of assisting others to sacrifice, of giving alms and of receiving gifts. To defend the people, to give alms, to sacrifice, to read the Veda, to shun the allurements of sexual gratification, are in a few words the duties of a Kshatriya. To keep herds of cattle, to bestow largesses, to sacrifice, to carry on trade, to lend at interest, are the duties of a Vaisya. One principal duty the Supreme Being assigns to a Sudra, namely, to serve the before-mentioned classes without depreciating their worth." [1]

The three first of the above-named castes, embracing the priests, warriors, merchants and agriculturists, were at some subsequent period designated *dvija*, "twice-born," and were entitled to wear a sacred thread across the breast and over one shoulder as a badge of their nobility. They also

[1] *Manu*, i. 87–91.

enjoyed the exclusive privilege of studying the holy Vedas, the Sudras being permitted neither to open a page of the sacred book, nor even to listen to the reading thereof. All strong priesthoods have, for very good reasons, been averse to admit the masses to a knowledge of their sacred books, and the Brahmans in shutting out the Sudras from all knowledge of the Vedas, only followed the usual safe course dictated by worldly wisdom.

Even after death the great distinctions of caste are to be maintained. The virtuous Brahman goes to the abode of Brahma; the good Kshatriya to that of Indra, and the worthy Vaisya to that of the Maruts, and the dutiful Sudra to that of the Gandharvas.[1]

To give the imprimatur of divine sanction to this convenient arrangement, a myth duly found its way into the sacred Veda to the effect that in the beginning the Brahmans proceeded from the mouth of the Creator, the Kshatriyas from his arms, the Vaisyas from his thighs, and the Sudras or servile class from his feet.[2]

Dissimilar and contradictory accounts of the origin of the four castes are to be found in other later sacred books of the Hindus, but they do not appear to have troubled the placid minds of the Indians, and we need not concern ourselves with them here.[3]

It has obviously been to the interest of the superior castes, particularly the hereditary priesthood, to strenuously and persistently uphold the integrity of the system just outlined; but, even so, no one could possibly anticipate the insolent arrogance with which the Brahmans have asserted their own unapproachable superiority and their right to

[1] The Márkandáya Purana, cited by Dr. John Wilson, *Indian Caste*, vol. i. p. 437.

[2] The Parusha sukta, being the 90th hymn of the 10th book of the Rig Veda. "This celebrated hymn," says Dr. Muir, "contains, as far as we know, the oldest extant passage which makes mention of the fourfold origin of the Hindu race."—*Original Sanskrit Texts*, vol. i. p. 7.

Writing of this hymn Professor Max Müller said: "There can be little doubt, for instance, that the 90th hymn of the 10th book . . . is modern both in its character and diction."—Quoted by Muir, *Original Sanskrit Texts*, vol. i. p. 13.

[3] Muir, *Original Sanskrit Texts*, vol. i. pp. 138-140, 159, 160, and 220, 221.

regulate the affairs of men, for it is surely without parallel in human history, as the following passages from Hindu Scriptures will show:—

> "The son of Ita then inquired: Tell me, Vayu, to whom the earth, with its wealth, rightfully belongs, to the Brahman or the Kshatriya? Vayu replied: All this, whatever exists in the world, is the Brahman's property by right of primogeniture: this is known to those who are skilled in the laws of duty. It is his own which the Brahman eats, puts on, bestows. He is the chief of all the castes, the first-born and the most excellent. Just as the woman when she has lost her (first) husband, takes her brother-in-law for a second: so the Brahman is the first resource in calamity; afterwards another may arise" (Mahabharata, Santiparvam, verses 2755 *et seq.*).
>
> "No blame accrues to Brahmans from teaching or sacrificing or from receiving money in any other way; Brahmans are like flaming fire. Whether ill or well versed in the Veda, whether untrained or accomplished, Brahmans must never be despised, like fires covered with ashes. Just as a fire does not lose its purity by blazing even in a cemetery, so too, whether learned or unlearned, a Brahman is a great deity. Cities are not rendered magnificent by ramparts, gates, or palaces of various kinds if they are destitute of excellent Brahmans. The place where Brahmans, rich in the Veda, perfect in their conduct, and austerely fervid, reside, is (really) a city (*nagara*). Wherever there are men abounding in Vedic lore, whether it be a cattle-pen or a forest, that is called a city, and that will be a sacred locality" (Vanaparvam, 13436 to 13540).
>
> "Through the prowess of the Brahmans the Asuras were prostrated on the waters; by the favour of the Brahmans the gods inhabit heaven. The ether cannot be created; the mountain Hamavat cannot be shaken, the Ganga cannot be stemmed by a dam; the Brahmans cannot be conquered by anyone upon earth. The world cannot be ruled in opposition to the Brahmans; for the mighty Brahmans are the deities even of the gods. If thou desire to possess the sea-girt earth, honour them continually with gifts and with service."[1]

In the Kriyá-Yoga-Sára of the Padma Purana it

[1] Muir, *Sanskrit Texts*, vol. i: pp. 129, 130.

is said: "Whatever good man bows to a Brahman, worshipping him as Vishnu, is blessed with long life, sons, fame and wealth. . . . The bearer of a drop of water which has been in contact with a Brahman's foot has all the sins of his body thereby destroyed. Whoever carries on his head the holy things touched by a Brahman's foot, verily, verily I say, he is freed from all sins."[1]

As a result of these extravagant pretensions we find the Brahmanical law recommending liberality to the Brahmans as the highest of virtues, and at the same time conferring upon that favoured caste remarkable rights and privileges, as compared with the inferior castes. For criminal offences a graduated scale of punishments is laid down by which the Brahman is let off with the least penalties, the Kshatriya fares better than the Vaisya and the Vaisya than the Sudra.

Under no circumstances whatever may a king order the execution of a Brahman.[2]

The immeasurable inferiority of the Sudras is illustrated by the law which prescribes that a man of the twice-born castes having intercourse with a Sudra woman is to be banished; a Sudra having connection with a woman of the superior castes is to be put to death.

It is needless to add that these ordinances are now as inoperative in India as are the Levitical laws in Christendom; yet the study of them is instructive as throwing light upon the past. But it may be well to realise in connection with these obsolete Hindu laws that class or caste privileges have been common enough in Europe, and that the feelings which dictated the sanguinary law against a Sudra cohabiting with an Arya woman finds practical expression even *now* in the cruel lynching of negroes for offences against white women in the great American Republic, where all are equal and where all are free!

From such facts and legends regarding the origin and working of the institution of caste as are revealed some-

[1] Dr. John Wilson, *Indian Caste*, vol. i. p. 426.

[2] This recalls to mind the old English law according to which priests, deacons, and clerks condemned to death could be *claimed* by the bishop of the diocese, and so escape punishment.—John Brady, *Clavis Calendaria*, vol. i. p. 363.

times deliberately, sometimes quite casually in the literature of the Brahmans from the ancient Vedas, through the Brahmanas, Upanishads, and Sutras to the famous Indian Epics—the Ramayana and Mahabbharata—may be learned how insidiously the Brahmans magnified their own importance and privileges, and how their arrogant self-assertion often brought them into serious conflict with the Kshatriyas, who, if we are to believe the priests, were *entirely* extirpated by Parasharama because of their opposition to the Brahmans. The legend to this effect is accepted by many living Pandits, who maintain that no lineal descendants of the original Kshatriya caste are existing at the present day. It is admitted, however, in the Mahabharata, that the Kshatriya race in a renewed form resulted from intercourse between Brahmans and Kshatriya women who were evidently not exterminated along with their menfolk.

That the four original castes, if ever there were such, have not been, and indeed could not have been, kept pure, has been recognised by the Hindus from the remotest antiquity,[1] and the literature of the past, especially the Epics, present us with pictures of life in the heroic age when the functions of the primitive castes seem already strangely confused, Brahmans, Vaisyas, and even Sudras being amongst the most distinguished military leaders in the fratricidal war which came to an end on the bloody battlefield of Kurakshatra. Nor is the idea of the exercise of even kingly power by a Sudra unknown to the law-books.[2] Changes of occupation amongst Hindus are also casually recorded in the old Buddhist literature.[3]

It is also admitted that the priestly class became subdivided into several sub-castes according to their supposed respective patriarchs (*gotras*), and that another cause of fission was the adoption by distinct families of the duty of collecting, arranging, and transmitting the various parts

[1] Muir, *Sanskrit Texts*, vol. i. pp. 135–137 and 281–283.

[2] M. Emile Senart, *Les Castes dans l'Inde*, pp. 118, 119.

[3] The Jatakas, cited by Professor T. W. Rhys Davids, *Buddhist India*, pp. 56, 57.

(known as *shákás* or branches[1]) of the Vedas; and of conducting the different ceremonials, particularly sacrifices connected with their ancient Scriptures.

According to the orthodox view, a great many well-established castes owe their origin to regular or irregular alliances between members of the four primitive castes, and between the descendants of such unions. A table of the parentage of one hundred and thirty-one such mixed and degraded castes are given by the Rev. Dr. John Wilson in his book on Indian Caste.[2]

Hindus further believe that irregularities and confusion have resulted in some cases from men of a lower caste pretending to belong to a superior one; *e.g.*, Kshatriyas and Vaisyas having set up claims to Brahmanhood, and obtained a more or less doubtful footing in the great sacerdotal caste. But after the above-mentioned mythical and other causes assigned in explanation of the origination of the primitive or of new castes have been allowed for, there remain many features of the existing system which require elucidation, and will repay investigation.

[1] "A *shákà* (branch), it must be remembered, is a definite literary Vedic treasure as held in the memory of its possessors and taught by repetition to others."—Dr. John Wilson, *Indian Caste*, vol. ii. p. 13.

[2] Vol. i. pp. 65-70.

CASTE IN INDIA—*continued*

SECTION III.—**The existing Hindu caste system contrasted with the theoretical system of the old books.**

CASTE, as we have seen, is mentioned in some of the oldest Hindu Scriptures; but in view of the unreliability of Indian texts and the uncertainties of Indian chronology, it may be worth stating that the Greeks noticed the existence of the caste system in India, and that Megasthenes, Greek ambassador at the court of the Hindu King Sandracottus (B.C. 306–298), enumerates seven Hindu castes as follows:[1]—

1. Philosophers.
2. Husbandmen.
3. Shepherds and Hunters.
4. Labourers, or those who work at trades, or vend wares.
5. Fighting-men.
6. Inspectors charged with the supervision of all that goes on.
7. Counsellors and Assessors of the King.

At the present day instead of the *four* castes of the Hindu Scriptures, or the *seven* referred to by Megasthenes, we have something very different, for no less than "2378 main castes and tribes and 43 races or nationalities" are included in the tables appended to the Report on the last Census of India. Everywhere, throughout the country, we find at the top of the social scale the Brahmans as of yore; but no longer of pure Aryan race, and sometimes far more akin to the Dravidian or Mongolian than the Aryan stock from which they claim descent. Further, we

[1] Dr. J. W. M'Crindle, *Ancient India*, pp. 47–53.

find the Brahmans represented by a variety of sub-castes between which intermarriage is not allowed. Below the Brahmans we find a medley of castes wearing the cord which is the special and distinguishing badge of the twice-born, thereby claiming to be, and popularly accepted as, the modern representatives of the traditional Kshatriya and Vaisya castes.

> "The ancient designation Sudra," writes Mr. Risley, "finds no great favour in modern times, and we can point to no group that is generally recognised as representing it. The term is used in Bombay, Madras, and Bengal to denote a considerable number of castes of moderate respectability, the higher of whom are considered 'clean' Sudras, while the precise status of the lower is a question which lends itself to endless controversy. At this stage of the grouping a sharp distinction may be noticed between Upper India and Bombay and Madras. In Rajputana, the Punjab, the United Provinces, the Central Provinces, Bengal and Assam, the grade next below twice-born rank is occupied by a number of castes from whose hands Brahmans and members of the higher castes will take water and certain kinds of sweetmeats. Below these again is a rather indeterminate group from whom water is taken by some of the higher castes, but not by others. Further down where the test of water no longer applies, the status of a caste depends on the nature of its occupation and its habits in respect to diet. There are castes whose touch defiles the twice-born, but who do not commit the crowning enormity of eating beef; while below these again in the social system of Upper India are people like Chamārs and Doms who eat beef and various sorts of miscellaneous vermin. In Western and Southern India the idea that the social status of a caste depends on whether Brahmans will take water and sweetmeats from its members is unknown, for the higher castes will as a rule take water only from persons of their own caste and sub-caste. In Madras especially the idea of ceremonial pollution by the proximity of a member of an unclean caste has been developed with much elaboration. Thus the table of social precedence attached to the Cochin Report shows that while a Nāyar can pollute a man of a higher caste

only by touching him, people of Kammālan group, including masons, blacksmiths, carpenters, and workers in leather, pollute at a distance of 24 feet, toddy-drawers (Iluvan or Tiyan) at 36 feet, Pulayan or Cheruman cultivators at 48 feet, while in the case of the Parāiyan (Pariahs) who eat beef, the range of pollution is stated to be no less than 64 feet."[1]

A large number of castes devoted to or connected with special occupations are to be found all over India, and have attracted considerable attention from Europeans, so much so that it has even been held that "function and function only was the foundation upon which the whole caste system of India was built up,"[2] a view which conflicts with the irrefragable fact that of no occupational or trade caste can it be said that even within a restricted area its members enjoy the privilege of marrying into all the other groups devoted to the same pursuit, carried on in exactly the same way.[3]

Changes in the component parts of the vast caste system have been, and continue to be, far more common and natural than is generally supposed. Disintegration and reconstruction have been going on perpetually. Under the pressure of circumstances and new conditions, the number of social groups is always changing, and their boundaries are ever shifting. The castes of to-day are not necessarily identical with those of the past, even the comparatively recent past. No doubt from the earliest times, the division of the Indian population into caste groups has been a noticeable feature of Hindu society, and it is so to-day; but there have been endless changes in the component parts of the system which is not and never has been more permanent than other human institutions. Yet *the idea of caste*, respect for the institution and *its recognition as an indispensable feature of Indian society*, has been strong and persistent amongst Hindus from remote antiquity up to the present day; and so has the broad principle that the internal affairs of each

[1] *Census of India Report*, 1901, p. 540.

[2] John C. Nesfield, M.A., *Brief View of Caste System of the North-Western Provinces and Oude*, p. 38 (Allahabad, 1885).

[3] *Census of India Report*, 1901, p. 553.

caste should be regulated by its own customary law, which even the king should uphold.[1] Revolts there have been from time to time, and in another book[2] I have pointed out that the principle of caste has often been called in question in India, and that, as a rule, the Hindu founders of new religious sects have manifested a decided hostility to the system by admitting men and women of all castes indiscriminately into these communities on a footing of equality; but that the practical result of such latitudinarianism has, in the long-run, been merely the creation of new castes, and not the abrogation of the system.

My plan being to deal merely with the more prominent characteristics of a very complex system, I am precluded from entering into details about the different castes, their organisation, customs, and peculiarities. But since a general survey of the Hindu caste system of to-day reveals the fact that on the whole the Brahmans are still, as formerly, the venerated spiritual and social leaders of the people in most parts of India, certain features of their present constitution may well arrest our attention for a moment.

As previously stated, the Brahmans do not now form a single monogamous caste, if ever they did so. Nor do they now pursue a single calling, many groups or sub-castes being devoted to various secular occupations.

Some Brahman sub-castes have arisen owing to particular families devoting themselves, as spiritual advisers (*gurus*), to special sections of the lay community. Thus there are several such sub-castes amongst the Gujarati Brahmans, *e.g.* the *Kunbigors* who act as *gurus* to the agriculturists, the *Mochigors* who look after the spiritual welfare of the shoemakers, and so on.[3]

Brahmans have been, and are still, employed in all State departments; they are throughout the country engaged in the administration or practice of the law and in mercantile and other secular pursuits. Brahmans serve as Sepoys in the Indian Army, and some have fought against us like the

[1] M. Emile Senart, *Les Castes dans l'Inde*, p. 117.

[2] *The Mystics, Ascetics, and Saints of India.*

[3] Dr. J. Wilson, *Indian Caste*, vol. ii. p. 93.

famous Tantia Topi and the still more famous Rani of Jhansi, whose names are indelibly associated with the great Sepoy revolt of 1857–58.

Many Brahman tribes till the soil with their own hands, as, for example, the Gaur Brahmans of Delhi, Rohtak, Gurgaon, and Karnal. Others live by trading, and great numbers are cooks even in *Sudra* households.

In Bengal there is a caste of Brahmans—known as Kulins, already referred to on page 28—many members of which seem to have little business in life beyond marrying and marrying, and marrying again, an unlimited number of times, and without reference to age, till they have in some cases been known to possess as many as 350 wives. They receive a substantial pecuniary consideration with each wife, without incurring the obligation of supporting her. I have myself heard one of these Kulin Brahmans say that he was going to marry another wife, and ascertained that he contemplated this step because he lacked money wherewith to complete a house he was building for himself. It is fair to add that some Kulin Brahmans do not exercise their polygamous privileges, and find other and more honourable modes of earning a living, supporting themselves, and building their dwelling-houses.

At least one Brahman caste is looked upon as positively disreputable. They are known as Burá Brahmans (evil Brahmans), and are a terror to the people, claiming as a right the clothing, bedding, and *lotah* (drinking vessel) of the dead. In such abhorrence are they held that to meet one of them in the morning is regarded as a very bad omen.

The missionary Mr. W. Ward, writing about a century ago of the Bengali Brahmans of his time, says: "The Shastra expressly forbids their selling milk, iron, lac, salt, clarified butter, sesamum, etc., yet many Brahmans now deal in these things without regard to the Shastra, or the opinion of stricter Hindus, and add thereto the sale of skins, spirits, and flesh. . . . I have heard of a Brahman at Calcutta who was accustomed to procure beef for the butchers; many traffic in spirituous liquors."[1]

[1] *A View of the History, Literature, and Religion of the Hindus*, vol. i. pp. 85, 86.

With the diversity in their avocations, there is to be found a corresponding diversity in many of their customs, arising out of the nature of their occupations, *e.g.* Trigula Brahmans who are employed in the cultivation of the pepper-betel do not, we are told, hesitate to destroy insects, which other Brahmans would not do.

In the matter of food the differences between the various Brahman castes is striking. The Javala and Shenavi Brahmans, for example, eat fish. Several castes amongst the Saraswata Brahmans eat both fish and flesh, the Sakhtas amongst them indulging in spirits also. The Gouda Brahmans of Central India also partake of animal food; while the Nepalese Brahmans "eat goats, sheep, and some kinds of wild fowl, but abstain from venison."[1]

Notwithstanding that some Brahmans, as just instanced, do eat animal food, we may take it as a general fact that abstention from *beef* is a requirement applicable to *all* Hindus in these days, though it was not so in the remote past.

So much for the Brahmans. If we pursue a like inquiry with respect to the present-day occupations of the castes which claim to represent the traditional Kshatriyas, we shall find similar diversities, showing that the caste system of to-day, and its practical working, differs greatly from the ideal—it could never have been anything more—which the Hindu lawgiver desired to place under the sanction of Holy Writ. Yet caste is *still* the most distinctive feature in Indian life, each caste being a hereditary group of families, more often than not ethnologically related, bound together by common religious and social practices, and, in many cases, devoted to a distinctive trade or occupation. For every Hindu the customs of his caste determine the details of the social intercourse he may have within the group or with outsiders, and limits strictly and inexorably for each man or woman the possible field of matrimonial alliances. Tampering with caste rules is, in the case of the wealthy

[1] For the facts stated above regarding the avocations and food of various Brahman sub-castes, I am indebted to Dr. John Wilson, *Indian Caste*, vol. ii. pp. 26, 27, 30, 68, 134, 137, 163, and 198.

and better educated, becoming more frequent perhaps than formerly, but still, for the country as a whole, caste retains its vitality, a fact which will not, however, surprise us if we clearly grasp the idea that the customs of each caste have been derived from *within*, not imposed from without, and that they preserve, though not unchanged, the religious conceptions and practices of a remote ancestry. With this key to its real inwardness, we can understand and appreciate the stability of the caste system through so many centuries, and the pride that each member of a caste takes to scrupulously maintain its boundaries intact, this being his primary duty as a religious, moral, reputable person. If a man respect not his caste he is worthy only of contempt and detestation. That he should be born in one caste instead of another, in one station of life instead of another, is due to his *Karma* (actions in previous existences), and therefore inevitable,[1] and it is this belief which enables him cheerfully to do his duty "in that state of life unto which it shall please God to call him"; the Brahman hierarchy being thus more successful than the Christian priesthood in attaining an end which both have kept in view, and still desire to see accomplished.

Note.—A word about Muslim castes may be added. The Muhammadans, as such, form a class apart, and as conquerors in India were strongly differentiated from the "infidels"; but the idea of caste distinctions amongst Mussulmans themselves is alien to the spirit of Islam, yet, under certain circumstances, castes may and do arise amongst Muhammadans. The origination of a Muslim caste out of a heretical sect is evidenced by the case of the Nakhawilahs of Medina, regarding whom Sir R. Burton writes:

> "They are numerous and warlike, yet they are despised by the townspeople, because they openly profess heresy, and are moreover of humble degree. They have their own priests and instructors, although subject to the orthodox Kazi; marry in their own sect, are confined to low offices, such as slaughtering

[1] "Fate," said the lawgiver Yājnavālkya, "is (the result of) a man's acts performed in a previous body."

animals, sweeping and gardening, and are not allowed to enter the Harim during life, or to be carried to it after death. Their corpses are taken down an outer street called the Darb al Janazah—Road of Biers—to their own cemetery near Al-Bakia."

Burton adds in a footnote, that this sect believe "in a transmigration of the soul, which, gradually purified, is at last 'orbed' into a perfect star! They are scrupulous of caste, and will not allow a Jew or a Frank to touch a piece of their furniture. . . ."[1]

Amongst Indian Muhammadans there are, it appears, two main social divisions: the Ashrāf or Sharāf, meaning noble, and the Ajlāf or Kamina, base or mean. "The former section," writes Mr. Gait, "is made up of all undoubted descendants of foreigners and converts from the higher castes of the Hindus."[2] The rest of the community falls into the second section. "In some places a third class, called Arzāl or 'lowest of all,' is added. It consists of the very lowest castes, such as the Halalkhor, Lālbegi, Abdāl, and Bedīya, with whom no other Muhammadan would associate, and who are forbidden to enter the mosque or to use the public burial-ground."[2]

Except in very exceptional circumstances, no member of the Ashrāf class will give his daughter in marriage to a man of inferior grade.

Indian converts to Muhammadanism and their descendants forming the lower section of the community have fallen quite naturally into endogamous groups, governed, as regards social life, after the manner of the regular Hindu castes.

[1] *Pilgrimage to Al-Madinah and Mecca*, vol. ii. p. 2. From their belief in metempsychosis, the Nakhawilahs were probably of Indian origin.

[2] *The Census of India*, 1901. Report, pp. 543, 544.

CASTE IN INDIA—*continued*

SECTION IV.—Caste outside the Hindu system—A digressional study.

NO little amused wonder and supercilious criticism on the part of Europeans has been aroused by the caste system of India, which has generally been regarded as an absurd, unhealthy, social phenomenon, without parallel elsewhere.

The system, it must be admitted, has very marked peculiarities of its own, but caste prejudices, and institutions based on such prejudices, are not wholly absent from social life outside India, even in highly civilised states of the Western World. And a little consideration of such indications of caste feeling will help us to account in some measure for the more salient characteristics of the Indian system, or at any rate serve to clear our minds of certain unfounded prejudices and offensive cant.

I am well aware that an attempt to establish any resemblance between the class distinctions which exist in Europe and the hereditary caste corporations of Hinduism, though it might be viewed with favour by educated Indians, would be scouted by the ordinary Englishman, who prides himself upon the homogeneity of his people, his free institutions, and his democratic ideals; and it must be admitted that *heredity* does not, at present, except in rare cases, form an indispensable feature of the classes into which European society is divided; but it is nevertheless undeniable that, even in Europe, certain genuine *hereditary caste distinctions* have at various times been maintained by law, and are to be found there even at the present day.

One much derided peculiarity of the Hindu caste system

is the hereditary character of trades and occupations, and in this connection it is interesting to recall to mind that at certain epochs the law in Europe has compelled men to keep, generation after generation, to the calling of their fathers without the option of change.

An instance in point is the organisation of the State under the laws laid down by the Emperor Diocletian and his successors.

> "This organisation established in the Roman world a personal and hereditary fixity of professions and situations, which was not very far removed from the caste system of the East. . . . Members of the administrative service were, in general, absolutely bound to their employments; they could not choose their wives or marry their daughters outside of the collegia to which they respectively belonged, and they transmitted their obligations to their children. . . . In municipalities the *curiales*, or members of the local senates, were bound, with special strictness, to their places and their functions, which often involved large personal expenditure. . . . Their families, too, were bound to remain; they were attached by the law to the *collegia* or other bodies to which they belonged. The soldier, procured for the army by conscription, served as long as his age fitted him for his duties, and his sons were bound to similar service.
>
> . . . .
>
> "In a constitution of Constantine (A.D. 332) the *colonus* is recognised as permanently attached to the land. If he abandoned his holding, he was brought back and punished; and anyone who received him had not only to restore him but to pay a penalty. He could not marry out of the domain; if he took for wife a *colona* of another proprietor, she was restored to her original locality, and the offspring of the union were divided between the estates. The children of a colonus were fixed in the same status, and could not quit the property to which they belonged."[1]

To the foregoing may be added that in England an ancient enactment required all men who at any time took up the calling of coal-mining or drysalting, to keep to that

[1] J. K. Ingram, LL.D., *History of Slavery and Serfdom*, pp. 74–78.

occupation for life, and enjoined that their children should also follow the same employment. This law was only repealed by statutes passed in the 15th and 39th years of the reign of George III.; that is in the lifetime of the fathers of many men who are with us to-day.

A more striking European example of a compulsory hereditary calling, common enough in the Middle Ages and down to the last century in Russia, is that of the serfs bound to the soil from generation to generation. Then again there existed through long periods of European history, the institution of hereditary slavery, with all its abominations.

In the social fabric of all countries are to be found certain classes which owing to various circumstances, political or other, are possessed of hereditary privileges, titles, and offices giving them precedence over the rest. These constitute the *aristocracy,* and at the bottom of the social scale in Europe, as elsewhere, are the *workers.* In India, for reasons explained later, it is the sacerdotal caste which is at present, and which has long been the hereditary Hindu aristocracy.

Below the aristocracy and above the proletariat we everywhere find a medley of classes, yet tolerably well defined; each with its pretensions stoutly asserted and jealously guarded. Such, for example, are the divisions based upon landed proprietorship; educational distinctions, as the learned professions lay and clerical; and those which are connected with mercantile affairs and trade pursuits.

Between the different grades of the social scale there exists a *matrimonial taboo,* and a woman of any recognised class who "marries beneath her," marries a man lower down in the social scale, is rejected of the class in which she was born, and is regarded by her former friends with aversion and contempt far greater than they feel for any member of the class to which she has descended.

Men who marry women of inferior social grade suffer in a similar way; but by no means to the same degree as women who marry below the rank in which they were born. Yet it may be noted that amongst the very exclusive German ruling classes and higher aristocracy a *mésalliance* on the part of a prince or noble is visited with the gravest penalties, including social ostracism and deprivation of rights. Herein we have caste prejudice strongly displayed.

Of the feelings which find expression in the well-understood social laws just glanced at, *pride of blood* is the most important, usually implying a claim to dominance at some time or other; such claims being often of a somewhat shadowy nature, as where an English family pride themselves upon the fact that a direct ancestor of theirs *came over with William the Norman,* the implication being that their ancestor was one of the conquerors of alien race from across the sea who subdued the native Anglo-Saxons in the eleventh century, and ruled over them.

Amongst men of kindred races professing the same faith and practically of the *same colour*, caste distinctions though they may be set up after conquest by the dominant nationality cannot, except in the case of serfs or slaves, be long maintained, because the offspring of women of the subject race by men of the conquering tribes or nations are able, without attracting special attention, to assume the status and enjoy the privileges of their fathers.

With the decline of the warlike spirit, the exaltation of commercialism, and the pronounced worship of wealth, a new source of pride has been introduced arising out of *the power of exploiting others* which the possession of money confers, though it must be admitted that this same commercialism has also tended to the discounting of hereditary class distinctions. Of the arrogance which is based upon the possession of a long purse no illustration is needed.

Besides the social barriers arising out of birth, opulence, knowledge, or occupation, there are others due to *religious differences* which are serious, often insuperable, obstacles to intermarriage, and tend to disseverance. Here the priesthood plays an important rôle. For the jealous maintenance of their own jurisdiction and power, but ostensibly for the protection of their flocks from deadly spiritual contamination by misbelievers, the priests of each religion or sect strenuously interdict, and visit with social penalties, all marriages between members of their own Church or denomination and outsiders, even of the same religion. Where powerful enough to impose their will on the laws of the country, intermarriages between members of divergent sects are made illegal. Hence, as is well known, unions between Roman Catholics, the followers of the orthodox Greek Church, and Protestants, generally are discouraged, or even actively opposed by the priests, and are, on that account, not very frequent. Even amongst Protestant sects the tendency to endogamy is apparent; for example, we have the Quakers, who since the formation of the sect about two hundred and fifty years ago, have intermarried mostly within the sect.

However, as already noted, it is not in communities made up of races of the same colour that prejudices giving rise to social or caste distinctions are most in evidence. It is when the contrast in colour between rulers and ruled is accentuated that such prejudices are rampant. Good contemporary examples are to hand in the relations subsisting between white men and negroes in the Southern States of the American Union; between European intruders and the black indigenous peoples of South Africa, and between the British in India and their brown or black subjects. Each of these examples differs materially from the others in many important respects, but all three have certain common features and may be studied with advantage.

If we consider the condition of society in the United States of America, a racial problem of surpassing interest presents itself to us. We are confronted with the results of the dominance of race over race in a definite and most instructive form. There four distinct varieties of human kind, differentiated from each other by anatomical peculiarities, by colour, and by civilisation, dwell together—a dominant white population of mixed European races; remnants of the so-called Red-Indian race; certain colonies of Chinese and Japanese; and a compact mass of about twelve millions of the black descendants of West Africans imported into the country as slaves, not conquered but kidnapped or else bought with gold, and only emancipated from bondage as recently as 1863.

Here the dominant whites disallow all matrimonial relations between their women and men of the other races, more especially the black. To such a degree is this sentiment encouraged that in the Southern States of the Union, an outrage by a black man on a white woman is generally avenged by the death of the negro at the hands of infuriated whites, who very rarely suffer any punishment whatever for such lawless acts.

Whites and blacks, even though they happen to belong to the same Christian sect or denomination, do not worship together, they do not attend the same schools,[1] do not dine together, or even sit at the same tables, do not travel in the same cars, and are buried in distinct cemeteries. The white man does not object to his food being cooked or served up for him by the black man; nor is he polluted by the black man's touch; but, these points being waived, the resemblance between the relations of white men and negroes in the Southern States of the Union is strikingly similar to that of the highest and lowest castes amongst Hindus in India.

Repression of the blacks in the United States and elsewhere is usually explained and justified by attributing it to an inherent and unalterable physical repulsion, *i.e., instinctive and unconquerable race antipathy.* That striking differences between races, as respects physiognomy, colour, temperament, intellectual attainments, and customs must necessarily lead to social incompatibility is obvious; but what has been persistently preached regarding deep-seated, instinctive, and uncontrollable race antipathy would be more convincing if the white man shrank with repugnance from the black or red woman. But this is not so! White men had for

[1] In 1904 an Act was passed in the State of Kentucky, imposing a fine of fifty dollars a day on any white person attending a negro school, or any negro attending a school for white persons.

Following the example of their rulers, the Redskins find their racial susceptibilities outraged by negro children being allowed to attend schools where *their* children are taught, and two years ago made representations to the United States Government on the subject.

In California Japanese children are, at the present time, excluded from the public schools; but the Japs, victorious over the Russians, are not likely to put up for long with such an indignity.

centuries formed irregular unions with their black female slaves, the result being an addition to the *slave population* of persons of mixed descent.

When in the fulness of time the slave population was at length endowed with political freedom, at a date within the memory of many now living, the members of this mixed race preferred to mate with their own kind rather than with the pure blacks, and, more than that, the mixed race exhibited a marked tendency to subdivide into more or less exclusive groups, those least related by consanguinity to the despised black stock claiming racial and social superiority.

That white men have nowhere shuddered at the embraces of black women is an indisputable fact; but on the other hand, that white women of a dominant nationality, being fully aware of the social degradation involved in any union, whether regular or irregular, with men of a subject and more particularly a black subject race, should shrink from them is at least understandable, but such aversion has nothing whatever to do with *instinctive race antipathy.*

Where distinct races, differentiated by colour, come into contact as conquerors and subjects, and more especially when the rulers, almost invariably invaders and aggressors, are, as is commonly the case, in the minority, the dread of losing their *right to exploit* the subject peoples by amalgamating with them ever so little is so keen, that caste feelings are fanatically fostered even to the extremes seen to-day in certain parts of South Africa—Transvaal and Natal, for example—where the natives are denied all political rights in their own land, are compelled in urban centres to live in appointed sites quite apart from their over-lords, subject to many galling restrictions,[1] where even temporary illicit connections between immoral white women and black, brown or yellow men, are punishable under the law, and where men of non-European race are subjected to the humiliating indignity of being obliged to walk in the roadway, while the footways are reserved for whites alone. This

[1] For example, to keep within doors after a certain fixed hour not long after sunset, and to carry passes with them to prove their identity, etc.

last is an almost identical reproduction of the treatment which used to be experienced by the *pariahs* in Southern India under Hindu rule, and which scandalised good Europeans so much in the past. That an Aryan Brahman from Central Asia should despise an aboriginal Pariah seemed a ridiculous and outrageous display of caste prejudice; but when it comes to the case of Europeans and Kaffirs, the matter seems to present a different aspect.

The position of the British Indian in the Transvaal and other parts of South Africa is peculiarly instructive. He has no political rights, and possesses neither social nor commercial equality. His *racial inferiority* is the ostensible cause of the position assigned to him; but it is acknowledged, even officially, that the British Indian owes his unfair disabilities to his marked success as a tradesman to the pecuniary detriment of his white competitors.

How mere industrial competition engenders race-hatred is exemplified by a quite recent and novel incident, the immigration of some 2500 Sikhs into British Columbia, regarding which Col. Falk Warren writes in November 1906, that although the conduct of these immigrants has been entirely exemplary, "a campaign of calumny and vituperation has been and continues to be engineered against them, to which the politicians who seek to maintain the labour vote are forced to submit."[1]

In India the British form a distinct caste, the most exclusive and haughty *varna* in the land. Though, theoretically, Englishmen laugh at and condemn caste, they, like others, are sticklers for it whenever their own interests are concerned, and, whatever their official utterances may be, Anglo-Indians are well pleased that the caste-ridden Hindus are what they are. To members of the ruling race in private life, no one is more distasteful than the denationalised Hindu gentleman, whatever his rank, who, putting aside his caste prejudices, and willing to conform to European social laws and etiquette, would seek to establish intimate friendly relations with the disinterested exiles, who devote their lives to the thankless task of governing and uplifting their Indian fellow-subjects.

[1] *Pioneer Mail* (Allahabad), 11th January 1907.

I have made it clear, I hope, that the feeling of race antagonism, which is at the root of caste distinctions, lies *primarily* in a sense of the danger to life, authority, privileges or trade profits likely to ensue from any fusion or friendly intercourse between the rulers and the ruled, as such blending or association would inevitably undermine the assumed natural superiority of the ruling race (usually a minority), damage their prestige, curtail their exclusive privileges or commercial gains, and be subversive of the existing dominancy, whether political or economic.

It may be urged that in the United States of America the blacks are numerically inferior to the whites, and are now *free citizens of the Great Republic*, and that the repulsion felt towards them by the whites is therefore not that of rulers towards a more or less dangerous subject race. Without admitting—for no one *could* do so—that the negro in the United States of America is a free man, with the rights and privileges of a citizen, since he is kept from the polls by actual violence or fraud, I would point out that the emancipated slave is, by reason of his emancipation, thrown, as a wage-earner, into unavoidable competition with free white labour of all kinds, and this renders him more personally odious to the white man than ever he was before. Besides, the white employer has now lost the power of exploiting the negro as he formerly did, and the white business man can no longer ignore him as a competitor, however heavily handicapped, in the general struggle for wealth, which means power. Moreover, the very fact that the negroes in the States were, not so long ago, a servile race, only widens the gulf between whites and blacks, for, laws or no laws, the taint of their long slavery still clings to the negro race, and will continue to do so. However, it is undoubtedly the industrial competition of the *free* negro and the free white which is *at present* the most important factor in encouraging and embittering the race-hatred which disfigures the relations of the whites and the negroes in the United States.[1]

[1] That under certain reasonable economic and administrative conditions white men and negroes can live together in harmony and to their mutual advantage, is evident from the present state of Jamaica, as has been shown by Mr. Sydney Olivier in his little book *White Capital and Coloured Labour.*

From a general survey of the matter it may be asserted that, carried away by conceit, a dominant race naturally arrogates to itself a fundamental, inherent, and permanent superiority, and Western science explains such claims by setting up anthropological standards based on morphological, and especially craniological peculiarities; and offers various plausible theories of race evolution, leading to the foregone conclusion that any mixture of the superior with inferior races can result in nothing but degeneration, and should therefore be avoided by the superior stock at all costs, even the persecution and, if necessary, extermination of the inferior. Much has been written on these subjects, but it is perhaps worth recalling to mind that, practically, as the world's history shows, the *superior* of two races at any period is the one that, having subdued the other, finds itself in a position which enables its members to swagger as *masters* and *better men* in comparison with the vanquished, and, for *the time being*, the claim is undoubtedly tenable.

If what has been already stated be correct, the comprehension of the problem of the genesis and evolution of *race prejudice* does not present insurmountable difficulties.

Assuming as a permanent fact that the climatic conditions—temperature, sunshine, moisture, soil, and elevation above sea-level—of various portions of the earth's surface will always present marked differences, it will, no doubt, be granted that any tribe, or body of men established for a *long* period of time on any particular locality would develop, in response to its environment, such special morphological and psychological characteristics as would differentiate it from the races or types of men evolved elsewhere under dissimilar climatic conditions. Now, if rivalry and competition, whether political or commercial, arise between such *distinct* peoples of alien civilisations, unbearable irritation and fierce antagonisms are generated, feelings which find expression in acts of hostility, conquest, and oppression on the part of the stronger; such acts being justified before the world by exaggerated vilification of the down-trodden people, who, filled with resentment, indulge in what reprisals they can or dare attempt. The vilification just referred to reiterated, generation after generation, comes to be accepted as embodying irrefragable verities, and breeds a settled contempt and aversion for the weaker, vanquished people in the minds of men and women of the dominant race; the prejudice thus established and perpetuated being easily mistaken for a *fundamental instinct* due to subtle causes traceable to eternal and unalterable laws of nature.

The foregoing studies bearing on caste in the social life of communities outside India and outside Hinduism, although deliberately kept within very narrow limits, reveal the existence of certain notable lines of social cleavage, traceable to various causes, the most important being: *Racial pride* on the part of members of tribes or nationalities which are, or have at some time previous been predominant, such pride being greatly accentuated by differences of colour when they exist; *pride in hereditary privileges*, offices, and titles indicative of ancestral superiority; and *greed* evidenced by a strong desire on the part of a ruling class to exploit the conquered for their own advantage.

Among minor causes of social cleavage in communities may be instanced: Incompatibility, and often animosity arising out of *religious differences; educational inequalities* as affecting whole classes; for example, the priestly and learned professions as compared with the working classes; and, lastly, the nature of the *occupation* followed for a livelihood.

Out of the sentiments, motives, and circumstances just detailed, arise in all societies many well-defined religious groups, and many clearly marked social ranks with certain arbitrary, perhaps unreasonable conventions of their own, the disregard of which is visited with penalties or disabilities more or less pronounced. The conventions I refer to have their *raison d'être* in the selfish and most natural desire of each group or rank to maintain, as far as may be possible, the social barriers between its own and other *lower* sections of the community, and consequently to discourage intimate or even friendly intercourse, and more particularly marriage, between members of distinct groups. That such conventions or caste prejudices are considered indispensable for the stability of communities, may account for their universality.

India could not, of course, be exempt from the operation of so general a law; but India exhibits the social phenomena of caste in a peculiar form. Its caste divisions are multitudinous and well defined. All of them, and not only a few as elsewhere, are hereditary, and their maintenance has the semblance of a *religious* duty, inasmuch as it is strongly supported in the case of each group by the Brahmans, who guide the spiritual life of each separate community. In this last stated fact lies the salient distinguishing feature of the Hindu system. It is a *quasi-religious system*; hence independent of secular laws, and instead of being a cause for heart-burning and jealousy, is more often than not a source of pride even amongst members of the humbler castes. So deeply is caste feeling rooted amongst the Indian people that not only do Hindus respect the caste system, but, as explained already, Hindus converted to Islam also, to some extent, surrender themselves to its potent hereditary influence, and often, too, Christianised Indians cannot quite emancipate themselves from its thraldom.[1]

[1] The native Christian headmaster of a mission school was asked in a court of justice what his religion was.

He replied: "Brahman-Christian."

The European judge, not recognising such a sect, asked for more information.

The headmaster then reiterated his former statement that he was a "Brahman-Christian," adding with some warmth: "I cannot call myself simply a Christian when that *Choorah* (sweeper) there is also a Christian. I am a Brahman-Christian, sir," and he said this by way of asserting his claim to racial superiority, not desiring that it should be forgotten because he had adopted a new creed.

CASTE IN INDIA—*continued*

SECTION V.—An attempt to throw some light upon the genesis and evolution of the Hindu caste system.

HOW the Hindu caste system really originated we do not actually know, and never shall know. But by the laborious researches of many capable inquirers and the intelligent investigations of many competent English officials, aided by native staffs, a great store of facts relating to the present state and past history of the Hindu caste system has been gradually accumulated, and several attempts have been made to derive from the data thus made available some more or less satisfactory explanation of the origin and development of the system. We have proof that it is of old standing, that it has not been exempt from mutation, and that it has been of gradual development. We are, moreover, able to trace the formation of certain new castes in India within quite recent times. The long past history of the world is not to be read like an open book; but, as in the science of geology, so in history, a close study of recent and contemporary happenings may help us to gain an insight into operations and events of which no direct or reliable records are available.

The preliminary studies, to which the previous section was devoted, show there are certain social and political conditions which, wherever they exist, have, quite irrespective of Hinduism, tended towards the genesis of hereditary caste distinctions. With this knowledge to guide us, and by the light of such fragmentary traditional and historical data as are available, we may not unreasonably hope to arrive at more or less satisfactory ideas regarding the origin and growth of the exceedingly complex caste system as it exists to-day in India.

As stated previously, the Sanskrit word for caste is *varna*, meaning *colour*, and this gives us at least one important clue to the solution of the problem, for it shows clearly that the Hindu caste system arose primarily out of the contact of races strongly differentiated by colour. What such contact leads to, even amongst nations contemporary with ourselves, we have already seen. But the conditions and circumstances of the old-world racial conflict, out of which emerged by gradual development the Hindu caste system, were widely different from those which have obtained in the United States of America, or in South Africa, or in India under British rule.

At a remote period, perhaps 1500 B.C., certain Aryan[1] tribes coming from Central Asia commenced invading the north-western corner of the already partially inhabited territories now known as India, bringing with them a religion which may be characterised as a vague physiolatry, represented more or less, at a later stage, by four collections of hymns known as Vedas.[2] Their form of government seems to have been constructed on *clan lines*. It

[1] From certain resemblances and affinities which the study of languages has revealed, philologists infer that the most important European races on the one hand, and the inhabitants of Persia, Armenia, Afghanistan, and Northern India on the other hand, had a common origin, and the name *Aryan* has been used to designate this group of Indo-European nations. As to where the original home or cradle of the primitive Aryans lay, the philologists have not been able to agree. Some find it is Central Asia, others in Europe.

[2] The Vedas are the *Rig*, the *Sama*, the *Yajur*, and the *Atarva*. The first of these and the most important is a collection of some 1028 hymns addressed, for the most part, to personified powers of Nature, such as Agni (Fire), Surya (The Sun), Indra (The Atmosphere), etc. The *Sama* and the *Yajur Vedas* are composed almost exclusively of the hymns of the *Rig* Veda arranged for sacrificial purposes. The *Atarva* Veda, of later origin than the others, is a collection of hymns taken from the *Rig* Veda intended to serve as charms to prevent or to cure diseases, to drive away demons, t frustrate sorcerers and enemies, to ensure victory in battle, to promote virility, to obtain a husband or wife, to arouse the passionate love of a man or a woman, to guarantee safety at an assignation, to allay jealousy, to stimulate the growth of the hair, and to secure a hundred other advantages both trivial and important; often, of course, at the expense of others.

was in fact a *clan organisation*, a federation of separate tribes, sub-tribes, and clans under their own chiefs.[1]

And, if the learned M. Senart is correct, the social organisation of these Aryan invaders was based on principles which underlie the later caste system of the Hindus. Unfortunately, however, there is no direct evidence for this conclusion, which is based upon certain resemblances and analogies in the social customs relating to marriage and food amongst the Greeks and Romans on the one hand, and the Hindus on the other.

The races and tribes inhabiting India when the Aryans came into the country had, of course, their own peculiar cults and languages, and also their polities, which last were probably, in most cases, tribal and not unlike that of the Aryans themselves.

One tribe of Aryan invaders would naturally be followed by another, and yet another, one clan would drift after another as the attractions of the sunny plains to the south of the Himalayas became known in the home lands of the Aryan race. Two distinct streams of Aryan invaders or immigrants composed of distinct tribes and clans seem, according to our best authorities, to have penetrated the new territories; one from the north-west into the Punjab and the other through Gilgit and Chitral into the plains watered by the Ganges and Jumna,[2] and there can be no doubt that following the line of least resistance, or attracted by special natural advantages of soil or climate, the separate clan organisations or even the distinct clans *squatted* where they could, and often out of touch with each other.

The proportion of women which each immigrant clan could bring along with it would naturally depend upon many circumstances; but in any case there would be a deficiency of Aryan women in each intrusive group; just as there is at the present time a paucity of European women in colonies planted abroad in newly acquired territories.

During the long centuries of conflict which followed

[1] B. H. Baden-Powell, *The Indian Village Community*, pp. 192–195.

[2] This latter stream of immigrants was suggested by Dr. Hoernle to account for the Aryo-Dravidian type of the inhabitants of the United Provinces.

these invasions and witnessed the successful, but very gradual, progress of the Aryans eastward and southward, contact with alien forms of belief and unavoidable miscegenation must have tended to modify the original religion and the social life of the Aryan invaders. Desirous of preserving their national faith, and above all their racial ascendancy amidst the dangers with which they were surrounded in their new southern home, the invaders appear to have recognised with instinctive wisdom the important truth that for the attainment of these ends a first and most essential step would be the establishment of a *hereditary priesthood* for the efficient performance of rites and sacrifices, and as custodians and interpreters of the law, and of a *hereditary class of warriors* always ready for the fight.

Professional pride and the requirements of their respective callings caused these two important classes to become exclusive communities within the body politic. The remainder of the Aryan invaders naturally fell into a third noble class, mostly concerned, as agriculturists and tradesmen, to promote the creation and accumulation of wealth; while the conquered tribes would, without doubt, supply the servile element in the community, and so constitute a fourth class of decidedly inferior status, debarred from meddling with matters religious, and denied the privilege of carrying arms.

When established as conquerors, the Aryans would, of course, comport themselves like other successful races in their dealings with subject peoples, and endeavour to secure for themselves the maximum amount of contributions and service from the conquered. Their own polity would suggest that the subject peoples should, for revenue and other governmental purposes, be considered and held responsible by tribes, clans, and even occupations, and this we have reason to believe was the plan actually adopted by the Aryans in their dealings with the Indian aborigines.[1]

As a consequence of their predominance, and by way of justification of their high-handed dealings with the subdued tribes, the ruling race would naturally vilify the latter, and

[1] B. H. Baden-Powell, C.I.E., *The Indian Village Community*, chap. v. sec. ii.

in the old Hindu literature the black autochthones are represented as disgusting monsters and vile demons.

The various detachments of Aryans who, from time to time, under the pressure of circumstances moved forward amongst the aborigines would become smaller and smaller as they divided off to find suitable locations, while the proportion of Aryan women amongst these dwindling bands would also be reduced, so that the immigrants would, to a large extent, be forced to take wives from the people amongst whom they intruded themselves. But, as Mr. Risley has pointed out, miscegenation would be discontinued as soon as each mixed tribe had a sufficient number of women to provide itself with wives. At this stage, intermarriage with the aborigines would be strictly tabooed. Thus endogamous communities of mixed descent would be formed in the midst of the aborigines. But finality is impossible in human institutions. The very attainment of a position of security and dominance would call into play forces which in all societies tend to produce distinct classes and grades, such forces being strengthened in the case of Aryan immigrants by their already well-established caste ideals. Under the influence of these general and special causes, as well as for administrative purposes on the clan system, the settled community we have had in view would naturally fall, or be divided into many minor groups, each group being made up mostly of allied families united by a *common occupation.*

The various Aryan mixed tribes in their new and often widely separated homes would be differentiated from one another owing to various causes, such as the length of time they had been cut off from the parent stock, the ethnical peculiarities, religions, and civilisations of the particular aboriginal races amongst whom they had established themselves, and the extent to which they had intermarried with these natives. Each of these distinct Aryan settlements would become the centre of a new group of castes.

In their isolation, the members of each little band claiming Aryan descent would draw closer the bonds of clanship, and though of mixed blood would become prouder Aryans, and greater sticklers for exclusiveness than their stay-at-home kindred. And we find this very peculiarity to-day. Fanatical respect for the observance of caste regulations does not exist in an equal degree throughout India. There is, as might have been expected, no uniformity in this respect, since the racial peculiarities, the political history, and the prevailing conditions of life are extremely dissimilar in the different countries which constitute the sub-continent which we designate India; but at the same time more laxity in certain points is observable in Aryan centres, the Punjab for example, than would be tolerated in the more remote provinces of Madras and Bengal, where the Aryan element is present in the Brahman caste alone.

However great may have been the martial and political successes of the Aryans in the extensive regions south of the Himalayas, they are probably credited with more than they achieved; an idea which derives support from the absence from India of slavery of the kind conquerors have not uncommonly imposed upon the peoples they have subdued.

The ethnological facts at our command show clearly that the Aryans were not able to destroy or even displace the Dravidian and other races, which probably formed the bulk of the population of the lands they invaded. To this day the Dravidian retains a very conspicuous and important place amongst the races of India, either in a pure state or mingled with the Aryans, Scythians, and Mongolians. Towards the south and east of the peninsula is the stronghold of the Dravidians, whilst the influence of Aryan blood is most marked in Kashmir, the Punjab, and Rajputana, and, in a less degree, in the territory now known as the United Provinces.

According to the ethnological map which accompanies the latest Indian Census Report, the Indo-Aryan race has not even a preponderating place in modern India, its ethnic influence being, as already stated, confined to Kashmir, the Punjab, Rajputana, and the United Provinces. Yet even where the population is non-Aryan the Brahmanical religion is honoured, and Brahmans hold the highest place in the social scale. It has to be noted, however, that the Brahmans in non-Aryan centres, though they usually exhibit Aryan characteristics, in some cases belong undoubtedly to the aboriginal stock, *e.g.*, Mongolians in Assam, and Dravidians in Madras.[1]

If we turn our attention from the Brahmans to the religion associated with them, we find that the Hindu religion and the gods worshipped are by no means identical over India. Hinduism as we find it to-day is a congeries of many and various indigenous cults, supplied with suitable myths and legends designed to link each with the others in some more or less direct way. Hinduism everywhere requires veneration of the cow, supports the caste system, and assigns the highest place in the body politic to the hereditary Brahman priesthood. Behind the local Brahmanical cults we have a background of Pantheism, with belief in reincarnations and the doctrine of *Karma*, this latter being unknown to the Indo-Aryans of the Vedic age. How these momentous doctrines were evolved, is a question still in obscurity. Were they thought out by the Indo-Aryans in their new home, or did they find the germs of them already developed amongst one or other of the more advanced Dravidian races of the South? Certain it is that the belief in reincarnations and *Karma*—an essential feature of Hinduism as well as of Buddhism, Jainism, and Sikhism—is held by a very large proportion of the world's inhabitants, not only in India but far beyond its borders.

Three points in the foregoing statements call for special consideration: the remarkable position accorded to the Brahmans throughout India even in vast territories where the Aryan race is not ethnically represented; the fact that Brahmans are not always of the Aryan race; and that under the common name, Hinduism, are embraced many very dissimilar cults.

Now the very exceptional position of the Brahmans is a fact of the greatest significance, for it suggests that it was the Aryan priestly caste which made an intellectual conquest of lands where the fighting Aryans never established themselves. That the Brahmans by intermarrying with the alien races lost their pure nationality in the course of time need not be doubted; but the fact that

[1] Dr. J. N. Bhattacharjee, *Hindu Castes and Sects*, pp. 58, 59, and 96.

in the Dravidian and Mongolo-Dravidian countries of India Brahmans are sometimes not of Aryan race at all is, I believe, due to the assumption of the Brahmanic name, with its status and privileges, by non-Aryans; a surmise which is supported by the case of the numerically insignificant caste of Amma Kodagas or Kaveri Brahmans of Coorg, who being the indigenous priesthood devoted to the worship of the Goddess Amma, have set up Brahmanical pretensions.[1] To this may be added the case of the Bhojakas of Jvalamukhi in the Punjab, who, although claiming to belong to the Hindu priesthood, are believed to be descendants of a servile class connected from of old with the famous temple there.[2]

The heterogeneity of Hinduism is to my mind a result of the *Brahman conquest of India.* As missionaries, the Brahmans would receive into their fold, as indeed they have been known to do in quite recent times, any tribe or clan that agreed to accept their spiritual guidance and leadership. They would, with rare liberality, find places in the Hindu Pantheon for the gods of the tribes won over to Brahmanism, and would guarantee the integrity of time-honoured tribal customs, especially those regulating marriage.

By these means the Brahmans would facilitate the spread of Brahmanism, while securing the allegiance of their new disciples. For the maintenance of the position and influence of the priestly order over their flock, it was of the highest importance that their hereditary superiority should be acknowledged and upheld. Nothing could possibly conduce more to that end than the acceptance by the people of a divinely sanctioned caste system of which the priests should be recognised as the unapproachable heads, and it would be for these priests to encourage the formation and perpetuation of such a caste system by every means at their command.

Each group of Brahmans successful in a new territory would desire to exploit the tribes which they had been instrumental in bringing within the pale of Brahmanism,

[1] Dr. John Wilson, *Indian Caste*, vol. ii. pp. 72, 73.
[2] *Idem*, vol. ii. p. 133.

and to ensure that such tribes should belong, as it were, to their own particular family for ever. Nothing could further these objects better than that annexed tribes should be crystallised, as it were, into distinct groups owning allegiance to their own special Brahmans, and separated by social barriers from other tribes annexed and exploited by other successful Brahman missionaries.

For the better understanding of the situation which I have endeavoured to picture, let us imagine that in Europe and America all contributions towards Foreign Christian Missions ceased; so that the missionaries abroad in Asia and Africa would have no pecuniary or other support from home.

The Christian missionaries in India, faithful to their labour of love, would, we may presume, continue to live in the land of their adoption, for the good of that land; but notwithstanding their unselfishness they would be driven to make what living they could out of the generosity of their several flocks. Now these flocks, though all professing Christianity, would belong to distinct and sometimes hostile denominations. To ensure their own subsistence, and that of their children, the missionaries of each sect would endeavour, even more than they do at present, to keep their respective flocks uncontaminated by intermarriage or intercourse with the unconverted, and they would strenuously guard their spiritual children from adopting the dangerous opinions and objectionable practices of other Christian sects. Common prudence would dictate these feelings, and self-interest, coupled with paternal solicitude, would suggest to each missionary group the desirability of making their spiritual calling hereditary. Cut off from the home land, the Christian missionaries of alien race would, under the imagined conditions, doubtless form a distinctive caste. Left to their own resources, *uncontrolled by a central authority*, they would soon learn for their own advantage to relax the rules for the admission of converts to their fold, and many customs and even beliefs would then be tolerated and even accepted, which under existing circumstances are rigorously excluded.

Now to my thinking the position of the Brahman

missionaries in the midst of the aborigines of Dravidian stock was in many respects analogous to that of the Christian missionaries in the hypothetical situation in which I have just envisaged them.

Imitation on the part of the Dravidian tribes, clans, or groups of families won over to Brahmanism would facilitate the establishment of the clan or caste system, as the aborigines would naturally adopt the customs and more especially the prejudices of their spiritual guides, and strive to fit into the new system such endogamous or other marriage rules as obtained amongst themselves. Even to-day this process of transformation and the origination of caste is going on, especially in the eastern parts of India, and ought to be taken into account.

Of imitation, which in such cases is so powerful an agent in the moulding of habits and customs, we see something in the contemporary doings of native Christians, who are developing a marked tendency to adopt the manners and especially the prejudices of their European models.

Some castes probably originated in offshoot immigrant bands being entirely cut off from communication with the parent stock or other branches of the family. Unable to preserve the purity of their blood, language, or religion, such bands would in their isolation form exclusive communities of their own, falling as usual into occupational groups.

From the particulars which I have placed before the reader, it would appear that the genesis and evolution of the diverse castes which now exist in India, or have existed in times past, are due not to one, but to a multiplicity of different, subtle, and concurrent causes, some too illusive to be ascertained or gauged. But on the other hand there are undoubtedly a few of these causes so fundamental and of such general application that their influence and effect can be clearly traced throughout the long history of caste development. Nationality is one of these, for it cannot, I think, be questioned that a number of the different Hindu castes originated, in all probability, in the first instance from distinct if minor nationalities, tribes, or clans, having their own customs and psychological characteristics. Some local castes are obviously aggregations of families having a common hereditary occupation or trade; while other castes have undoubtedly arisen from religious (sectarian) schisms.

Mr. Risley's view that caste in India has an ethnic basis and arose out of conflicts between white and black races in the olden time, is to my mind substantially correct; but I believe that what I have urged regarding the deliberate and conscious action of the hereditary Brahmanic priesthood, in promoting and consolidating the caste system for the enhancement of their own power and pecuniary advantage, is as important a factor in the case as any other, and is indeed the vital peculiarity of the Hindu caste system, while giving it a quasi-religious dignity. Brahmans wherever they went amongst the aborigines *claimed the first place in society* by virtue of caste, and in so doing had necessarily, for the maintenance of their own pretensions, to build up or encourage the growth of a social system in which *caste* should be the fundamental feature. Only in a recognised caste system could their pretensions be treated with deference. Much religious and ritualistic latitude had to be conceded in order to secure and maintain the Brahmanic ascendancy, especially in places far removed from the Aryan homeland; and it is, I believe, to this enforced tolerance of local cults, and the absence of any *central authority*, that the great diversity of religions embraced under Hinduism is attributable.

CASTE IN INDIA—*continued*

SECTION VI.—**Caste considered with respect to its political and economic aspects and its probable future.**

CONTRASTING aristocracies with democracies, Dr. John Beattie Crozier, in his book *Civilisation and Progress,* makes certain remarks bearing upon the Indian caste system which as they represent the ordinary European views on the matter may profitably detain us a moment.

> "Besides in democracies," says Dr. Crozier, "where the least possible restraint is put on freedom of action, only such restraints are put on freedom or expression of thought as are indispensable for common morality; whereas, in aristocracies, besides these restraints, there is the more minute and circumstantial pressure, imposed on each individual, by a host of unwritten customs, prejudices, sentiments, and traditions. Take India and America as examples; one, of the most rigid of all forms of aristocracy, that of caste; the other, of the purest and most advanced of democracies; and what do we find? In India, the tyranny of custom, opinion, and mode of life is so great, that the slightest infringement is followed by a loss of caste, and the loss of caste is tantamount to a sentence of execution; and, from old habit and custom, this tyranny is worn so easily and smoothly that men walk about to all outward appearance as if they were really free. But in America freedom of thought and sentiment is so complete, that you have the spectacle, hitherto unknown, of Catholics and Protestants, Atheists and Mormons, Freelovers, Shakers, and Quakers all living quietly side by side in peaceful toleration; and the sense of liberty

> so acute, that the slightest restraint galls the spirit and raises aloud the cry of tyranny and oppression, which the effete aristocracies hearing from a distance regard with secret satisfaction as the forerunner of disruption and ruin."[1]

With what feelings "the effete aristocracies" may regard American protests against the slightest restraint imposed by authority does not concern me, but I feel strongly that the contrast which Dr. Crozier has instituted, in the above-quoted extract, between "America," which I presume means the United States, and India, is extremely infelicitous, for whatever may be the "freedom of thought and sentiment" enjoyed at the present time in the United States, quite as much "freedom of thought and sentiment" as regards philosophical and religious matters is now and has always been enjoyed in caste-ridden India, where for ages the greatest variety of sects and of religions also—not excluding various forms of Christianity—have existed peacefully, even as they do at the present time, while many practices, polygamy for example—fully sanctioned by the Old Testament—are recognised as lawful in India, though not tolerated in free America, where the Mormons have been forced to give it up. Again, it is an undeniable fact (as shown in a previous section) that in the United States *caste prejudices* on the part of the white races arising out of industrial competition between them and the black and yellow races are even more conspicuous, vehement, intolerant, and inimical to true liberty and equality than they are in India even under foreign rule. Further, Dr. Crozier's idea, which appears to be a very common one, that the slightest infringement of caste customs in India is visited with loss of caste, which "is tantamount to a sentence of execution," is, as we have already seen, absolutely incorrect. Permanent loss of caste is an infliction of *very rare* occurrence, and, though socially a very serious trouble, it does not, as I shall presently show, involve under British rule the loss or impairment of any civil or legal rights. Looking at all the facts without prejudice I am inclined to hold that a larger proportion of men and women lose their places irreparably in the ranks

[1] *Civilisation and Progress* (1888), pp. 356, 357.

of Western than of Hindu society, because amongst the Hindus there are prescribed methods—suitable religious ceremonies, purificatory rites, and reparation—by which lost status might be regained, whereas no such authoritative or recognised provision is made for the rehabilitation of the offender against society in the West.

The cool assumption of freedom from petty prejudices and from the tyranny of custom which Westerns commonly make in their supercilious criticisms of Oriental social and religious life would be amusing were it not grossly inaccurate and needlessly offensive. The tyranny of custom is not peculiar to India or to the East. Occidental or Oriental, each has his own more or less minute and rigid rules for the conduct of domestic life, the regulation of social intercourse, modes of eating and drinking, and the ordering of official functions. Each has his own canons with respect to dress, behaviour, etiquette, and honour, far more complicated perhaps in the West than in the East. But the Western, while conforming docilely, even slavishly, to the conventions which govern private and official intercourse at home, contemplates with raised eyebrows the dreadful burden which the Eastern bears unmurmuringly. But the Asiatic's burden is in ordinary life no heavier than his own; only it is different. That is all!

Amongst the more important forces now at work in determining the future of the caste system is the British Government in India, whose attitude in this matter deserves attention. As a rule, the British Indian Government ignores and thereby discourages all caste distinctions, and by placing all Indians upon a legal equality declines, no doubt rightly, to concede any special privileges to men of the superior castes in their relations with their fellow-countrymen. It has further by law deliberately undermined the coercive power of caste as a recognised *legal* institution, for Act XXI. of 1850 rules as follows:—

> "So much of any law or usage now in force within the territories of the East India Company as inflicts on any person forfeiture of rights and property, or may be held in any way to impair or affect any right of inheritance by reason of his or her having been

excluded from the communion of any religion or being deprived of caste, shall cease to be enforced as law in the Courts of the East India Company and in the Courts established by Royal Charter within the said territories."

In other words, no man, whatever be his offences against his caste, shall, on account of merely such offences, suffer any forfeiture of rights or property, even after being expelled from the society of his caste-fellows. That the law in question has seriously weakened the power previously enjoyed by both Hinduism and Islam for the restraining or punishing of apostasy is obvious. This point has been acknowledged, discussed, and justified by that well-known jurist Sir James Fitzjames Stephen.[1]

This attitude of the paramount authority towards the ancient caste regulations, due though it be to a natural want of sympathy with Hindu ideals, may possibly have proved acceptable to some sections of the lowest castes of the community. By the rest it has been ordinarily accepted and endured with the meekness which is characteristic of the Hindus; but beneath the calm exterior of patient acquiescence there may always be found a sensitiveness not far removed from suppressed irritation, and occasionally some positive act of culpable official ignorance or high-handedness has so outraged the deep-seated caste prejudices of a section, or it may be of the entire Hindu community, that the resentment aroused by it has had deplorable results. It would not be difficult to cull from the records of the past many examples to illustrate this statement; but it will suffice to take only the most startling instance of all, the great Sepoy revolt of 1857–58, writ large in blood-stained characters across the pages of Indian history.

Although this is not the place for a discussion of the many causes which led to that great upheaval, such as interference with immemorial religious customs and breaches of political faith on the part of the British in India, I may be permitted to state my conviction that the Mutiny would never have attained the formidable proportions it did had

[1] "Legislation under Lord Mayo," being chapter viii. vol. ii. of Sir W. W. Hunter's *Life of the Earl of Mayo*.

it not been for the *egregious and criminal folly* which led to the cartridges issued to the Sepoys from the Government manufactories being greased with the fat of *both cows and pigs*, the former abhorred by all Hindus on account of their veneration of the cow, the latter repugnant to all Muhammadans because of its impurity and condemnation by their Prophet.

For the comprehension of the matter it is necessary to bear in mind that the muskets for which the cartridges were supplied were all muzzle-loaders, that the cartridge case, which held the gunpowder and bullet in two compartments, was simply made of strong paper (known, for this very reason, as *cartridge* paper) well greased to exclude damp from the gunpowder. The military regulations required that the paper over the gunpowder end of the cartridge should be *bitten off* by the Sepoy before inserting the cartridge into the muzzle of the barrel, in order that the powder might be set free to run down to the nipple fixed at the lower end. The bullet with the paper case, of course, descended on top of the gunpowder, and both were driven home with the ramrod. Thus every Sepoy was forced, each time he loaded his musket, not only to handle, but actually to introduce into his mouth the fat of both kine and swine.

Now although the tendency of the caste system is undoubtedly to break up the body politic into more or less discordant communities, there is yet one deep-seated religious sentiment common to all Hindu castes alike, and that is profound, unreasoning veneration of the cow as a sacred animal, with the consequent horror of introducing beef into the mouth in any form, and, strange to say, it was this one universal caste prejudice which was contemptuously outraged by the greased cartridges issued to the Sepoys, amongst whom were serving a number of Brahmans.

Some, I am aware, discredit the story of the greased cartridges; but since the momentous days of 1857–58, which I passed in Calcutta, I have myself had no doubt about the matter, and was, therefore, not surprised to read the following in Lord Roberts' important book, *Forty-one Years in India:*

"The recent researches of Mr. Forrest in the records of the Government of India prove that the lubricating mixture used in preparing the cartridges was actually composed of the objectionable ingredients, cow's fat and lard, and that incredible disregard of the soldiers' religious prejudices was displayed in the manufacture of these cartridges. When the Sepoys complained that to bite them would destroy their caste, they were solemnly assured by their officers that they had been greased with a perfectly unobjectionable mixture. The officers, understanding, as all who have come in contact with natives are supposed to understand, their intense abhorrence of touching the flesh or fat of the sacred cow or the unclean pig, did not believe it possible that the authorities could have been so regardless of the Sepoys' feelings as to have allowed it to be used in preparing their ammunition; they, therefore, made this statement in perfect good faith. But nothing was easier than for the men belonging to the regiments quartered near Calcutta to ascertain, from the low-caste native workmen employed in manufacturing the cartridges at the Fort-William arsenal, that the assurances of their officers were not in accordance with facts, and they were thus prepared to credit the fables which the sedition-mongers so sedulously spread abroad, to the effect that the Government they served and the officers who commanded them had entered into a deliberate conspiracy to undermine their religion."[1]

After what has been stated in previous sections of this paper in respect to the pollution which a Hindu suffers from even involuntary contact with forbidden viands, it is unnecessary to enlarge upon the feelings of burning resentment and fanatical hatred which would be kindled in the breast of any Sepoy at finding that, by what would seem to him to be the deliberate act of the constituted authorities, he was being daily subjected to a process of defilement which, while degrading him in his own estimation, rendered him unfit to hold personal intercourse even with his own kindred and friends in his native village, whence he had willingly come forth to fight for rulers who, without provocation on his part, treated him and his religious

[1] Lord Roberts, *Forty-one Years in India*, vol. i. pp. 431 and 432.

scruples with immeasurable contempt. Who can wonder at the result?

The events just discussed show clearly that caste in India is a political force to be reckoned with; but I would direct attention to the fact that the circumstances connected with the case of the greased cartridges are so very extraordinary and exceptional, that the recurrence of anything even remotely resembling them is highly improbable. The general effect of the caste system has been to subdivide the nation into so many distinct and independent, often antipathetic social groups, that vigorous and sustained combined action for any great common object has been rendered extremely difficult, except in the very rare cases where the caste system itself seemed to be endangered or caste feeling cruelly outraged. On the other hand, the pride and exclusiveness of caste—not dependent on wealth or worldly position, but on an inalienable birthright—may have kept the Hindus during many centuries of foreign dominion from sinking to the dead level of serfdom; and it is quite conceivable, indeed not at all improbable, that the various caste organisations controlled by recognised caste leaders may be employed most effectively for special political ends, especially as already certain important castes hold regular congresses and conferences of their own. Nevertheless it cannot be denied that living always within and for the caste, with little interest beyond it, has hitherto tended to circumscribe each Hindu's outlook to such a degree that the idea of nationality is not natural to his understanding nor the sentiment of patriotism to his heart.

Mr. Oscar Browning, a cultured impressionist, "thinking imperially," says in a recent book:

"My visit to India persuaded me to tolerate purdah and to have an admiration for caste, and I should be sorry to hear either of them had been overthrown."[1]

Yes, and many another *imperialist* would, no doubt, be sorry to see the caste system die out in India, for such a change would inevitably add very considerably indeed to the task of governing and retaining England's immense Empire in the East.

[1] *Impressions of Indian Travel*, p. 230.

Besides the political there are other aspects of the Hindu caste system which call for attention. Considered from the industrial point of view, the Indian trade castes, though differing in many respects from the trades guilds of mediæval Europe, have played the part of such guilds in respect to the Indian handicrafts, and helped the preservation of ancient arts in no small degree, and to-day the value of the Indian caste *as a co-operative society in full working order* has been so far recognised that the official Registrar of Co-operative Credit Societies in the United Provinces recently suggested that the caste should be made the unit of co-operation.[1]

Viewed from the ethical standpoint, we are bound to allow that the organisation of the Hindu castes and sub-castes of closely allied family groups has proved an effective agency for the suppression of immorality and vice. That it has been very useful in the support and relief of the destitute poor is equally undeniable. In connection with this latter point I would make a passing reference to what was said, not long ago, by Mr. J. D. Rees at a meeting of the Society of Arts, to the effect that there was a larger proportion of people in receipt of relief at the expense of the State in England, in a normal year, than there was in India during the height of the (recent) famine.[2] To obviate any misunderstanding of the significance of this statement, and to place it in its proper light, it should be added that there are no poor rates for the support of paupers in India. If such rates were available, I should not like to predict what the result would be.

Turning to quite another aspect of the caste system, it may be noted that by it has been kept alive for ages the doctrine of the dignity of the hereditary priesthood, and incidentally of *learning* as represented by that privileged class. Caste, through its stubborn conservatism, has probably been the most efficient practical means of safeguarding Hinduism and maintaining its principles, traditions, and customs against religious reformers within its own body, and also against the aggressions of alien religions, being,

[1] *Agricultural Journal of India*, No. 2, 1906.

[2] *Journal of the Society of Arts*, 3rd March 1905.

as the Rev. Dr. John Wilson, of Bombay, wrote, "the grand obstacle to the triumph of the Gospel of Peace in India"; because, as a recent writer quaintly puts it, the keen Hindu mind perceives that "Redemption must mean loss of caste."[1]

Consequently, and very naturally, the Hindu caste system has incurred the unqualified condemnation of Christian missionaries, and of all who are interested in the Christianisation of India. And, without doubt, the inter-relation between caste and the foundations of Hinduism is both intimate and peculiar.

We may not know how or when certain hymns were written or incorporated with the sacred books of the Hindus, but it is none the less undeniable (*vide* page 50) that the advocates of the caste system can now appeal for support to the earliest of the Hindu Scriptures, the Vedas themselves, as regards the establishment of the four great *varnas*. Hence if the Vedas were to be given up, caste would lose its earliest recorded sanction; but who would expect the privileged hereditary castes to resign their advantages? Therefore while these advantages are worth fighting for, the sanctity and authority of the Vedas and the Scriptures based upon them will be strenuously maintained.

However, under the pressure of the new political and commercial conditions, a change is coming over the spirit of India. The worship of wealth is affecting the Indian in a striking degree. "It is depriving us," said a young Hindu to me, "of our Brahmans, who now rush into secular employment as the only means of obtaining the respect to which they have been accustomed."

As the British Government has honours only for the well-to-do, a desire for the possession of wealth is assuming a larger and larger place in the Indian mind, although it is, I understand, still true that in Indian society at social gatherings members of the same caste sit together, high and low, rich and poor alike, without too invidious distinctions, and that an indigent member of the clan may still be handed the hookah from

[1] Amy Wilson-Carmichael, *Things as they are: Mission Work in Southern India*, p. 20.

the lips of the prosperous man. But it may be safely predicted that respect for poverty and *Brahma Vidya* amongst this people will rapidly disappear, as, stimulated by Western example, the worship of Mammon takes a stronger hold upon him.

Amóngst the forces inimical to caste at the present time are the railways, which under British management do not show any favour to that institution. Promiscuous travelling now prevails throughout the country, and, every day in the year, hundreds of thousands of *twice-borns* sit in contact with Sudras, outcasts, and *Mlecchas* on the levelling benches of the railway cars, conveniently closing their eyes to the terrible contamination which such contiguity involves, or else enduring as best they can the really considerable hardships to which they are exposed.[1] Whether promiscuous railway travelling will in the long-run affect Hinduism itself we may well doubt, but it must lead to a relaxation or a more liberal interpretation of the stringent rules of the caste system as regards the specific issue of the contaminating effect of contact with men of inferior castes, and non-Hindus. We may trust the astute Brahmans to find a way of reconciling convenience with duty in this matter.

Like the railways, public hospitals and jails are institutions which, in their way, are inimical to the caste system, as within their walls the claims of caste are deliberately ignored, sometimes, I believe, more than ignored. In schools and colleges too, persons of all castes, except the lowest, and of different religions sit together in the same classrooms, join in the same games on the playground, and often reside in the boarding-houses attached to some of these seminaries.

[1] A couple of years ago at a public meeting, held in Bangalore, a Pandit of Benares discussed the inconveniences suffered by Brahmans while travelling on railways. The Pandit stated that the Brahman, unlike the other passengers, would not eat in cars or drink water when there were present men of other castes. Consequently the Brahman had to starve during the journey. The majority of the Brahmans travelled in third-class cars, and their condition was the more miserable as they had to mix with unclean people. What he wanted was the provision of separate cars for the use of Brahman passengers, as had long been provided for Europeans and Eurasians travelling third class.

There is in the Sepoy army a mingling of different castes, at any rate during the performance of military duties, and many minor prejudices no doubt get rubbed away by daily association with other than caste mates; and the more so when, as comrades in arms, common dangers and death itself are faced by them together.

Every year hundreds of Indian gentlemen visit Europe for purposes of study or mere pleasure, and in doing so wittingly transgress a well-established caste rule prohibiting Hindus from crossing the ocean or, indeed, any of the boundaries of India. While abroad these gentlemen fling to the winds many of the cherished prejudices of the caste system in which they have been reared, and although when they return home these *samu-drayais*, after purification, resume the obligations of the system, it can never be to them what it once was.[1] If, however, in this connection I should be expected to state that with the spread of English education the caste system will disappear, I must say I am by no means prepared to go so far, for I have known many Indian gentlemen, highly educated and holding very good positions in State departments, who were in no-wise anxious to free themselves or their children from the restraints of the caste system, and it does not seem to me that education alone will effect the great things which are expected of it.

Hindu Governments always did uphold caste distinctions and caste privileges, and when practicable they do so now, as in Nepal. But under British rule it is quite different, and able and worthy men of inferior caste rise to official positions in which they have men of higher castes under their orders. Such successful men, and their caste brethren also, naturally belittle the pretensions of the superior castes, and even scoff at the presumptuous claims of the Brahmans. I have myself known them to do so.

Then the administration of justice in India under its

[1] Some of the more recent religious codes are very severe upon Hindus who cross the sea. "Caste communion it is maintained . . . is not to be held with a person who has passed the sea in a ship, even though he may have performed penance for it, and, therefore, connection with such a person in this *Yuga* is reprehensible."—Dr. Wilson, *Indian Caste*, vol. i. pp. 403 and 405.

British rulers, with its recognition of the rights of the individual irrespective of his caste or creed, may tend to weaken the caste sentiment by awakening aspirations amongst the inferior castes.

In the Roman Empire the law "did much negatively to break down the walls of separation between Greek and Barbarian, Jew and Gentile, patrician and plebeian, master and slave."[1] And there is not the slightest doubt that the pretensions of the superior castes will under the present *régime* be more and more discredited, and the artificial barriers between caste and caste get gradually demolished. Thus indirectly and unintentionally, but none the less surely, does British rule in India, by its discouragement of the caste system, foster the growth of the national sentiment amongst the people.

Under the influence of the many causes I have alluded to, and no doubt many others which are less obvious, there has become apparent within the past twenty or thirty years a marked disesteem of the rigid caste system in India, at any rate in the ordinary talk of many educated Hindus. Contempt for an old-world system is too often in itself an indirect claim to enlightenment and emancipation from ignorant prejudices; but, before allowing credit in this case for such enlightenment, it should be remembered that the contemners of the old system are frequently men of quite inferior caste, outside the pale of the twice-borns, and that there may possibly be some measure of truth in the statement made by Mr. Shoshee Chunder Dutt that a "love of food and drink proscribed by the Shastras and a morbid craving for promiscuous intercourse with females of all orders," are mainly responsible for the hostility to the caste system prevailing at the present time.

If we regard the caste system from the point of view of the still influential Brahmans, it is evident that with individual exceptions they will very naturally cling all the more, with outraged pride, to the hereditary importance derivable from their dominant and enviable place in that ancient time-honoured institution of their native land, and the end of the contest between the old forces

[1] Caird, *The Evolution of Religion*, vol. i. p. 15.

and the new is not yet, and certainly not within sight.

But though the system may not be obsolescent, it is, as I have explained, being assailed at the present time by so many disintegrating forces, that changes are inevitable, and, in my opinion, many concessions for facilitating social intercourse between the different castes and even between Hindus and non-Hindus may be looked for, even in the near future; but, on the other hand, the recognised time-honoured limitations with respect to the sphere within which marriage may be contracted—that most essential feature of Indian caste—will, I think, be more enduring and prove, for a long time to come, almost unassailable by either progressives or reformers.

THEISM IN BENGAL

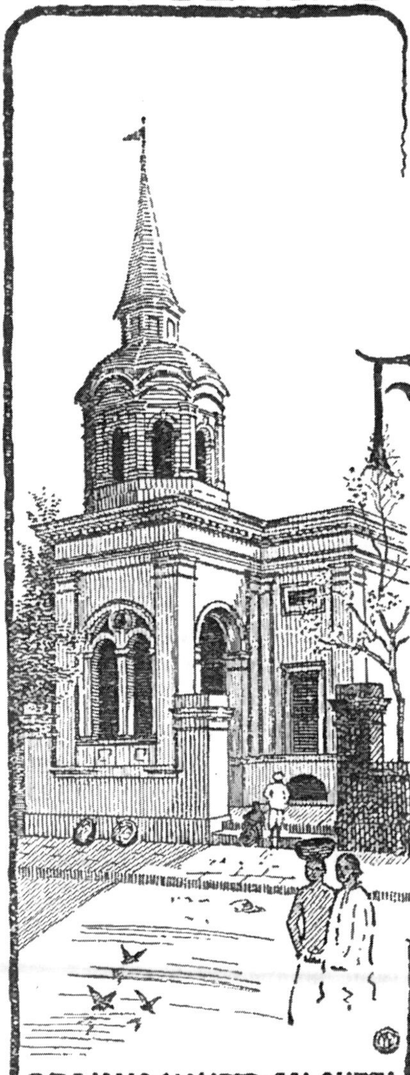

·BRAHMO·MANDIR·CALCUTTA·

CHAPTER III

THEISM IN BENGAL

SECTION I.—Ram Mohun Roy, the Bengali Theistic Reformer—His life and work.

FROM the long and often embittered conflict of world-religions in India, many diverse sects have arisen, especially out of Hinduism. Vigorously assailed as that ancient faith has been for centuries by the forces of Islam and Christianity, representing in both cases the religions of powerful dominant nationalities, it has responded to the aggressive forces confronting it by repeated outbursts of religious enthusiasm within its own borders, conducted by Hindu reformers of many types.

Of the sects which this war of creeds has called into being in the fertile religious soil of Hindu India, the Brahma Samaj (written also Brahmo Samaj and Brahmo Somaj) is one which will repay study, for its history reveals the influence of both Islam and Christianity, and its development the salient mental and moral characteristics of the keen-witted, highly emotional Mongolo-Dravidian stock to which the Bengali race belongs. Indeed, the Brahma or Brahmo movement displays in a high degree the preponderating influence of racial psychology on national faiths, and is for this, as well as other reasons, deserving of the attention of thoughtful men.

At the present time the Brahma sect, consisting of three distinct sections, is a purely theistic one, without any sacred book to appeal to and without any miraculous legend as evidence of the truth of its faith, or of the doctrines it professes. But it was not always so. During the seventy-five years of its existence the sect has gradually undergone a progressive development, passing from a purified form of Hinduism to its present independent position. In the year 1774, while Warren Hastings was still pursuing his ambitious projects of empire in India, Ram Mohun Roy, the original founder of the sect, was born in the quiet little village of Radhanagar, in Bengal, some fifty miles from Calcutta.[1] His parents were high caste, and thoroughly orthodox Brahmans in easy circumstances. In his birthplace Ram Mohun received the ordinary village-school education of the day in his mother tongue, after which he was put to study Persian, at that time the language of all the civil and criminal courts of the country. He also took up Arabic. His progress in all branches of study was very rapid, but to ensure a more complete and thorough mastery of the Persian and Arabic languages, the boy was, at the age of twelve years, sent to Patna to continue his education under the erudite Moulvis at that seat of Muhammadan learning. His studies at Patna opened up to the inquiring mind of Ram Mohun Roy the theology and philosophy of

[1] G. S. Leonard, *History of the Brahma Samaj.*

the Mussulmans. The young student took advantage, with passionate eagerness, of every source of knowledge within his reach. He anxiously weighed and considered the conflicting opinions which came under his notice, and, while still a mere lad, was powerfully attracted towards the Sufi[1] philosophy and monotheistic doctrines, without, however, being led at any time to adopt the Muhammadan religion, against which he wrote in later life, objecting strongly to the anthropomorphic conception of God which the Koran encouraged. To counteract the tendency of these studies his parents sent him to Benares, to learn from orthodox Hindu teachers the sacred literature of their Sanskrit ancestors. But Ram Mohun Roy was already too strongly tinctured with monotheistic sentiments to be won back to idolatry and the gross Puranic faith of his parents. However, in the Vedanta Philosophy[2] of the Hindus he found, or thought he found, a confirmation of the conclusions he had already reached; and at the early age of sixteen he wrote, but did not publish, a paper against the idolatrous practices of Hinduism.

The hostile attitude he had taken up towards his ancestral religion, and the very decided opinions he had formed, made his position under the parental roof anything but comfortable, and with the consent of his parents, he set out on a course of travels and visited many parts of India. Most Indian religious reformers travel extensively, studying the local languages, and paying special attention to the religious tenets and practices of the people. Ram Mohun Roy even, it is said, adventurously crossed the Himalayas and visited Tibet to study the Buddhist religion as actually existing in that country. In his twentieth, some say twenty-second, year, he commenced to learn English, and in time acquired a good knowledge of that language. When about twenty-eight or twenty-nine years of age, he published, in Persian, a book in which, while denouncing

[1] Sufi Philosophy. This system, which is but a Muslim adaptation of the Vedanta school of Hindu philosophy (Hughes, *Dictionary of Islam*, Art. "Sufi") is one that naturally commends itself to the Indian mind.

[2] Vedanta Philosophy. One of the orthodox systems of Hindu philosopby, which may be styled Hindu Pantheism.

polytheism and idolatry, he also boldly objected to the doctrines of incarnation and revelation. Shortly after the publication of this work, Ram Mohun Roy, in 1803, entered the service of the British Government as a subordinate Revenue official, and in ten years "acquired as much money as enabled him to become a Zemindar,[1] with an income of ten thousand rupees (equivalent in those days to at least £1000) a year."[2] How this money was obtained cannot now be known, but its acquisition enabled him, in the fortieth year of his age, to give up the public service, purchase a residence for himself at Calcutta, and settle there in 1814. His easy leisure appears to have been devoted to religious studies, to discussions and controversies with Hindus, Muhammadans, and Christians, and in agitating for various social reforms, for instance the abolition of Sati.[3]

Two years after settling in Calcutta he published in English *A Translation of the Abridgment of the Vedant or Resolution of all the Veds.* After a diligent study of the Bible, he brought out in 1819 a book entitled *The Precepts of Jesus, the Guide to Peace and Happiness.* Although this work was eminently appreciative of the character and teaching of Christ, it gave rise to an attack from the missionaries of Serampore, and a controversy followed, in the course of which Ram Mohun Roy studied Greek and Hebrew, the better to stand his ground against his assailants. Strange to say, he so far converted his tutor Mr. Adam (himself a missionary) to his own way of thinking, that that gentleman relinquished his spiritual office, became editor of the *Indian Gazette*, and was generally known in Calcutta as "the second fallen Adam."[4]

This occurred in 1828. Ram Mohun's controversy with

[1] Landed proprietor.

[2] *A History of the Brahma Samaj*, by G. S. Leonard, p. 20.

[3] Whatever credit may be due to Ram Mohun Roy for his efforts to have the rite of Sati abolished, it must be remembered that in his crusade against this cruel practice he could count upon the moral support of every Englishman in India, and that the matter had been officially considered by the Marquis of Wellesley in 1807. (See Dr. George Smith, *Life of William Carey*, pp. 279–285.)

[4] Dr. George Smith, *Life of Dr. Alexander Duff*, vol. i. p. 118.

the advocates of Christianity has its own peculiar features. Unable to deny the shortcomings of Hinduism, as based upon the modern text-books of that faith, he took refuge in the mysterious Vedas, works venerable by their antiquity, and as yet jealously guarded from the contamination of European eye or hand; but there is reason to believe that the Hindu controversialist was himself but little, if at all, acquainted with these writings of a very remote past. On this point we have the opinion of Professor Max Müller, who says:

> "Now it may sound strange, but I feel convinced that Ram Mohun Roy himself, when, in his controversies with his English friends, he fortified himself behind the rampart of the Veda, had no idea of what the Veda really was."

And again:

> "When Ram Mohun Roy speaks of the Vedas, and of the Monotheism taught by them, he almost invariably means the Upanishads not the Brahmanas, not the mantras or hymns of the Veda. Both the Brahmanas and the hymns teach a polytheistic, or, more accurately, a henotheistic, but not a monotheistic religion; yet they form the great bulk of what is called Veda, while the Upanishads form only a kind of appendix."[1]

Such tactics, although unfortunately too common amongst polemical writers, can only by a misuse of language be held to consist with an honest seeking after truth.

The fourteen years that had elapsed since Ram Mohun Roy settled in Calcutta, had been fruitful in events calculated to produce a lasting impression on the ideas of the people of India. Not the least of these was the establishment of the Hindu College, in January 1817. Much good work had been done in that institution in bringing the native mind into contact with the treasures of European literature; but very stirring times in the intellectual world of native society in Calcutta were at hand. In March 1828, Mr. H. L. V. Derozio joined the teaching staff of the Hindu College, and under the bold guidance of this youthful Eurasian professor, a man of some genius, and a free-thinker,

[1] Professor Max Müller, *Biographical Essays*—"Ram Mohun Roy."

an enthusiasm of inquiry had been raised which has seldom been equalled. Keen and eager students flocked round the young master, and unsatisfied with the ordinary hours of study, and the instruction of the classroom, followed him to his home, there to renew the discussions, and to probe to their depths the most cherished dogmas of philosophy and religion.[1]

The natural result of these full and free inquiries, conducted no doubt with more zeal than judgment, was a widespread scepticism amongst the Hindu students, who carried their new ideas into the family circle. "The convulsion," says a Bengali writer, "caused by Derozio was great. It pervaded almost the house of every advanced student. Down with Hinduism! Down with orthodoxy! was the cry everywhere."[2]

This open and aggressive scepticism of the rising generation created a panic in the heart of orthodox Hindu society, which rose up against the new ideas, and succeeded eventually in getting Derozio removed from his place in the College. But an important work had already been accomplished. The vast region of European speculation in metaphysics and ethics had been opened out to the Calcutta students by Derozio in a manner which probably no other Professor of Philosophy in an Indian College would have done, and a shock was given to Hinduism in Bengal, the effects of which were apparent on all sides.

Profiting by the disintegrating labours of Mr. Derozio, Dr. Alexander Duff, the enthusiastic Scotch missionary, made a vigorous, well-timed effort at proselytising. Offering, with persuasive eloquence, to the young sceptics of the Hindu College a refuge from their doubts in the bosom of Christianity, he succeeded in attracting into the Christian fold a few of those to whom the condition of doubt was intolerable, or who had already irretrievably compromised themselves, and been expelled from Hindu society.[3]

[1] Mr. Derozio's connection with the Hindu College lasted from March 1828 to April 1831.

[2] Peary Chand Mittra, *A Biographical Sketch of David Hare*, p. 16.

[3] Between August 1832 and April 1833, Duff made four converts to Christianity.

At this time also the great political questions which arose out of the storm of discussions and controversies on the Reform Bill began to teach the mild Hindu the "rights of man." This awakening of the Eastern mind, under the stimulating influence of occidental ideas, marks an epoch in the intellectual history of India, a *renaissance* destined to lead to the most important consequences, of which as yet only the *beginnings* are apparent.

During the period of speculative fermentation of which we have been writing, Ram Mohun Roy, assisted by a few friends and disciples, founded the Brahma Samaj or Society of God. A suitable house of prayer was opened in 1830, designed for congregational worship, itself an important innovation upon Hindu customs in religion. The service in the new theistic church consisted in the recital of the Vedas by two Telegu Brahmans,[1] the reading of texts from the Upanishads, and the expounding of the same in Bengali. The Samaj, thus constituted, looked for its sanctions to certain Hindu Scriptures of great antiquity and acknowledged authority, and it was at this time practically, although an unorthodox, still a Hindu sect, true to the all-important institution of caste. Indeed, in establishing this sect Ram Mohun Roy professed to be leading his countrymen back to the pure, uncorrupted monotheistic religion of their Vedic ancestors; but his monotheism, based as it was essentially upon the Vedanta philosophy, was in reality but a disguised Pantheism, enriched as regards its ethics by ideas derived from Muslim and Christian literature and theology.

At about this period the French travelling naturalist, M. Victor Jacquemont, made the acquaintance of Ram Mohun Roy at Calcutta, and he devotes several pages of his book of travels in India to an appreciative account of the reformer's history, acquirements, and character. As M. Jacquemont was received on intimate terms into the very best Anglo-Indian society, his opinions naturally reflect the opinions of his hosts, and are strong evidence of

[1] Telegu or Madrasi Brahmans were employed because there are no pure Brahmans in Bengal to whom the sacred task could properly be entrusted.

the high esteem in which Ram Mohun Roy was held by his English contemporaries in India. With regard to his private life, our French traveller says that he dispensed in charities the whole of the fortune which he had inherited from his father, living himself with the strictest economy in order that he might have the more to give away.[1]

On the other hand, the impression produced on the famous French missionary, the Abbé J. A. Dubois, by Ram Mohun Roy was not at all favourable. He formed no high opinion either of his learning or his originality, considered that the reformer's talents were much overrated, and derided his efforts to bring back his countrymen to the religion of their ancestors. Especially objectionable did Ram Mohun Roy appear to M. Dubois when, at an entertainment given by the reformer to the Spaniards living in Calcutta, he made an elaborate speech, with reference to the recent revolution in Spain, on the advantages of religious and political freedom. "In fact," says the French missionary, "to see a Brahmin decorated with the *treble cord*, that indubitable badge of the most oppressive and most degrading despotism, turn the apostle of freedom, is so shocking an anomaly, that persons acquainted with the subject will find it difficult to reconcile themselves to such a contradiction."[2] But this harsh and not quite reasonable criticism on the part of the good Abbé—usually so very fair minded—may well be attributed to the *odium theologicum* aroused in the militant French hierophant by the sight of a hated priestly opponent commanding public attention and receiving, as in this case, respectful hearing even from Europeans.

In 1830 the titular Emperor of Delhi, himself a Muslim, conferred the title of *Rajah* upon the Bengali reformer, and induced him to proceed to England on a mission to the Home Government, deeming, in all probability, that the high estimation in which Ram Mohun Roy was held by Anglo-Indians marked him out as the fittest advocate of his cause in England.

Of distinguished appearance, agreeable manners, and

[1] Victor Jacquemont, *Voyage dans l'Inde*, tome premier, pp. 183–188.

[2] *Letters on the State of Christianity in India*, pp. 165, 166.

undoubtedly great ability, the envoy from the Mogul court, "the first Brahman who had ever crossed the sea,"[1] was everywhere warmly welcomed in England, and the more cordially, perhaps, because, from his professed admiration of Christ and His teaching, it was felt that he was one almost persuaded to become a Christian. But Ram Mohun Roy, who has been described by Professor Sir Monier Williams "as the first earnest-minded investigator of the science of comparative religion that the world has produced,"[2] had done more than look into the various religions which claim the allegiance and sustain the hopes of men, and was by no means a likely convert.

It is one thing to avow admiration of the exalted character and teaching of Christ, it is quite another thing to subscribe to the *dogmas of a particular Christian Church, undergo baptism in order to be received therein, formally renounce one's old faith, and incur all the social penalties of apostasy.* And this unqualified acceptance of specific dogmas, together with the public and complete repudiation of one's national religion, is what the conversion of a Hindu or a Muslim to Christianity actually involves.

Without questioning for a moment the genuineness and sincerity of the estimation in which the Bengali reformer might hold the pure and elevated teaching of Christ, it is probable that in their eager desire to regard him as a Christian in all but open profession of faith, his kind hosts attached more importance to his words than they really deserved. Be this as it may, Ram Mohun Roy never embraced the Christian religion, but died in England in 1833, a Hindu to the last, clinging tenaciously to all

[1] "The immense difficulty of the enterprise at that period is proved by the fact that we do not hear of any other Hindoo of high caste visiting this country since the death of Ram Mohun Roy until in 1841 or 1842 his friend Dwarkanath Tagore came to England, and in 1845 four native Indian medical students, accompanied hither Dr. Henry Goodeve, the founder of the Medical College in Calcutta."—Mary Carpenter, *The Last Days in England of the Rajah Ram Mohun Roy*, p. 67.

Needless to add that hundreds of Indians are now studying in Britain, and that many thousands of Indians of all ranks, castes, and creeds have visited England within the last seventy years.

[2] *Journal of the Royal Asiatic Society*, January 1881. Art. "Indian Theistic Reforms."

the observances and restrictions of his caste. The Rajah was buried in Bristol, and a monument erected by his friend and disciple Dwarkanath Tagore marks his last resting-place in Arno's Vale Cemetery.

Ram Mohun Roy was a keen-witted man of high capacity, whose studies had satisfied him that the orthodox Hindu system was not without defects. In this he was not singular. Reformers like Kabir and Nanak had lived and taught before his days, but Ram Mohun Roy's work was done in the broad light of the nineteenth century, and much of it in such a fashion as to attract the attention, sympathy, and countenance of Europeans. Throughout his career, though at one time subjected to much social persecution, the reformer seems to have managed to steer a safe and tolerably comfortable course. Although he had written against Muhammadanism, he was selected as the envoy of the Mogul Emperor to England; although he carried on a controversy with the Serampore missionaries, he seems to have won the confidence of Christians, for we learn that the first person the Scotch missionary Alexander Duff was, on his arrival at Calcutta, advised to consult about his mission, was no other than Ram Mohun Roy; while by his strict adherence to caste rules, and the obligatory ceremonies of Hinduism, he fully maintained his claim to be regarded as a Hindu to the end of his life. In all things he was a shrewd man of the world. His clear intellect could see that reforms were urgently called for in the Hindu religion and society, and he worked towards the desired end, without exposing himself to very serious risks or inconvenience. He took a prominent part in agitating for the suppression of Sati, and strongly advocated a practical scientific education for his countrymen, instead of the traditional Sanskrit learning, which he, in the fulness of knowledge, held in no great esteem.[1] On the whole, Ram Mohun Roy was a man of conspicuous ability and much tact, with a rare liberality of sentiment and a practical turn of mind. As the first Indian reformer whose writings reflect the Christian influence introduced from the West, he has naturally been dealt with in a kindly

[1] Peary Chand Mittra, *Biography of David Hare.*

and appreciative spirit by European writers, and has perhaps been exalted by some of them into a position beyond his deserts. In estimating the originality and liberality of his views, it has to be borne in mind that some of his proposed social reforms, for example the prevention of Sati, were probably suggested by his European friends in high position, and that his religious views may have owed their catholicity to the genius of Hinduism, strengthened perhaps by his familiarity with the ideas of the French and English sceptics of the eighteenth century, and their successors.

THEISM IN BENGAL—*continued*

SECTION II.—Debendra Nath Tagore and the Adi Brahma Samaj—The first important schism led by Keshub Chunder Sen.

RAM MOHUN ROY died in debt, and after his demise the Brahma Samaj languished, its money capital amounting to only six thousand and eighty rupees.

This amount was clearly inadequate to the support of the institution, and it owed to the liberality of a single man, Dwarkanath Tagore, the payment of its very moderate monthly expenses of some eighty rupees. By 1841, after an existence of eleven years, the Brahma Society could not count more than five or six persons who cared to attend the religious services at the *Mandir* (place of worship), and there was but *one* regular attendant, a relative of the gentleman by whom the place was kept up. In this moribund condition, the Samaj was taken in hand by Debendra Nath Tagore, a son of Dwarkanath, and by his devotion, energy, and ability, some new life was infused into the almost extinct Society. In 1843, Debendra Nath instituted a form of initiation into the Society which involved the signing of a covenant by the initiate, affirming his adoption of the Vedantic faith, and *renunciation of idolatry.* At that time the Samaj could number only eighty-three members. By Debendra Nath's zeal, branches were established in many of the towns and villages of Bengal. Up to this time the Brahma Samaj professed to derive its doctrines, and to rely for its sanctions upon the Vedas. But, as subsequent events proved, a pure theistic church could not be firmly built upon such foundations.

Opposition and criticism awakened honest inquiry and investigation. Four learned Pandits were sent in 1845 to Benares at Debendra Nath's expense, to copy out and make a special study of the Vedas. After two years they returned to Calcutta. Debendra Nath devoted himself, with their aid, to a diligent and critical examination of the sacred books, and eventually, after much controversy, and even danger of disruption, the Samaj came, under his guidance, to the important decision that the teaching of the Vedas could not be reconciled with the conclusions of modern science, or with the religious convictions of the Brahmas,[1] a result which soon led to an open and public denial of the infallibility of the Vedas. There is nothing in the Brahmic movement more creditable to the parties concerned than this honest and careful inquiry into the nature of the doctrines and precepts of the Vedas.

The conclusion arrived at was a momentous one in the history of the Society, for at a later period it led, and necessarily so, to a complete and uncompromising rupture with Hinduism on the part of all those who were prepared to follow to their logical consequences the principles which they publicly professed. The sect now fell back upon Natural Religion, but, needing some sort of text-book explanatory of their creed and practices, one was compiled in 1848 by Debendra Nath himself, entitled *Brahma Dharma Ghrantha*, a collection "of Theistic Texts containing selections from the Shastras and the Shastras only"; that is from such of the old oracles of the Hindu faith as the Upanishads, Manu, the Mahabharata, and the like. A Bengali translation of the selected texts, and a commentary thereon, formed an essential part of this book. Having given up the infallibility of even the most sacred of all the Hindu Scriptures, the Vedas, it is clear that a few passages culled from later sacred books of the Hindus, in support of a particular doctrine, could not be, in any sense, authoritative; but the leaders of the Society appear to have held that its theism, though founded on intuition and reason, was still in consonance with the highest teach-

[1] Pandit Sivanath Sastri, M.A., *The New Dispensation*, p. 6. T. E. Slater, *Keshab Chandra Sen*, p. 36.

ings of Hinduism, and they desired to emphasise this opinion, and keep it before the minds of their countrymen.

At this time the creed of the Brahmas was embodied in the following four articles:—

> "(1) One only God before this was, and nothing else was co-existent with him. He has created whatever there exists.
>
> "(2) He is eternal, intelligence itself, infinite, all-good, all-apart, without parts, one, without a second, all-pervading, governing and supporting everything, omniscient, omnipotent, perfect, immutable, without a likeness.
>
> "(3) His worship alone ensures all present and future bliss.
>
> "(4) Love of him, and doing the works he loves, is his worship."[1]

Here I may call attention to the fact that in these articles of faith, no reference is made to the doctrines of successive reincarnations and of *Karma*, so characteristic of Hinduism in its subtler aspects.

Henceforward the apostles of the Brahma Samaj openly taught that they had no written scriptures, but based the doctrines of their faith upon the laws of nature, and the primitive convictions implanted in the mind of man.

With all their outward profession of austere monotheistic doctrines, it appears that, at this time, the Brahmas in their domestic life differed little, if at all, from their idolatrous countrymen.

To avow a theoretical belief in the unity of God, and to pass a sweeping condemnation upon idolatry of every kind, was far easier than to avoid participating in idolatrous practices, interwoven as these were with every ceremony and detail of public and private life. It was clear that if the new ideas were really to bear fruit, vigorous action was necessary in lieu of dreamy speculation. Zealous young reformers desired the total suppression of all idolatrous rites. To reconcile their conduct with their creed in the matter of religious ceremonies, without unnecessary innova-

[1] G. S. Leonard, *A History of the Brahma Samaj*, p. 91.

tion, was a delicate matter, but had to be attempted if the sect was not to become a byword. Under the stimulus of pressing necessity, rules for the conduct of all the principal ceremonies were at length drawn up for the guidance of Brahmas, retaining as much as possible of the time-honoured usages and practices of Hinduism, and Debendra Nath himself was the first to set the example of performing a Hindu rite without any proceedings savouring of idolatry. But these concessions were not sufficient for the extreme radical party in the new sect. The more conservative members still clung to Hinduism, and regarded themselves as *Hindu reformers*, while the *progressive* Brahmas, as they styled themselves, were minded to go a good deal further. That party was prepared to break altogether with Hinduism. It was determined to abolish the use of sect marks, to allow marriage between members of different castes, and it was ready to welcome into its ranks converts from every caste and creed. The conservatives were led by Debendra Nath Tagore, a man learned in the Shastras and Sanskrit literature, averse to Christianity, and deeply tinctured with the Sufi-ism of the Persians.

The radicals were headed by a young man of the Vaidya caste, named Keshub Chunder Sen, who had joined the Samaj in 1859 and been appointed *a minister* by Debendra Nath Tagore in 1862. Educated in the Presidency College at Calcutta, more familiar with English and the Bible than with the Sanskrit language and Vedic literature, he was filled with deep enthusiastic admiration of the beauty of Christ's character and teaching. A schism in the Society was an unavoidable consequence of these differences of opinion. Under the energetic leadership of Babu Keshub Chunder Sen, the progressive party seceded from the original Society, and set up a Samaj of their own, which was publicly established in November 1866.

With the secession of Keshub Chunder Sen and his followers a complete and permanent separation was effected between the conservative and progressive parties in the Samaj, which owed its origin to Ram Mohun Roy. Each went its own way, the former being henceforth known as the *Adi* (original) *Brahma Samaj*, while the latter assumed the somewhat pretentious title of "the Brahma Samaj of India."

Before dealing with Keshub's very conspicuous and somewhat erratic career, I may devote a couple of pages to the interesting, though uneventful, story of the *Adi Samaj*.

Under the guidance of its founder Debendra Nath Tagore, who was born in 1818 and died so recently as January 1905, the Adi Brahma Samaj has continued to uphold theism as a cult in harmony with the national religion. It professes indeed to be a Hindu sect whose special mission is to abolish idolatry and propagate theism. To the Hindu caste system the Adi Samaj maintains an attitude of toleration, trusting that reforms in respect to this matter will, in course of time, follow the full acceptance of its fundamental principles. Debendra Nath—who has been succeeded as chief minister of the sect by his eldest son Babu Dwijindra Nath Tagore—was a man of great ability, a fine orator, a careful man of business, a wise father, a man of scrupulous integrity,[1] and eminently religious from quite youthful days. In his old age Debendra Nath Tagore led the life of a recluse. To a spot, situated about a mile from the Bolpur station of the East Indian Railway, now known as the *shantiniketan* of Bolpur, Debendra Nath was wont to retreat in order *to hold communion with God,* in other words *to practise Yoga.* He used to pitch a tent there and give himself up to religious meditation in the shade of a particular tree. Eventually he secured about six and a half acres of land, built a dwelling-house on it, and, later on, a chapel and a *Brahmavidyala* or school.

> "The sanctuary or chapel is a marvellous edifice," says a pious Bengali pilgrim. "The roof is tiled, but the enclosure is of glass, some of which are painted and some coloured. The Crystal Palace, London, is a glass house. We have not heard of any other house besides it made of glass. Although in magnitude the *shantiniketan* sanctuary cannot be compared with the

[1] C. E. Buckland, C.I.E., *Bengal under its Lieutenant-Governors*, vol. ii. pp. 1035–37.

famous Crystal Palace, it gives the people some idea as to what sort of edifice the latter is. It undoubtedly is an attraction to the villagers, who come to see it in large numbers. This glass hall is about 60 feet long and about 30 feet broad. The pavement is of white marble. There are suitable inscriptions in it in Sanskrit. It has four gates from four sides of the garden. Towards the eastern gate, there is a beautiful portico with a tower over it, and the word *OM* in Bengali, like the figure of the cross in Christian churches, flourishes over the topmost pinnacle. Suitable inscriptions, both in Sanskrit and Bengali, are inscribed on beautiful pedestals for flower vases, and placed at the approach to the holy place. There is a beautiful artificial fountain, which plays on special occasions, and on the two pillars near it are stuck two large pieces of marble, the one bearing an inscription in Sanskrit and the other in Bengali, describing the blessedness of heaven—of which the place assuredly is the foreshadow."[1]

In the chapel described as above by a devout Bengali admirer, religious services are held regularly twice a day, in accordance with the liturgy of the Adi Brahma Samaj, by a Brahman appointed for the purpose. Within the precincts of the *shantiniketan* animal food is interdicted. There is a *holy of holies* in the sanctuary, the spot where Debendra Nath used to practise *Yoga* under a great chittim tree. Here stands a small elevated seat made of white marble—the *Vedi*—upon which, lost in contemplation, the minister used to hold communion with God. The *Vedi* is deemed so sacred that no one but the *Master* has ever presumed to occupy it. The chittim tree at Bolpur is in the belief of Debendra Nath's followers destined to become in after years as famous as the Bodhi tree at Buddh Gaya, which some four-and-twenty centuries ago witnessed Gautama's great temptation and his final triumph over Mara the Evil One.

By his disciples Debendra Nath was styled *Maharshi*—grand Rishi or Saint—and he was highly esteemed by all classes in Bengal. The ceremony of the Cremation of the *Maharshi's* body at the Nimtollah Burning Ghat was the

[1] From *Unity and the Minister*, 13th October 1901, reproduced in *Tattwabodhini Patrika*, vol. xv. part iii.

occasion of an unprecedented display of sympathy and respect on the part of his countrymen of all denominations. Yet the sect which Debendra Nath Tagore founded, and practically maintained at his own expense, is still numerically insignificant. According to information received by me in July 1905 from a Bengali gentleman (Babu Jogindra Nath Bose) interested in the Samaj, the entire sect numbered only "three hundred people, men, women and children all told."

THEISM IN BENGAL—*continued*

SECTION III.—Early troubles of the "Brahma Samaj of India;"—Act passed by Government to legalise Brahma marriages.

THE leader of the progressive party, Babu Keshub Chunder Sen, who was only twenty-eight years of age, had shown a strong passion for the stage, and loved nothing better than the plays of Shakespeare. He was fond of performing himself, and especially delighted in appearing in the rôle of magician before his family and friends. One of his biographers even gives him the credit of having revived dramatic performances in Bengal.[1]

At an early age he studied the Bible with the Rev. T. H. Burne, domestic chaplain to Bishop Cotton, and imbibed ideas and feelings which made a lasting impression on his mind.[2] Although decidedly clever and self-reliant, Keshub does not appear to have made a figure either at school or college, probably on account of his distaste for mathematical studies, and his irrepressible individuality. At the age of twenty-one he began life as a clerk on a small salary in the Bank of Bengal. Endowed with an emotional temperament, earnest piety, a very ambitious spirit, unusual energy, a gift of ready speech, and a strong leaven of vanity, Keshub Chunder Sen found the sober, monotonous duties of a bank clerk intolerable, and very soon sought a more congenial field for the exercise of his abilities. The reform movement set on foot by Ram Mohun Roy attracted his attention,

[1] *A Biographical Sketch of Keshub Chunder Sen*, printed at the Vedanta Press, Calcutta, 1884. This sketch was written by an ardent admirer of the reformer, and one apparently well acquainted with him and his family.

[2] *Idem*, p. 7.

and, as already stated, he formally joined the Brahma Samaj in 1859. He was now in his proper element, and, as we have seen, became before long an acknowledged leader in the Society.

At the inaugural meeting of the new Brahma Samaj of India, of which Keshub was the founder, texts from the sacred Scriptures of the Christians, Hindus, Muhammadans, Parsees, and Chinese were publicly read, in order to mark, and to proclaim to the world, the catholicity of spirit in which the new sect was formed. And thus the Brahmas, although denying the inspiration of any of the writings held sacred by the professors of existing creeds, still use them as a common storehouse from which to borrow whatever seems most suitable to point a moral, to strengthen an argument, or to support a thesis. And the same sermon or lecture may bristle with quotations from the Ramayana, the Koran, and the Bible, all brought forward with curious impartiality, and referred to with equal veneration.

From the time of his secession from the parent Society, Keshub by his writings and public lectures kept himself prominently before the Indian world, enlisting the sympathies of the Viceroy, Sir John Lawrence, who took a deep interest in the work of the native reformer, particularly as Keshub had spoken publicly of Christ in terms which seemed to justify the belief that he was a Christian in all but open profession of faith.

In 1868, Keshub visited Simla in order to have an interview with the Viceroy, and there, for the first time, I heard him deliver to an appreciative audience one of his popular lectures, displaying much showy eloquence and emotional fervour.

By this time several marriages had been performed according to the revised ritual of the Brahmic Church. They had given great offence to orthodox Hindus, and had exposed the participators in these novel rites to much obloquy. The legality of marriages thus contracted had even been questioned.

This was an important epoch in the history of the sect. Here was a real stumbling-block in the way of the propagation of Brahmaism. If marriages conducted according to the Brahmic ritual were null and void, and if Brahmas could not, without doing violence to their consciences or public professions, conform to the ceremonials of orthodox Hinduism, it was to be feared that the young Church, apparently making for Christianity, would be stifled in its very infancy. The State alone could afford relief to the distressed Brahmas in this serious difficulty, while at the same time the granting of such relief would undoubtedly give offence to the great Hindu community as tending to facilitate apostasy from their ancient faith.

Fortunately for the cause of the Brahmas the ruling power in India was ready to give encouragement to what it considered the healthy moral and social development of the people. Aware of, and relying upon, such sympathy, formal application was made to the Government in 1868, by the progressive Brahmas, under the leadership of Babu Keshub Chunder Sen, for an act legalising Brahma marriages.

Sir Henry Maine was at that time legal member of the Viceroy's Council, and speaking in the Council Chamber on the 10th of September, he said that after due inquiry he

> "had convinced himself that the creed of the Brahmas lacked stability. The process by which the sect was formed might be increasing in activity, but there seemed also to be a growing disinclination to accept any set of common tenets. It would be difficult for legal purposes to define a Brahma, and if no definitions were given, there might shortly be petitions for relief by persons who were in the same legal position as the present applicants, but who declared that they could not conscientiously call themselves Brahmas."

Sir Henry Maine, however, recognised the case in point as one in which relief could not be withheld by Government, and to meet the difficulty introduced a Bill, which was, in fact, a Civil Marriage Bill. The proposed enactment met with opposition in many quarters, and was modified so as to meet the specific case of the Brahma Samaj. But at this stage an unexpected difficulty presented itself. The conservative Brahmas of the Adi Samaj, deeming themselves Hindus, deprecated any special legislation. To quote the words of Sir James Fitzjames Stephen, who succeeded Sir Henry Maine as Legal Member of the Viceroy's Council:

> "The Progressive Brahmas have broken far more decisively with Hinduism than the Conservatives. The object of the Conservatives is to pour the new wine into old bottles so that the one may not be wasted, nor the other broken. The Progressive Brahmas undertake to provide at once new wine and new bottles. As regards marriage, the difference between the two parties appears to be this: the marriage ceremonies adopted by the Progressive Brahmas depart more widely from the Hindu law than those which are in use amongst the Adi-Brahmas. The Adi-Brahmas indeed contend that by Hindu law, their ceremonies, though irregular, would be valid. The Progressive Brahmas admit that by Hindu law their marriages would be void. Moreover, the Progressive Brahmas are opposed both to infant marriage and to polygamy far more decisively than the Conservative party."

Eventually the relief to Brahmas took the form of an Act providing, to use Sir James Fitzjames Stephen's words,

> "a form of marriage to be celebrated before the Registrar for persons who did not profess either the Hindu, the Muhammadan, the Parsee, the Sikh, the Jaina, or the Buddhist religion, and who are neither Christians nor Jews."

This Act received the sanction of the Legislature on the 19th of March 1872.

The effect of such legislation as the above is, in the opinion of Sir Alfred Lyall, following Sir H. S. Maine, to arrest the process of constant change which has been going on in Hindu social and religious life since the earliest times.[1] In other words, the tendency of British Indian law is to destroy the remarkable elasticity of the Hindu religious system, which has for ages enabled it to retain within its pale sects holding the most divergent theological opinions and observing the most dissimilar customs. Henceforth pronounced heretics of the Brahma type will have to openly

[1] Sir Alfred Lyall, *Asiatic Studies*, First Series, pp. 8, 9.

acknowledge themselves to be *non-Hindus*, a fact which will make their reabsorption, at any future date, into the old national faith a matter of considerable difficulty. Whether the conditions thus created by the operation of British Indian law will be prejudicial to Hinduism or the reverse, is an open question, which Time alone can decide.

THEISM IN BENGAL—*continued*

SECTION IV.—Keshub Chunder Sen worshipped by some followers—His views in respect to his own mission—Visit to England—Result.

HOWEVER, the career of Keshub was not without its dark days. Dazzled, I may say burthened, by the eloquence of their leader, and by the figure he was making in the world, many of his followers began to worship him as an incarnation of the Deity, and to supplicate his intercession on their behalf.

Certainly this was nothing new in the history of Indian sects, for the worship of living religious leaders and teachers (usually called by the general name *Guru*) is common all over India.

What the recipient of these divine honours did to discountenance them is not very clear, but two of the missionaries of his own Church, presumably with sufficient reason, published in a Calcutta newspaper a letter, which I reproduce without abridgment, on account of the side-light it throws on certain phases of religious development:

A NEW DEITY.

"SIR,—For the information of that section of your readers who are Brahmas, please publish the following protest against a mischievous and unBrahmic practice of certain Brahmas of Calcutta and the Mofussil:

"We are astonished and grieved to observe that some Brahmas have begun to acknowledge Baboo Keshub Chunder Sen, *as a saviour of men*, commissioned by God. They accordingly call him 'Good Lord, Redeemer, etc.,' and pray to him for salvation in this wise:

"'Good Lord! I am a great sinner, have mercy on me and save me. Lead me to the feet of thy merciful father. O don't forsake me!'

"Even to divine service they have given an objectionable form. They now offer up their prayers to God, through Keshub Baboo. We have heard a Brahma pray to Keshub Baboo thus:

"'Good Lord, I am a great sinner. I cannot entertain a hope that God will hear my prayer. Do pray for me to your merciful father.'

"This sort of proceeding on the part of certain Brahmas has given a shock to almost all Brahma Samajes, as has been brought to notice during a tour in the Mofussil, and many are jumping to the conclusion that Keshub Baboo is propagating his own worship and not that of God. But we would advise them to wait till we hear anything from him for or against this practice.

"In conclusion, we beg of our Brahma brethren, who have thus begun to worship Keshub Baboo, to think what they are about; what a dangerous doctrine they are preaching to the world, a doctrine which has been the cause of all bitterness and antipathy between religious sects, and which has ultimately led men to pseudo-divine honours. We also beg of Keshub Baboo to direct his efforts to put a stop to the above practice, and disabuse the public mind that is prejudiced against him.

"JADOO NATH CHUCKERBUTTY,
"BIJOY KESSEN GOSWAMEE,
"Missionaries of the Brahma Samaj of India.

"CALCUTTA, *20th October* 1868."[1]

The threatened storm blew over. Explanations were apparently given and accepted. Some pretended to pooh-pooh the whole thing, and to regard the matter, so far as it affected the conduct and character of Keshub, as mere idle calumny. However, there are peculiarities in Keshub Chunder's views of his own mission, which are of some interest in this connection. In 1866, in a lecture on "Great Men," he propounded the doctrine that God manifests Himself in history through great men, who "are great on account of the large measure of the divine spirit which they possess and manifest."

[1] *Indian Daily News*, 28th October 1868.

It is only fair to add that while Keshub considered that the prophet should be "honoured[1] as a teacher," he himself declared that the "idolatrous bending of the knee before man is an insult to Heaven, and an audacious violation of that entire loyalty and allegiance to God which is demanded of every true believer."[2]

Regarding his ideas at this time we can probably form a fair conception from his public lectures delivered in 1866–69,[3] which are somewhat more sober and substantial, less metaphysical and frothy, than those which in later years dazzled by their rhetoric, but mystified by their transcendentalism the thousands who pressed to hear him year after year in the Town Hall of Calcutta.

He believed in the unity of God—"One without a second," and laid special emphasis upon His *immanence*. "God the Creator," he said, "should not be considered apart from God the Preserver, He is the immanent power of the world, its indwelling life." The immortality of the soul he firmly believed in, and a future state of rewards and punishments.

God, he held, makes Himself known to us through His wonderful works; through "great men who are sent into the world to benefit mankind" when the necessity for their appearance arises; and lastly, "through the soul or conscience of each individual."

He strongly maintained the doctrine of justification by faith, saying: "A man is justified by faith, and not by deeds, however excellent." Indeed *bhakti,* or living faith in the Supreme Being, was one of the strongest and most notable characteristics of the great men already sent into the world by God to benefit mankind. Jesus commanded Keshub's highest love and admiration. He certainly makes allusion to Chaitanya, the great Bengali prophet, whose doctrines of justification by faith, and the necessity of ecstatic union with God (Krishna), seem to have been in

[1] Lecture on "The Future Church," January 1869.

[2] Lecture on "Great Men," 1866.

[3] The lectures were—(1) "Jesus Christ; Europe and Asia," 5th May 1866. (2) "Great Men," 28th September 1866. (3) "Regenerating Faith," 24th January 1868; and (4) "The Future Church," 23rd January 1869.

complete harmony with his own ideas and feelings,[1] but Christ was apparently the object of Keshub's special homage. No one who denied the divinity of Christ could speak of Him with more love and reverence than did Keshub, who seems to have been deeply touched and powerfully influenced by his study of the Bible, and especially the Gospel history. His attitude towards the Bible was somewhat peculiar for a non-believer, since he seems to have accepted without doubt or cavil the historicity of the entire Bible story, from the fall of man in Eden to the founding of Christianity amongst the Gentiles by St. Paul.

There was, however, no existing form of Christianity which Keshub was prepared to adopt. He was apparently impressed with the idea that he was himself a "great man" of the kind he had spoken about, and that he had a special mission of his *own* to accomplish. But there was nothing very novel or striking in this. Vain men and dreamers have, in all ages, been apt to flatter themselves with such notions. A new Church, Keshub told the world, would arise, which, repudiating idolatry, pantheism, and man-worship, would "uphold the absolute infinity and unity of the Divine Creator." This new Church would be "the result of the purer elements of the leading creeds of the day, harmonised, developed, and shaped under the influence of Christianity."

In Keshub's opinion both Hinduism and Muhammadanism, and probably all other religions, contained certain central truths, surrounded by errors. In his "Church of the Future"—which he predicted would be unsparingly destructive of idolatry, pantheism, and prophet-worship—all that is good in the different religious systems would be rescued and preserved, while *un*-important differences would be swallowed up in a community of feelings and interests. In this Church of the Future, which would eventually be embraced by all mankind, each nation would retain its own peculiar style and ceremonial. There would "be unity of spirit, but diversity of forms." With respect to essentials, there could not, of course, be any difference.

[1] For an account of Chaitanya and his sect, see Professor Monier Williams, *Religious Thought and Life in India*, pp. 138–145.

Divested of its rhetorical adjuncts and reduced to its proper proportions, Keshub's idea was simply this. In the course of time men would gradually refine their respective creeds by eliminating, one by one, the errors which disfigured or obscured those central truths, which all possessed in a more or less degree. By this process of elimination the professors of all the leading creeds would eventually arrive at a pure form of theistic religion, which, in regard to essentials, would be the same everywhere.

The realisation of the Future Church was seen as something far off, but Keshub was apparently impressed with the belief that his mission was to hasten the desired result.

Holding the ideas and opinions which I have attempted to summarise in the preceding pages, Keshub visited Britain early in 1870. He preached or lectured in all the principal cities of both England and Scotland. Men and women of all ranks and opinions crowded to hear the dusky but eloquent speaker from the Far East, and vied with each other in expressions of genuine admiration of the mental and moral gifts of their remarkable visitor. The Babu was lionised a good deal, and even Royalty made a point of noticing this unofficial representative from England's Indian Empire. From his *Diary in England*,[1] it appears that Keshub saw a good deal of the leaders and influential members of the Unitarian Church in England, both Christian and purely theistic, and he could not have failed to learn from themselves or their published writings, the peculiar tenets of the several sections into which theists in England and America have separated themselves. He preached in many Unitarian chapels, and was everywhere listened to with deferential attention. After learning all about the Unitarians both within and without the pale of Christianity, and obtaining an insight into the dogmas and constitution of "the countless and conflicting sects" of Christians in England, a subject to which he made pointed allusion in a speech at Birmingham, Keshub returned to his native land, a "confirmed Indian" and a confirmed theist.

At the end of his six months' tour in England, Keshub

[1] Published by the Brahma Tract Society, 1886.

gave a farewell address at Southampton, in which, after affirming his belief in the Fatherhood of God, and the Brotherhood of Man, he proceeded to say:

> "The true kingdom of God will not be realised, unless the East and the West are joined together, for it has been said, and every day, through inspiration, we may hear the voice from God, that the East and West, the North and the South, shall sit down in the kingdom of God. The West, with all its thought and culture, its social purity and domestic sweetness, is but half the circle of human civilisation and progress. The East is the other half. I admire the earnestness and firmness of purpose which I have seen here; I admire those stupendous works of noble and disinterested charity in which thousands of pure and generous-minded English men and women are daily engaged. I admire the force of will and the strength of character which I see in your nation; I feel that you have nerves of adamant, with which you overcome any amount of opposition, and surmount obstacles that may come in your path; but this is not all that God requires of us. When I turn to my country and the East, I find warmth of heart, solitary contemplation on her hills and mountains, deep communion with the indwelling and omniscient spirit of the One Supreme God; I see a voluntary and deliberate withdrawing of the heart from all anxieties and cares of the world for a time, in order to engage in uninterrupted contemplation of the attributes of God; I see the heart in all its fervour and sympathy directed in daily communion towards the one loving Father. I see there the heart of man, and in England the mind of man,—there the soul, here the will; and as it is our duty to love God with all our heart and soul and mind and strength, it is necessary that all these four elements of character should be united. I do not mean to say that there is no such thing as religious fervour in this nation, nor do I mean to say that there is no such thing as practical righteousness in the nations of the East, but that each nation, so at least I believe, represents only one side of truth, and represents it with peculiar fidelity. The truths which are represented in England and Western countries generally, are those which refer to force of character, earnestness of purpose, conscien-

tious strictness, noble charity, practical duty, whilst the truths which I find peculiarly developed in Indian —developed to a greater extent than anywhere else— and in Eastern countries generally, are those which have reference to sweetness of communion, sweetness of temper, meekness, and resignation to God. Is it not then our duty as brothers to unite England and India, the East and the West, that the East may receive some of the truths of the West, and the West some of the grand ideas of Eastern countries?"[1]

The contrast between the busy, practical West and the dreamy, meditative East—drawn with so much insight and expressed above with so much propriety—seems to have made a strong impression on Keshub Chunder, and we find him, on his return to India, vigorously initiating and carrying out various measures of social reform, suggested by the new ideas he had brought from Europe. Of course it is not to be supposed that his journey to Europe had simply directed Keshub Chunder's energies towards the realisation of practical aims. The effect produced upon his character, his self-esteem, and his future work by the reception he received in England must have been considerable. It is a far cry from Calcutta to London. In Keshub's case it was no small thing for him to have been taken about to this place and the other by an ex-Viceroy of India, to have dined with Dukes and Cabinet Ministers, to have been escorted hither and thither by admiring English ladies, to have had his acquaintance sought by men like Dean Stanley and John Stuart Mill, to have been consulted by members of H.M. Government, to have had his photograph asked for by Royalty, and last, but by no means least, to have had his opinions on religious and even political matters received in England as the opinions, not of a merely well-informed person, but of a leader and teacher of men.

[1] *Keshub Chunder Sen in England.* (Brahma Tract Society, Calcutta.) Second Edition, 1887, pp. 388–390.

THEISM IN BENGAL—*continued*

SECTION V.—Keshub Chunder Sen's proceedings, which lead to a new schism and the founding of the Sadharan Brahma Samaj.

IT may be difficult to judge what effect all the well-meant attentions he received in England may have had on the character of Keshub, but he must have been more than human if he did not come back to his native land with an exalted opinion of his own place in the world, and of his mission for the regeneration of mankind. His first step on his return to Calcutta was to found the "Indian Reform Association," composed of Hindus, Muhammadans, Parsees, and Europeans, with a view to promote the moral and social betterment of the natives of India, by especial attention to the amelioration of the condition of women, by the spread of education and cheap literature, and the discouragement of intemperance. In furtherance of the proposed objects, a female normal and adult school and a theological seminary were established.

A newspaper was started at the low price of one pice the copy. A boarding house for Brahmas was opened at Calcutta, and other institutions inaugurated.

But Keshub, once the fiery leader of the extreme radical party, was already too conservative for the younger generation. They desired to do away with the *purdah* which screened the women during worship at the Mandir. This innovation was not to the reformer's taste, for, as one of his biographers says: "He was always against the kind of female emancipation in vogue amongst the Europeans,"[1] a fact which, had they known of it, would have been dis-

[1] *A Biographical Sketch of Keshub Chunder Sen*, especially prepared for the Students' Jubilee. (Vedanta Press, Calcutta.)

appointing to the ladies who so kindly took Keshub by the hand in England. However, a compromise was made. Seats were placed outside the *purdah* for such ladies as might care to use them.

To obviate any misapprehension with respect to Keshub's attitude towards woman in the abstract, I should add that:

> "To him woman was the incarnation of divinity. He never proposed to compare the superiority or inferiority of man and woman. In woman he saw God. The tenderness of a wife or a mother was to him a celestial fact; and seeing God in woman, he honoured woman with all the Christlike honour—all the tenderness and sweetness—the lingering memories of which pierced like barbed arrows the hearts of many faithful and true women he left behind him."[1]

The quondam worshipper of Kali and Durga might well see divinity in woman, but the worldly-wise Oriental realised the undesirability, at any rate in Bengal, of freely associating women with men even in divine worship.

The period at which we have arrived seems to have been with Keshub one of restless religious excitement. In 1873 he brought the doctrine of *Adesh*, or special inspiration, rather prominently forward, declaring emphatically that inspiration is not only possible, but is a veritable fact in the lives of many devout souls in this age.[2] This dangerous doctrine which, as subsequent events proved, could only too easily be made use of for unworthy purposes, met with many opponents amongst the more sober-minded Samajists. The year 1874 and two or three years following, witnessed a special development of that essentially Asiatic, and perhaps more especially Indian, form of religious feeling, which finds its natural satisfaction in solitary ecstatic contemplation. As a necessary consequence, an order of devotees was established in 1876, divided into three main classes, which in ascending gradation were designated Shabaks, Bhaktas, and Yogis. The lowest class, divided into two sections, is

[1] Mr. P. C. Mozoondar, "Aims and Principles of Keshub Chunder Sen": A sermon delivered in the Town Hall, Calcutta.

[2] Lecture on Inspiration, delivered on the 25th January 1873.

devoted to religious study and the practical performance of religious duties, including doing good to others. The aspiration of the Bhakta is "inebriation in God." He "is most passionately fond of God, and delights in loving Him, and all that pertains to Him. . . . The very utterance of the Divine name causes his heart to overflow, and brings tears of joy to his eyes." As for the highest order of devotees, the Yogis—"they live in the spirit-world, and readily commune with spiritual realities. They welcome whatever is a help to the subjugation of the entire soul, and are always employed in conquering selfishness, carnality, and worldliness. They are happy in prayer and meditation, and in the study of nature." This last addition about the study of nature appears, to say the least, extremely unpractical, if not foolish, for the Yogi is also admonished by Keshub to draw his feet, his ears, his eyes, and his hands away from the world, and to concentrate them *within his own soul*, a procedure not likely to lead to results in science, and is possibly a concession, though a mere verbal concession, to the spirit of the age. Initiations into these various ascetic orders were actually made by Keshub Chunder Sen, who, in his address on the occasion, informed the Yogis that there would be some difference between himself and the men who sat around him, as the message of light would come to them through him.[1] As for the Minister, he too went into retirement to give himself up to contemplation. As a necessary consequence of the predominance in the church of the spirit of renunciation and the practice of solitary communion with God, the business side of the Samaj suffered. The schools were neglected, some had to be closed, and other undertakings came, similarly, to an untimely end. Keshub had already passed the meridian of his intellectual and working life. The stimulating effect of his visit to England was wearing off. He and his followers were, in fact, drifting back into the hereditary Yogaism and pantheism of India, which, as I shall show further on, were assuming larger proportions in Keshub's mind. The religious tendencies exhibited by Keshub since his return from England, and especially his assumption of

[1] Miss E. B. Collet, *The Brahma Year-Book for* 1877, pp. 23–25.

autocratic superiority in all matters connected even with the secular business and arrangements of the Samaj,—his most ardent admirers admit that he could not brook opposition,—led to the estrangement of a small number of his followers, forming, apparently, a compact party in the Samaj, who raised their protests from time to time against the proceedings of their leader. The tension of ill-feeling growing out of rivalries and unsatisfied aspirations in the Samaj was gradually increasing, when a deliberate act of the reformer gave his opponents their opportunity, and called down upon himself the public censure of his followers, recorded in a resolution adopted at a public meeting held on the 22nd March 1878.

The resolution is sufficiently precise to need no commentary. It was couched in the following words:—

> "That in the opinion of the members of the congregation of the Bharatvarshiya Brahma Mandir, assembled in this meeting, Babu Keshub Chunder Sen, the Minister of the Mandir, by countenancing the premature marriage of his daughter, has violated principles accepted by himself and the *Brahma Samaj* of India, and by allowing Hindu rites to be observed in connection with that marriage, has sanctioned an idolatrous early marriage, consequently, in the opinion of this meeting, he cannot continue in the office of the Minister." [1]

An attempt was made to get possession of the Mandir, but Keshub invoked the assistance of the police, and frustrated his opponents.

The bridegroom in this case was, it should be added, a person of high rank, the boy Rajah of Cooch Behar, a fact which accounts for, though it cannot justify, the action of the reformer,[2] whose devoted followers however, believing

[1] G. S. Leonard, *A History of the Brahma Samaj*, p. 165.

[2] In connection with this marriage the following extract from a newspaper under native management, published at Lahore, will not perhaps be uninteresting:—

"The Maharajah of Cooch Behar has made the handsome present of Rs.5000 to the shrine of Kali-Ghat to propitiate the goddess on behalf of the new-born heir to the Raj. A similar sum has also been paid to the Kurta of the Muchooa Bazaar Street. But the Rajah, we were assured by Baboo K. C. Sen, was a staunch Brahmo."—*The Tribune*, Lahore, 20th May 1882.

in the doctrine of *Adesh*, asserted that in this, as in other matters, their leader acted under divine inspiration, acted indeed by God's direct command. The Prophet Muhammad, it is well known, often claimed to have been similarly favoured in matters domestic.

The events just narrated brought matters to a crisis. Another schism took place in the church, and a party of uncompromising theists, under the leadership of Pandit Sevanath Sastri started, on the 15th May 1878, a new Samaj, known henceforth as the *Sadharan* or Universal Brahma Samaj. The creed of this, the youngest of the Brahma sects is, briefly—

1. Belief in the immortality of an infinite creator.
2. Belief in the immortality of the soul.
3. Belief in the duty and necessity of spiritual worship of God.
4. Disbelief in any infallible book, or man, as the means of salvation.[1]

The Sadharan Brahma Samaj has set its face steadily against idolatry and caste. One of its rules is that "none but Brahmos who have entirely discarded idolatry and caste in their private lives can be office-bearers, ministers, missionaries, or members of the Executive Committee of the Samaj."[2]

As a precaution against the undue ascendancy or arbitrary action of individuals, the constitution of the Samaj has been laid down upon democratic lines, all disputed points being put to and decided by the votes of the members. The Samaj, which has been in existence for twenty-eight years, has been very active, and has achieved a fair measure of success in Calcutta.

Being a purely theistic sect of the type long known in Europe and America, the Sadharan Brahma Samaj has, of course, many friends outside India, but this very fact, together with the pronounced *non-Hindu* character of the Samaj, will undoubtedly prove prejudicial to its influence in its own country, and prevent its growth beyond very moderate limits.

[1] Pandit Sevanath Sastri, M.A., *The New Dispensation and the Sadharan Brahma Samaj*, p. 90.

[2] *Idem*, p. 108.

THEISM IN BENGAL—*continued*

SECTION VI.—Keshub believes himself to be a prophet—Proclaims the New Dispensation—Its aims and objects—Keshub's death—Subsequent history of the sect.

THE schism which culminated in the formation of the Sadharan Brahma Samaj was a very serious event in the career of Keshub Chunder Sen, and was met in characteristic fashion. To cover his recent defeat, he made more arrogant claims as a divinely appointed teacher than at any previous stage of his public life, and at the same time, in virtue ostensibly of a new commission from God, materially revised his teachings to suit his altered circumstances, and to meet the exigencies of his case.

Within a few months of the schism just referred to, the reformer took as the theme of a public discourse the question "Am I an inspired Prophet?" and came to the conclusion that "he was not as ordinary men are," that he was under direct divine inspiration, and "commissioned by God to preach certain truths," and that those who protested against his preaching protested against the dispensations of God Almighty. In a word, Keshub, while still sometimes affecting humility, declared himself a prophet in unmistakable words. Further, probably as a sort of apology or explanation of his inconsistencies and doctrinal caprices, he informed the world that the Lord had told him he was to have "no doctrine, no creed, but a perennial and perpetual inspiration from Heaven."

Now Keshub's hitherto ostentatiously professed leanings towards Christianity had undoubtedly militated against his popularity with his own countrymen, so he seems to have deemed it advisable at the present crisis to revise his creed

To face page 136

in this respect, and henceforth gave greater prominence to Hindu ideals and sentiments in his theology. Dr. Bhattacharjee has pointed out that the moment was peculiarly convenient for such a change; as Keshub's distinguished patron, Lord Lawrence, a man of deep religious convictions, who had done so much to bring the Bengali reformer prominently before the world as one about to become a Christian, had recently died in England. Released from the ties of gratitude which, through the friendship of the late Viceroy of India, had bound him to Christianity, Keshub remodelled his old opinions and taught quite a new doctrine.

The views which at this period Keshub expressed in regard to Christ and Christianity, divested of their mysticism and disentangled from the web of rhetoric which he spun round them, are both curious and interesting. He held, as the outcome of long years of study and meditation, that the Asiatic Christ of history, the man of Nazareth, is only partially understood in Europe, and, in important points, totally misunderstood. The Christ offered to India by the English missionary—a man of narrow dogmas and practical good works—was in Keshub's opinion an English version of the true Christ of Judæa. This true Christ, the Asiatic Christ, was a *pantheist* and a *yogi*!—a yogi of unblemished virtue, who retired to the mountains to *pray*. The memorable assertion "I and my Father are One" was, as Keshub understood it, but the expression of the doctrine of communion with divinity—that communion which necessarily follows from the total suppression of self, and is familiar to Hindu philosophy and theology. The claim made by Jesus in the words "Before Abraham was, I am," meant to Keshub no more than this: that Christ felt He had existed potentially in the Supreme Being from all eternity—"though the human Christ was born, all that was divine in Him existed eternally in God."[1] It will be noticed that Keshub Chunder Sen indulged in no critical objections to the authenticity of the Gospels. He accepts them in their entirety, but assumes

[1] Keshub Chunder Sen, Lecture "India asks, 'Who is Christ?'" 9th April 1879.

the right of interpreting the history of Christ's life and works in his own way, which is characteristically Indian, showing clearly what firm hold pantheism and Yogaism have upon the mind of India; and how necessary it is to keep them prominently in view when studying Indian life or estimating former or contemporary religious developments in India. In the days of his intellectual and physical vigour, before his visit to England, we find Keshub speaking of pantheism, "with its arrogant spirit of self-adoration," in terms of strong disapproval, and predicting that it, along with other evils, would find no place in the Church of the Future. But ten years later, 1879, this inspired teacher tells the world, "I am in spirit a pantheist, though I hate the errors of pantheism. I wish to encourage this spirit of pantheism in India";[1] and in another place:

> "Pantheism and mysticism are things of Asia, while positivism and all the sciences of the day are from Europe. My Church is an Asiatic Church. I am in my very bones and blood, in the very constitution of my soul, essentially an Asiatic. . . . Like a mighty river the stream of natural devotion comes into my Church from the Vedas and the Upanishads, the pantheistic books and mystic scriptures of ancient India."

As to Yogaism he says:

> "Though living in the nineteenth century, I go back to the mystic age to drink of the pure fountain of Yoga communion there. I go to the Aryan Yogis of ancient India to learn contemplation."

Keshub must have felt that he was called upon to prove his credentials by effecting something noteworthy—something that might satisfy the aspirations of his followers, and be an answer to his adversaries. Let us see what he attempted, and what success attended his efforts.

Out of the hosts of the Hindu Pantheon the Bengalis have, as explained in an earlier chapter, the goddesses Durga and Kali as the special objects of their worship, and throughout their religious development have manifested a marked leaning towards the adoration of *Sakti* or the *female energy*. *Naturally*, therefore, Keshub Chunder Sen,

[1] Keshub Chunder Sen, Lecture "Am I an inspired Prophet?"

under national and hereditary influences, recognised in the Supreme Ruler of the Universe, the *mother* of mankind. He proclaimed the motherhood of God in his usual impulsive, emotional, and extravagant way in the year 1879. Flags inscribed with the word "Mother" were hoisted upon the house-tops, and processions paraded the streets singing hymns to the Divine Mother, who is made to say, in the *Mirror* of the 12th October 1879: "Ye shall go forth from village to village, singing my mercies, and proclaiming unto all men that I am India's Mother."

Accordingly a band of Keshub's missionaries with some attendants made a short tour in Bengal, preaching the motherhood of God, and Keshub's devoted followers have ever since addressed their prayers to the Divine Mother.[1] This was only the beginning of the work entrusted to the new prophet.

Freed by the schism of May 1878 from the restraining influence of the more practical and sober members of the Samaj, and once fairly launched on the sea of innovation under the sway of the spirit of religious mysticism, there was no limit to the vagaries in which Keshub indulged, and to the blind obedience with which some of his adherents accepted his inspired dicta. He seemed determined to exemplify in his own person the idea to which he had given public expression: "That there is something remarkably irregular in the lives and career of great men, which ordinary facts and precedents cannot account for or explain. . . . Great men, like comets, move in eccentric orbits."

Towards the end of 1879, Keshub's *Sunday Mirror* announced the advent of one of those manifestations of the divine will, which occur at special times and under special circumstances, when the world is in need of a revival or upheaving. And the prophet himself followed this announcement by proclaiming to the world in January 1880 the birth of the "New Dispensation." And what is this New Dispensation?

[1] "Of late it has become customary to address the Deity as Mother."—*The Faith and Progress of the Brahma Samaj*, by P. C. Mozoomdar, p. 394. In this book, pp. 394-401, the Bengali feeling in respect to the "Divine Maternity" is well set forth by one who is both a Brahma and a native of Bengal.

> "It is the harmony of all Scriptures and Prophets and Dispensations. It is not an isolated creed, but the science which binds and explains and harmonises all religions. It gives to history a meaning, to the action of Providence a consistency, to quarrelling churches a common bond, and to successive dispensations a continuity. It shows by marvellous synthesis how the different rainbow colours are one in the light of heaven. The New Dispensation is the sweet music of diverse instruments. It is the precious necklace in which are strung together the rubies and pearls of all ages and climes. It is the celestial court where around enthroned Divinity shine the lights of all heavenly saints and prophets. It is the wonderful solvent, which fuses all dispensations into a new chemical compound. It is the mighty absorbent, which absorbs all that is true and good and beautiful in the objective world."[1]

Following this announcement, and within the same year, Keshub Chunder's organ, the *Sunday Mirror*, gave, as a Bengali Brahman remarked, "the following certificate of good character to the Hindu religion":[2]—

> "Hindu idolatry is not to be altogether overlooked or rejected. As we explained some time ago, it represents millions of broken fragments of God, collect them together and you get the individual Divinity. To believe in an undivided deity without reference to those aspects of His nature is to believe in an abstract God, and it would lead us to practical rationalism and infidelity. If we are to worship Him in all His manifestations we shall name one attribute—Sarswatee, another Lashmi, another Mahadeva, another Jagadhatri, etc., and worship God each day under a new name, that is to say, in a new aspect."

Such teaching was assuredly pure Hinduism, and utterly at variance with the tenets of earlier Brahmaism.

The New Dispensation having come into the world to harmonise conflicting creeds and regenerate mankind, must have its outward symbol, its triumphant banner, floating proudly on the joyful air of highly favoured India.

[1] Keshub Chunder Sen, "We Apostles of the New Dispensation." Lecture delivered in Calcutta on the 22nd January 1881.

[2] Dr. J. N. Bhattacharjee, M.A., D.L., *Hindu Castes and Sects*, p. 168.

A flag was therefore made, and formally consecrated as the "Banner of the New Dispensation." This emblem of "regenerated and saving theism" the new prophet himself formed with a yak's tail, and kissed with his own inspired lips. In orthodox Hindu fashion, his missionaries —apostles of the New Dispensation—went round it with lights in their hands, while his less privileged followers respectfully touched the sacred pole, and humbly bowed down to it.[1] In a word, the banner was worshipped as Hindu idols are worshipped any day in India. Carried away by a spirit of innovation, anxious to keep himself prominently before the world, and realising no doubt that since churches and sects do not flourish on intellectual pabulum only, certain mystic rites and gorgeous ceremonials were necessary to the success of the New Dispensation, Keshub introduced into his church various observances which attracted a good deal of attention, and did not escape criticism.

On one occasion he went with his disciples in procession, singing hymns, to a stagnant tank in Calcutta, and made believe that they were in Palestine, and on the side of the flowing Jordan. Standing near the tank, Keshub said, "Beloved brethren, we have come into the land of the Jews, and we are seated on the bank of the Jordan. Let them that have eyes see. Verily, verily, here was the Lord Jesus baptized eighteen hundred years ago. Behold the holy waters wherein was the Son of God immersed."

Addressing the water before him, Keshub said: "O Thou Great *Varuna*, Water of Life, Sacred Water, Mighty Expanse of Sea and Oceans and Rivers, we glorify thee; Thou art not God; but the Lord is in thee. . . ."

After explaining that Jesus plunged into the Jordan "because He saw the water was full of God," Keshub anointed himself with oil after the manner of the Bengalis, and immersed himself three times in the water, saying: "Glory to the Father, Glory unto the Son, Glory unto the Holy Ghost," and then took a fourth immersion to the glory of "Truth, Wisdom, and Joy in One."

[1] Pandit Sevanath Sastri, M.A., *The New Dispcnsation and the Sadharan Brahma Samaj*, p. 55.

We learn also that Keshub and his disciples attempted to hold communion with saints and prophets of the olden time, upon whose works and teachings they had been pondering in retirement and solitude.

On this subject the following notice appeared in the *Sunday Mirror*:—

> "It is proposed to promote communion with departed saints amongst the more advanced Brahmos. With a view to achieve this object successfully, ancient prophets and saints will be taken one after another on special occasions and made the subject of close study, meditation, and prayer. Particular places also will be assigned to which the devotees will resort as pilgrims. There for hours together they will try to draw inspiration from particular saints. We believe a spiritual pilgrimage to Moses will be shortly undertaken. Only earnest devotees ought to join."

This idea of the efficacy of contemplation to ensure communion with Deity or disembodied spirits, is one pre-eminently and characteristically Hindu. It is indeed the Indian idea of Yoga, which formed the subject of Keshub Chunder's latest writing.

The same year Keshub performed what is known as the *Hom* ceremony, a sort of adoration of fire.[1] Addressing the flames, he said, "O Thou blazing Agni (fire), Great are thou, great among the forces in creation. We shall honour thee and magnify thee because of thy greatness and majesty. Thou art not God; we do not adore thee, but in thee dwells the Lord," and so on.[2]

Attracted by the mystery of the Eucharist, the Brahma reformer seems also to have adopted this rite in 1881, using rice and milk instead of bread and wine. At an earlier date he had, in imitation of the practice of certain worshippers of Vishnu, danced a mystic dance with his followers, clad in gay garments around the invisible "Divine Mother" in the Brahma Mandir. Thus we have both Hindu and Christian rites and ceremonies alike finding favour with the prophet of the New Dispensation,

[1] Described in *Indian Life, Religious and Social*, pp. 95–97.

[2] *The New Dispensation and the Sadharan Brahma Samaj*, by Pandit Sevanath Sastri, M.A., pp. 50–59.

who in adopting them of course affected to give them a new spiritual allegorical meaning. As an instance we may cite the *Hom* ceremony, which, in the "Brahma Samaj of India represents burning the passions in effigy."[1]

What Keshub was trying to effect—what at least was his ostensible object at this time (May 1881)—may be judged from the following extract from a letter of his to Professor Max Müller:[2]—

> "The British public ought to know how the most advanced type of Hinduism in India is trying to absorb and assimilate the Christianity of Christ, and how it is establishing and spreading, under the name of the New Dispensation, a new Hinduism, which combines *Yoga and Bhakti*, and also a new Christianity, which blends together Apostolical faith and modern civilisation and science."

It may not be irrelevant to notice the fact that in 1880, or prior to Keshub's letter to Professor Max Müller, there appeared an article by Mr. Edward White in the *Calcutta Review*, explaining Edward von Hartmann's views in regard to the religion of the future, in which the following quotation from von Hartmann appears:—

> "Looking to the course of history, we find that the religion of the future must be realised through a synthesis of the Hindu and Judæo-Christian phases of religious thought. It must combine the advantages of both, and thereby become capable of explaining both, as a universal religion, such a pan-monotheistic system would be most in conformity to reason, and the best adapted to excite and satisfy the religious sentiments. It would afford the strongest metaphysical support to ethics, and approach nearest to giving that which men seek as truth in religion."

Strange as it may seem, it is not at all improbable that Keshub, in introducing into his Church heterogeneous rites and ceremonies borrowed from Christianity and Hinduism, was actually deluding himself into the belief that he was uniting the two religions, and carrying into effect the

[1] *The Theistic Review and Interpreter* of 1881, quoted in Count D'Alviella's *The Contemporary Evolution of Religious Thought* (1885), p. 287.

[2] Max Müller, *Biographical Essays*, p. 117.

glorious object of his New Dispensation. His rhetorical approval of Muhammadanism and Buddhism, of Zoroastrianism and the rest, began and ended in mere words. Keshub was indeed a Hindu strongly leavened with Christianity, and perhaps, in his earlier manhood, not without a tincture of rationalism. In his best days he was more Christian than Hindu—in his later life, more Hindu than Christian.

But consecrated banners, musical processions, pilgrimages to Jordan, mystic dances, the adoption of rites and ceremonies from other creeds, had not exhausted the resources or inventive powers of Keshub Babu, who, with his old love for the stage and stage effect, brought out, at the end of 1882, a moral play, written by one of his disciples, in which the prevailing vices of young Bengalis were satirised, and the triumph of the New Dispensation dramatically illustrated. In this performance the prophet, as we may well call him, appeared behind the footlights in his favourite character of a juggler, and to the delight of his followers fashioned instantaneously a single symbol, the symbol of the New Dispensation, out of the cross, the crescent, the trident of Siva, and other religious emblems of the older faiths of the world,—a childish trick at best, the levity of which certainly produces an unfavourable impression with respect to Keshub's wisdom, and his sense of the fitness of things.

Shortly after his performance on the stage, the prophet of the New Dispensation gave his last public lecture in Calcutta, entitled, "Asia's Message to Europe," from which it would seem that he had arrived at a more exalted opinion of the divine mission entrusted to him than any he had held before. Out of a cloud of pretentious rhapsody, confused thought, fantastic theology, and misunderstood history, we gather that Keshub Chunder accepting, in his own way, the doctrine of the universal atonement of Christ, indulged the ambitious and utopian dream of uniting, under the central banner of the New Dispensation, all the religions of the world, in a purified form, but each retaining its own individuality, each led by its trusted chief, and each marching under its respective Scriptures. In other words he wanted all religious sects to become catholic in sentiment, to give up sectarianism and yet retain all their own distinctive peculiarities!

The reader may, perhaps, think that the Brahmist leader must have meant something else, something less impracticable; but there is no room for doubt about the matter. The accomplishment of this task was, indeed, the special mission entrusted by God to Keshub Babu; it was the essence of the New Dispensation, and had been already proclaimed by him to the world in a lecture entitled "We Apostles of the New Dispensation," and had been reiterated in no uncertain terms by Keshub's organ the *Sunday Mirror*. "Our position," said that paper, "is not that truths are to be found in all religions, but that all the established religions of the world are true. There is a great deal of difference between the two assertions."

Yes, indeed, there is! And a great deal of difference too between this position and that held by the prophet himself fourteen years earlier, when he revealed to the world the character and constitution of the Church of the Future. Many reformers have cherished the fond hope of effecting a harmony of various cults by persuading the followers of such faiths that the root-ideas, the basal elements, of their respective creeds are essentially identical. Something of this kind seems to have been in Keshub's mind in the earlier days of his career, but his ideas had undergone a great change latterly, and grandiose dreams of uniting under one banner all the religions of the world, with little, if any, modification, was the final result of five-and-twenty years of his ministry. This was Keshub's last word to an expectant world, and though his aspiration may be impossible of realisation, it is so much in keeping with Hindu conceptions that it invites further consideration.

No Jew, Christian, or Muslim could ever have entertained Keshub's idea. As each one of these *along with his co-religionists* is chosen of God *to the exclusion of the rest of mankind*, and has special knowledge of the one and only way to propitiate God and attain heaven, so each one is fiercely intolerant of the faiths of the other two, and in a milder degree of all other religions also. Amongst Christians themselves we have experience of the bitter hostility of the various churches and sects towards one another, and with these familiar facts before us may well marvel at the kindly hope which animated the Hindu reformer's spacious dream of the union of all the faiths of the world under the banner of a single Church universal. Most certainly, as I have remarked above, the hope which Keshub Chunder cherished could never have occurred to the mind of such exclusives as Jew, Christian, or Muslim, and to the followers of any of these faiths must appear ridiculous if not impious. But the Hindu views this matter from quite another standpoint.

At the "Parliament of Religions" held in Chicago in 1893, the Bengali Sadhu Swami Vivakananda said, "that it was a Hindu principle to recognise all faiths as expressions of truth, and that from his earliest boyhood he had repeated a sacred text, used daily by millions in India, which says that as the different streams having their sources in different places, all mingle their water in the sea, so the different paths which men take through different tendencies, various though they appear, and crooked or straight, all lead to the one Lord."[1]

And in the Bhagavad-gita, Krishna, as the Supreme Being, says to Arjuna: "They also who worship other gods and make offering to them with faith, O son of Kunti, do verily make offering to me, though not according to ordinance,"—a transcendently lofty conception, which fortunately for humanity is now finding an echo in European and American thought. The Hindu, it is true, does not regard all modes of worship as equally admirable or efficacious, but he deems them all worthy of sympathetic countenance as being natural aspirations towards the Infinite God; and his sincerity is amply exemplified in the growth by accretion, and the heterogeneous constitution, of his own religious system, as we find it in the Hinduism of the present day.

Keshub's dream then was quite in harmony with Hindu ideals; but in utter discord with the pretensions and aims of the more exclusive and intolerant religions of the world. That there will ever be one universal world-religion, or even

[1] *The World's Parliament of Religions*, vol. i. pp. 242, 243.

a happy union of all the faiths of mankind under a common banner, is a vain hope; but time and an increase of knowledge, especially of the science of comparative religion, will assuredly promote amongst intellectual men in advanced nations a hitherto unknown religious toleration, not contemptuous but sympathetic.

What Keshub did accomplish, we need hardly say, was something very different from what he hoped for. He, who was always protesting against sectarianism, added, as if by the irony of fate, *one* more sect, one more religion if you like, to the hundreds already existing, weaving into the ceremonial law of the new society, rites and symbols borrowed without any sense of historical fitness or traditional propriety from both Hinduism and Christianity, under the belief, it would seem, that by so doing an amalgamation of these creeds was being effected under the banner of the New Dispensation. At the same time Keshub's fervent admiration of Christ's life and work, and his eloquent confession of devotion to Jesus, has probably made a deeper impression upon his countrymen than the preaching of a multitude of foreign missionaries could ever have done, although it cannot be denied that these foreign Christian missionaries created the moral atmosphere that gave birth to a desire for a pure form of worship, and made Brahmaism possible.

Within a few months of the date of his lecture "Asia's Message to Europe," already referred to, the Brahma leader died, on the 8th January 1884. His body was laid on a pyre of sandal-wood at the Nimtollah Burning Ghat, in the presence of a large concourse of persons, including some Europeans. As the sun was setting, Karvana Chunder Sen, eldest son of the deceased, ignited the pyre, uttering these words: "In the name of God I convey the sacred fire to these last remains. Let the mortal part burn and perish: the immortal part will revive. O Lord, the liberated soul rejoices in thee in thy blessed abode." The prophet's ashes, collected in an urn, were carried away, and interred in the little chapel adjoining his residence, known as Lily Cottage.

The ceremony of mourning for the dead to be observed

by his followers was thus prescribed by the *Apostolic Durbar:*

> "All who have taken to mourning for the late Babu Keshub Chunder Sen are enjoined by the *Apostolic Durbar* of the New Dispensation, to observe it for a fortnight in the following manner:—
>
> "(1) Every true believer in the New Dispensation shall wear on his person a piece of *gairu* cloth, striped in the manner prescribed in the New Sanhita.
>
> "(2) He shall abstain from animal food.
>
> "(3) He shall give up all manner of mirth and merriment.
>
> "(4) He shall study the life and teachings of the minister.
>
> "(5) He shall pray for the descent of the Holy Spirit, and practise communion daily with the view to realise the presence of the Divine Mother, with Her child, the minister, on Her lap.
>
> "(6) He shall try to assimilate the minister's character in his life with his daily food.
>
> "(7) He shall hold conversation with friends every evening on spiritual topics."

On the anniversary of his death the Brahma Tract Society sold their publications at half-price to commemorate *the ascension* of Keshub Chunder Sen. The death of the reformer called forth a great many appreciative articles on his life and character in the magazines and newspapers of the day. Professor Max Müller, writing on the occasion, gave Keshub Chunder Sen "the first place among his fellow-countrymen, and a pre-eminent place among the best of mankind."

"On more than one occasion," observed Count D'Alviella, "I have severely condemned his acts, and almost despaired of his future. But whenever I turned to his discourses and writings, I again fell in some measure under the charm which arose from his personality and genius."[1]

Although an admiring countryman believes Keshub to have been "one of the greatest thinkers, one of the greatest philosophers, and one of the greatest men of the world," I feel bound to say that he was none of these, but a pious

[1] *The Contemporary Evolution of Religious Thought*, p. 284.

mystic, endowed with a rare gift of expression, a marked individuality, a strong will, not a little worldly wisdom and a charm of manner which gave him a great ascendancy over the men with whom he came in contact.

There was one thing that Keshub believed in, and was never tired of teaching with all the glowing eloquence of a really gifted man—the immanence of the Creator. To Keshub, God was the ever-present sustainer of the universe an all-pervading Presence, the very life of the world. He tries to keep before himself and his hearers the idea of a personal God, but the vision seems to elude him; he slides almost unconsciously into pantheism, which after all is the natural and hereditary creed of India. With his fervent piety and passionate admiration of Jesus, which seems to have coloured his entire life, he might possibly, under other circumstances, have become a Christian, but he came to believe, sincerely perhaps, that he was himself entrusted by God with a divine mission. His confidence in himself was so great that men believed in him. His knowledge was apparently very limited, but his imagination was strong. He liked to make allusions to physical science, and always spoke with deference and approval of the work accomplished by scientists. He himself had a short cut to knowledge. He saw, he felt, and thus he knew, and what he knew he proclaimed.

In the later years of his ministry the Brahma Church of the New Dispensation was gradually developed into a distinct religion. It was no longer Hindu theism nor pure theism, but a new and very latitudinarian religion dating from the nineteenth century. A religion of sentiment, mysterious and ritualistic, with a strong leaning towards pantheism and Yogaism, admirably suited to the dreamy temperament of the Indian people, and in harmony with their past religious development.

Hardly had the earth closed over Keshub's ashes, when jealousies and rivalries disturbed the Brahma camp. The first cause of dissension was the *Vedi*, or marble pulpit in the *Mandir*, which the family of the deceased and several of the Brahma missionaries desired to set apart in memory of the prophet, whose spirit was supposed to occupy the accustomed place in the congregation of the faithful. On the other side, Babu Protab Chunder Mozoomdar, the secretary to the congregation, protested against the proposal as being contrary to rules and principles laid down by Keshub himself; but, if I am not mistaken, the pulpit, despite his remonstrances, remains empty to this day in memory of the prophet.

With time, disagreement and strife became so rife amongst the leaders of the Church of the New Dispensation that in 1901 Babu Suresh Chunder Bose issued a public appeal to the followers of the late reformer, exhorting them to support Babu Protab Chunder Mozoomdar, "who," said this advocate, "is verily our Minister, though his missionary brethren by disputing the fact have wrecked the church." Mozoomdar, who seems to have been a man of great earnestness and piety, visited England in 1874, and again in 1883 on his way to attend the "Parliament of Religions" at Chicago, where he represented the Brahma Samaj, spoke on several occasions, and created a favourable impression. He had been Keshub's companion and friend since their college days, and always expressed the highest admiration of the founder of the Church of the New Dispensation. Under his guidance the Samaj seems to have gradually drifted towards American Unitarianism, and to have been supported, in no slight degree, by funds from the United States of America. On this point the following appeared in the *Civil and Military Gazette* of Lahore on the 18th of May 1895:—

> "The fact that Baboo Protab Chunder Mozoomdar, the distinguished Brahmo missionary, who has visited Lahore many times on a missionary tour, is now dependent on his American friends for the support of his mission-work and himself, has caused surprise only to those who are ignorant of the dissensions and disputes that now obtain in the section of the Brahmo Church to which Mr. Mozoomdar belongs. In fact, the Brahmos of the New Dispensation are now divided into half a dozen small parties, or rather coteries, of one of which Mr. Mozoomdar is the recognised leader. He himself is not a man of means, and his followers are too poor to help him. When Mr. Mozoomdar

visited America as representative of the Brahmo Samaj to the Chicago Parliament of Religions, his American admirers proposed to start a fund in aid of his mission work, and this proposal has now been carried out, and from the 'Mozoomdar Mission Fund' in New York the Brahmo missionary is in receipt of an annual allowance. Mr. Mozoomdar's supporters in America are all Christians, chiefly of the Unitarian persuasion, who evidently regard him as one of themselves. The Brahmo missionary's well-known work entitled *Oriental Christ*, is the cause of his popularity among the ministers of the Unitarian Church in America."

On the 27th May 1905, Mozoomdar died at Calcutta, and in announcing his death the *Indian Review* remarked:

"Of recent years it has been growing more and more apparent that the hold which the Brahmo Samaj had on the mind of a considerable section of educated Indians during the lifetime of Keshub Chunder Sen, and even for some time later, has been steadily decreasing, and it is to be apprehended that the death of two such leaders like Devendranath and Mozoomdar leaves it in a poor plight indeed, seeing that, among the younger men, there are none who can fill the positions occupied by them in the eye of the public as well as regards the affairs of the Samaj with anything like success."

Since Keshub's death there has been a tendency towards the establishment of friendly relations between the different sections of the Brahmic Church, which was not possible during the lifetime of the prophet of the New Dispensation. I have before me the report (February 1896 to February 1905) of the "Brahmo Samaj Committee," in which all three Samajes are found co-operating with one another and *with Unitarian Societies in England* in philanthropic work in India, the funds for such work being nearly all derived from England. This arrangement shows the subtle potency of gold even in such an unlikely enterprise as the drawing together of hostile sects, and it reveals moreover the first steps of the inevitable ascendancy, in the perhaps not distant future, of the English and American Unitarians in the Brahmic Churches.

This, for aught I know, may be for the best; but however commendable a spirit of mutual toleration and fellowship between the different sections of the Brahma Samajes may be, the existence of such feelings amongst sectaries holding very divergent views on essential matters, seems only possible as the result of an increasing lukewarmness, and, if so, the beginning of the end of Brahmaism as a distinctive Indian institution cannot be very far off.

We have followed the history of the Brahmic movement from its beginning under Ram Mohun Roy to its latest developments, and it is but just to add that the succession of extraordinarily capable and exemplary men who have guided the fortunes of the sect in its various branches would reflect great credit upon any community whether in the East or the West, their lives and teaching bearing striking testimony to the high intellectual vigour and moral excellence which can be found amongst the Bengalis, a race only too frequently and too hastily condemned by Europeans.

THEISM IN BENGAL—*continued*

SECTION VII.—Summary and Conclusion.

FROM the foregoing brief sketch of the history of the Brahma Samaj, it is evident that the seeds of his subsequent theistic doctrines were first planted in the mind of Ram Mohun Roy by his studies in *Muslim literature* and theology.

Discovering later that his new ideas were at least not at variance with interpretations that might be put upon certain texts scattered through the ancient Hindu Scriptures, he, a Hindu and a Brahman, naturally leaned for support upon these national authorities, and taught a pure theism, claiming to rest upon the sanction of the Vedas, but borrowing ideas in no small measure from Christianity, of which he had made a careful and diligent study. Under Debendra Nath Tagore, however, the sect founded by Ram Mohun Roy, hard pressed on every side by the criticisms of the orthodox Hindus and others, reluctantly gave up their profession of faith in the Vedas as the authority for the theistic doctrines which they held, but with the conservative spirit so natural to the followers of an old religion, they continued to cling with tenacity to the sacred Scriptures of their country, and, with an amiable inconsistency, prepared for themselves a religious text-book by culling passages from works whose divine authority they had ceased to maintain. While renouncing idolatry, they adhered as closely as possible to the rules and customs of Hinduism. And this is still the position and attitude of the Adi Brahma Samaj.

With Keshub Chunder Sen new principles of thought and action were brought into play, giving, at first, a quite distinct and un-Hindu direction to the current of doctrines and events. At one time he seems indeed to have been in reality only an advanced Christian Unitarian, holding opinions identical with those professed by thousands of that sect in England and America. Later on he began to believe that he was himself entrusted with a special divine mission—the reconciling of all the existing forms of religion. As time went by he drifted further and further away from his old opinions, and, still clinging to "the Asiatic Christ" as a raft of safety, floated into the deep and tranquil waters of his own national mysticism and pantheism. But the voice of the restless nineteenth century, calling for deeds, demanding results, would not let the prophet lose himself in the ecstatic Yogaism into which he was now sinking. Roused by the voices of his friends and enemies, the prophet rushed into action with feverish excitement, waved aloft the banner of the New Dispensation, transformed into one device the symbols (alas, the symbols only!) of contending creeds, paraded the streets with flags and music, danced mystic dances in the Mandir, adopted some of the more prominent features and ceremonies of an alien creed, and finally passed away leaving behind him a disorganised sect and a place of worship of mixed European and Oriental architecture, adorned, or perhaps disfigured, with tablets, pictures, and statues copied from other churches, and let in haphazard into the walls of the new structure.

As the result of seventy-five years of theistic agitation and preaching developed from the germ originally planted by Ram Mohun Roy, we have at the present day—

1. A sect of *Hindu* theists—the Adi Brahma Samaj;
2. A sect of *non-Hindu* theists—the Sadharan Brahma Samaj, who take reason and conscience as their guide; and
3. The sect of the New Dispensation, strongly Hindu in its spirit and leanings, but practically believers in Keshub Chunder Sen as an inspired teacher or prophet.

The original sect of Ram Mohun Roy is quite extinct, the Adi Brahma Samaj of Debendra Nath Tagore is in a stationary condition; but the two younger Samajes still show signs of vitality and the spirit of propagandism. The numerical results of the entire movement, from which so much was expected and which has been watched with such keen interest in India and outside India, are quite insignificant, since only 4050 persons returned themselves as Brahmas when the last census of India was taken in 1901. The indirect results of the movement will be referred to in a subsequent page.

In considering, as we may now do, how far the political conditions prevailing in the British Indian Empire are favourable, or otherwise, to the establishment of a new religion capable of comparing in numbers and influence with the old-established faiths, we have to bear in mind that the cessation of all internal warfare, the recognised liberty of thought and complete freedom of expression enjoyed by all religious denominations, the facilities for rapid intercommunication afforded by railways, and the possession of a common language—English—by all educated natives throughout the country, make the quick and extensive propagation of new ideas an easy matter, and give the greatest encouragement and scope to that widespread missionary enterprise, which forms a remarkable feature of the Brahmic and other religious movements of the time. The common subjection to an alien government gives rise to a sense of fellowship amongst the subject races, and encourages a feeling of fraternity, beneath which, as in Keshub's doctrine of the "Fatherhood of God, and the brotherhood of man," we can detect the underlying idea of the equality of *all* men, that is of *conquerors* and *conquered alike.* The advantages just referred to, which are not confined to any one sect, and the bonds of union, more sentimental perhaps than real, amongst the educated classes, are not, however, sufficient to encourage the expectation of the establishment in India of a new religion on an extended scale in face of the deep-rooted, time-honoured religions which already occupy the ground, particularly as the wisdom and policy of the British Government preclude the idea of persecution of any kind, and new religious movements in India are likely to lack that fanaticism amongst the leaders, that loyalty and obedience amongst the followers, and that thorough organisation in the whole body which arise out of the presence of a common and pressing *danger*. Whether any form of Brahmaism will be found sufficient for the spiritual needs of a considerable portion of the Indian population, and whether the usual miraculous legends which accrete round the early history of religious movements, will make their appearance in connection with the initial struggles of any of the Brahmic Churches, time will show. But it may be safely predicted that unless such legends do spring up and flourish vigorously, the Brahma reformation will not give rise to any new and popular religion in India.

The austere tenets of the Sadharan Brahma Samaj preclude any such possibility in connection with that sect. But the *Maharshi* Debendra Nath might well become the semi-divine centre of a future Hindu sect of importance; and in Keshub's case the circumstances are more favourable and the probabilities of legendary developments still greater. Indeed, it seems to me that should it come to pass, when the haze of years casts a dim veil over the personality of the prophet, that his followers pay him divine honours as some have done already, then a *Keshubite* religion may attain a vigorous growth and possibly endure when the other Brahma sects have either been completely reabsorbed into Hinduism, or been refined into some one or other of the forms of Unitarianism or Rationalism established in Europe or America.

Socially considered, the Brahmic movement in its later developments is of importance, as it encourages the dissolution of the barriers of caste, staunchly and practically encourages the remarriage of widows, and makes it a professed object to raise the intellectual status and improve the social position of Indian women by giving them a freedom which the orthodox party would not for a moment countenance. And as I write this I call to mind how years ago the leader of the Sadharan Brahma Samaj at Lahore pointed out to me the adult unmarried ladies of his household, walking about unveiled in the gardens of beautiful Shalamar. The party of ladies was certainly not attended by members of the opposite sex, and probably before the complete emancipation of the Hindu female from the seclusion of the zenana can be safely carried out, and free social intercourse between the sexes allowed, "the moral tone of native society," as Babu Shib Chunder Bose has remarked, "must be immensely raised, its manners and customs entirely remodelled, and its traditional institutions and prescriptive usages thoroughly purified."[1] But the fact that the gentleman I refer to had the courage to have *adult* unmarried daughters, and to allow them to go about unveiled, proves sufficiently that the views and opinions of the Brahmas are not merely theoretical, but actually affect their habits and customs.

Of course social reforms cannot be carried out without opposition and reviling, and I have heard orthodox Hindus affirm that the Brahma sects were chiefly recruited from amongst men who were of low caste, or had through some cause or other lost social position, that, in fact, those who now give their warm support to the Brahmic movement are just such as a generation ago would most probably have been driven into the arms of Christianity.

One most important aspect of the religious situation remains to be noticed. I refer to *the powerful reaction in favour of Hinduism* created by a spirit of opposition to Christian and Brahmic teaching, and strongly stimulated by the political discontent of recent years.

> "There was a time," says an Indian journal, "when Brahmoism was regarded to be the only possible religion for every educated Hindu, who was eager to be loyal to his conscience. The untenableness of idolatry, judged from the liberated intellectual and spiritual standpoint of every man of culture, was made so clear and unmistakable by the labours of the Brahmo Samaj, that it was a disgrace to be an idolater. Unhappily this healthy public opinion has not lasted. In direct opposition to the teachings of the Hindu Shastras, which set down idolatry as only a low form of worship, fit only for the ignorant and the uncultured, a new cult has been founded which openly and defiantly dignifies idolatry into the only possible and practical form of religious worship, easily exciting

[1] Shib Chunder Bose, *The Hindoos as they are*, p. 7.

true religious emotion and developing genuine Bhakti or divine love. Again, there is another section of our educated countrymen who uphold *Adwaitism*, or the philosophical Pantheism of Sankaracharya.

"The reasoned idolatry and the abstract pantheism of the day which count among their votaries a large proportion of those Hindus of education and culture whom the Brahmo Samaj at one time hoped to attract to its fold, constitute the two prominent modes of rampart religious thought which it has at present to combat."[1]

The reaction referred to in the passage just cited is not a mere revival of the old Hinduism. The awakened mind of educated India will never revert to the veritable past, but will find temporary satisfaction for its religious needs in a reformed but progressive Hinduism, modified in many respects, but always haunted and even dominated by its essential old-time ideals.

With respect to the spiritual influence of the Brahmic Church, it doubtless extends far beyond the limits of its own professed adherents; but we need to guard ourselves against an exaggerated idea of the importance of this new religious and social reformation, which, after all, represents only one of the many results produced by Western thought acting upon the mind of India. Another and very necessary caution to be borne in mind is that the glowing narratives of Brahma successes, of religious awakenings, of passionate zeal and so forth, which may come from interested parties, should not be accepted too literally. "What we wrote did not represent what we did. Our writings exceeded our lives," was the confession which Keshub once made in a letter to Miss Collet, and would in all probability be appropriate in the mouths of most Brahma writers and statisticians.

The attitude of Brahmaism to Christianity is a subject of great interest to many earnest men. At one time the Christian missionaries appeared to think that Keshub was doing their work for them, and that the reformer himself would eventually come into the Christian fold. This was one reason why he was made so much of by Europeans of all

[1] *Tattwabodhini Patrika*, vol. xv. part i.

classes. Even now some Christian missionaries regard Brahmaism as but a step on the road to Christianity, but I am by no means of that opinion.

Whatever may be the modifications produced in Indian ways of thought and in the sentiments and customs of the people, by the stimulating contact of Western literature, philosophy, science, and religion, it may be safely predicted that the inherited tendencies of the people of India are too strong, and their national beliefs too subtle, comprehensive, and deep-rooted, to allow of their breaking away in any notable degree from their immemorial past. Under existing political conditions at any rate the religious evolution of the vast Hindu population will, I believe, take place along the already long-established lines of pantheism and yoga philosophy.

Brahmaism as a national theistic Church may, in one form or another, possibly have a future; but if foreign Unitarians, whether English or American, succeed in imposing their austere occidental views upon any considerable proportion of the Brahmas, and, aided by their money-bags, are able to assume the guidance of the Brahmic movement, it will acquire an exotic character, become unpopular, and inevitably die of inanition.

SOCIAL REFORM

·THE·PUBLIC·HOUSE·

CHAPTER IV

HINDU SOCIAL REFORMERS

INTRODUCTION.—Forces in operation tending to bring about changes in Hindu social life.

SO many stimulating forces of extraneous origin, such various culture-influences have come into operation throughout the land, so many novel ideas are circulating there, so much criticism sometimes just, sometimes supercilious and too often foolish, has for many years past been lavished upon the Indian social fabric, whether Hindu or Muslim, that a crowd of reformers both wise and unwise have, as an inevitable consequence, come into existence. For men who love notoriety, for speakers who desire to advertise themselves and are fairly pushing and thick-skinned, the rôle of the reformer is everywhere a congenial one, and present-day India has, perhaps, more than a fair share of such men. Besides these fussy self-seekers, there are others of another and better type, reasonably anxious for moderate changes in Hindu social customs to suit the altered times, and modestly doing what they can within their limited sphere to accomplish this end.

Europeans, impatient of the *political* aspirations of the Hindu people, direct attention to the wide field for urgent *social* reforms which Indian society provides, and in their zeal for the improvement of their "fellow-subjects" these well-wishers indulge in highly coloured contrasts between Western and Eastern customs, necessarily to the disadvantage of both Hindus and Muslims. Naturally the restrictions imposed by caste afford convenient texts for these alien reformers, and give occasion for much ill-considered speaking and writing addressed to the Indian native public. To give examples: The other day I found it stated or rather implied in a reputable Calcutta newspaper, desirous of improving native social arrangements, that Englishmen may marry where they please, and eat where and how they please; while the trained official, freeing himself for the nonce from the trammels of red-tape, lays it down with authority, in a State document too, that, "In the West the field from which a man can choose his wife is practically unlimited." (Census Report, p. 421.) But is all this quite true? Is the ordinary Englishman really so blessed? Is he so absolutely free? Without losing sight of the disabilities due to the Hindu caste system, we may be permitted to ask whether the Englishman, be he Hodge, or John Smith, or Mr. Aubrey de Vere, or the Marquis of Landsend, can marry into any class he likes? Whether his *chance* in matrimony (not always his *choice*) is not ordinarily confined simply and absolutely to such women *of his own class, within the small circle of his personal acquaintances*, as may be disposed to accept his advances? We may press the matter further and inquire whether it is not true that both men and women in England, notwithstanding the unlimited field of selection with which they are credited, often cannot get mated at all, even with the irregular help of matrimonial agencies. As to Englishmen being able to eat *where* and *how* they please, surely the anonymous writer I have quoted above, and taken perhaps too seriously, was thinking of Hampstead Heath on a Bank-holiday.

After all, the West is not quite so free from social restraints nor the East so enmeshed in them as some seem to think. It is not all blissful equality and happy social freedom on one side of the world and all hateful social tyranny on the other. Limitations and restrictions are essential features of social life everywhere, only the limitations and restrictions are not quite the same in the Occident as in the Orient. This is a point worth bearing in mind while studying the problems presented by Indian life.

Playing up to the party who advise the Indians to busy themselves with social rather than political questions, is a class of educated Hindus, conscientious men I dare say, not very numerous, it is true, but useful in their way and, happily for themselves, so thoroughly in sympathy with English official opinion that they cannot escape the appreciative attentions or the special rewards of a discriminating government.

Some of these, with almost touching confidence in the wisdom of their foreign rulers, seem desirous of placing their native reforming propaganda under the ægis of the British Government, suggesting to this end the formation of a special Imperial Legislative Council to deal with social and religious questions *under the guidance of the Viceroy.* But I fancy the good judgment of the rulers will keep them free from any such council, now or hereafter.

Last, but by no means least, amongst Indian reformers are certain important Indian feudatory princes and a few influential territorial magnates whose position and nationality enable them to profess and carry out reforms with less offence to the susceptibilities of their people than would be possible in the case of alien rulers.

So much for the reformers who are assailing from

Photo by W. Campbell Oman

THE NEW STYLE—"MR. CHAIRMAN AND GENTLEMEN"

(A TYPICAL NORTH-INDIAN AUDIENCE)

various points, with divers motives, dissimilar aims and different degrees of force, the fortress of long-established Hindu customs. But this ancient stronghold, built as it is on the rock of religious ordinances and traditions, supported by national sentiment and guarded by a powerful hereditary priesthood, is not likely to yield any positions without an obstinate defence. Indeed, we find that the reformers are everywhere confronted by a strong body of Hindu conservatives opposed to social changes, holding that innovations of every kind should be vigorously resisted, since departures from old ancestral practices have a tendency to revolutionise and even disintegrate society. This anti-reform party is not only recruited from the ranks of the more backward orthodox Hindus, but even from amongst the young men who have been educated in the State and other schools and colleges of the day. For the attitude which these educated Indians take against sweeping social reforms one reason at least is obvious and quite natural. It is the feeling that whatever may be the defects of these social institutions, they have stood the test of time and need not be hastily modified. In addition to this natural if not quite sufficient reason against introducing changes into Hindu customs there is, I know, a strong conviction in the minds of most educated Indians that European modes of life, particularly in regard to social intercourse between the sexes, are by no means free from many serious shortcomings and dangers too, which would inevitably appear and be seriously magnified in any purely Indian community which might be remodelled upon existing Western lines; and it is undoubtedly in the Western world that would-be reformers do mostly find the ideals which inspire their reforming zeal, however much they may try to conceal this fact from their fellow-countrymen. Further, the pride and patriotism of a vast majority of both Hindus and Muslims rebel against the thought of admitting that their national habits and customs, based on religious sanctions, are in any way inferior to those of their European masters.

However, under the existing political conditions of Indian life which bring the people into perpetual contact with the alien civilisation, religion, and literature of a powerful and dominant race, modifications of ideas and changes of customs are inevitable. For my own part, I must confess that an adequate treatment of this important and complex subject is entirely beyond me; yet I nevertheless hope that the particulars embodied in this chapter will give the European reader a fair idea of the direction in which contemporary Indian social reformers are working for what they consider social improvement. I also hope to be able, at the same time, to direct attention to some of the results of the new awakening.

HINDU SOCIAL REFORMERS

—continued

SECTION I.—Reformers in Council.

IMPERFECTION being inseparable from human institutions, the true reformer has never lacked, and will never at any time lack, opportunities of exercising his important if often thankless vocation; but the reforms preached and fought for at any given time and in any particular place are necessarily peculiar to and characteristic of the period and the country, and so naturally throw a flood of light upon the condition and civilisation of the people amongst whom they are advocated.

Fully appreciating this fact, I was glad when representative men from all parts of India assembled in the capital of the Punjab, primarily to discuss political questions, but willing at the same time to air their views on the most pressing social problems of the day.

As a pendant to the *National Congress* held at Lahore in 1893 for the furtherance of the political aspirations of the educated classes, there was a great *Social Conference* of delegates from the four quarters of the land, affording me a long-desired and excellent opportunity of learning what India was thinking about in regard to the great questions of social reform which had come to the fore in recent years, and I did not fail to attend the Conference for enlightenment on the present social needs of Aryavarta.

From a preliminary notice issued by the General Secretary, Social Conference, Madras, to the Secretaries of Social Reform Societies throughout the country, I learned that resolutions would be proposed embodying the views of the Conference in regard to many reforms which seemed desirable in existing native customs.

The meeting was held in a huge thatched pavilion called "the Pandal," specially erected for the National Congress, provided with bent-wood chairs for four or five thousand persons. Though the place had been crowded during the political meetings of the Congress, the gathering for the Social Conference did not exceed one thousand or at most twelve hundred persons. Before the proceedings of the day commenced I took stock of my surroundings, and noticed that by way of decoration a number of coloured glass globes had been hung from the framework of the roof, that red and green flags, and some shields with the British coat of arms emblazoned on them, had also been used to give a festive aspect to the pavilion. As a silent, visible declaration of loyalty to the Government, there was placed near the tribune a portrait of the Queen-Empress.

Old Mr. Dadabhai Naoroji, M.P., looking limp and worn-out, attired in his national Parsee costume, wearing loose maroon-coloured trousers and one of those peculiar Parsee hats so familiar in Bombay, sat on the platform, an embodiment of helpless discontent. Over him was held an umbrella to keep off the rain, which was leaking in everywhere, through a very imperfectly constructed roof. To such a degree were the audience incommoded, that Mr. Naoroji's umbrella was only one of many which were opened in the building. The scene, if quaint, was also very characteristic and decidedly depressing.

Only one Hindu lady graced the meeting with her presence. Dressed in print skirt and white chaddar, she sat on the platform with a little girl beside her, the two representing the fair sex on that occasion. As the business of the day, conducted entirely in English, went on, the lady, apparently wearied by the proceedings, of which she probably did not understand a word, quietly drew up one slender leg and then the other on the seat of the chair she occupied, covered herself with her chaddar as completely as possible, and composed herself to sleep, disdainfully regardless of the social problems of the day. After a while her slumbers were disturbed by rain-water leaking upon her from above, when some native gentlemen politely made a little room for her to shift her chair to another spot. Though the lady did not evidently appreciate the work of the Conference, she afforded many speakers that day the opportunity of saying "*Ladies* and Gentlemen."

All classes of the Hindu community, official and unofficial, were represented in the audience: from a Judge of the High Court of Bombay to quite junior clerks in Government and railway offices; from prosperous landed gentry to petty shopkeepers.

The proceedings were most orderly and business-like, but I missed the note of genuine earnestness throughout. Two important addresses were read—one by Dewan Narindra Nath, M.A., a gentleman of private means and holding an important official position in the Punjab; the other by Mr. Justice Ranade, of the Bombay High Court.[1] No doubt the speakers had thrashed out the subjects scores of times before, and while they spoke were uncomfortably conscious of the dead weight of ancestral prejudice and feminine conservatism which refused to be moved or modified by all their well-meant endeavours up to that moment.

As a result of the deliberations of the Conference, a dozen resolutions were carried after the usual speeches, and afford a glimpse of the many very important points which are engaging the attention of present-day reformers in India; for they embrace such questions as the following: Temperance, higher female education, infant marriage, extravagant expenditure at weddings, the remarriage of widows, intermarriage between sub-castes, and the improvement of the Hindu joint-family system. There were also resolutions touching foreign (beyond sea) travel, loud mourning at funerals in the Punjab, naughty nautch girls, and the prevention of conflicts between Hindus and Muhammadans in connection with religious processions and observances. Further, as bearing directly upon the business of the Conference, it was resolved that "social

[1] Both of these addresses are given in full in a bulky volume entitled *Indian Social Reform*, edited by C. Yajnesvara Chintamani (Thompson & Co., Madras).

reform funds" should be raised by social and other associations, and applications made to Government to exempt such associations from the operation of the rules laid down in Act VI. of 1882.

These resolutions afford good examples of the nature of the subjects which are engaging the attention of contemporary social reformers in India. Some of the matters taken up were, however, of merely local interest; for example, the question of the *Siapa* system of mourning aloud and beating the chest vigorously which prevails at present in certain parts of North-Western India. Others, again, were undoubtedly inspired by political rather than social considerations, the one, for instance, which relates to disturbances between Hindus and Muhammadans. That this was the case, the speeches I listened to left no doubt in my mind; certain speakers insidiously hinting that they *knew* where the real fomenting forces of these disturbances were to be found, but they had been advised not to speak on this point, and refrained from doing so. The impression which these orators wished to leave on the minds of the audience was that the Government itself desired to secretly encourage, for its own advantage, dissensions and divisions between the two great religious sections of the Indian community.

One result of the Conference must have been to strengthen the hands of the local reformers, for it would enable them to quote, in support of their labours, the deliberately expressed and authoritative opinions of men of culture and position in Hindu society drawn from all parts of India. To this extent, at any rate, the work of the Conference would be neither futile nor ineffectual.

A feature of more recent Congresses has been an Industrial Exhibition, which, however excellent and useful in itself, cannot but distract attention from the main purposes of the Congress, and tend to make of it a great annual *tamasha* (entertainment). "So much the better," many will say or think; but the yearly Conference is an institution of supreme importance to India, and it is to be hoped that its distinctive character may be preserved and its usefulness be increased and not impaired.

HINDU SOCIAL REFORMERS

—continued

SECTION II.—A typical reformer—A Yogi lecturer on "How to make a dead man alive."

FOLLOWING the plan I have deliberately adopted of bringing the reader, as often as possible, face to face, as it were, with living men and their doings, I now invite him to meet a typical present-day Indian reformer, and with *his* help to consider once more a familiar evil presented in a new and peculiar setting.

A lecture by a certain *Swami* of the sect of the Yogis, was publicly announced, the subject, as stated on the bills, being, "How to make a dead man alive." A Yogi—perhaps a Mahatma!—on such an important matter was irresistible, so without hesitation I resolved to attend the meeting and profit by the Yogi's wisdom.

Swami-ji appeared upon the platform at the appointed hour, with long wavy black hair carefully combed and oiled, a full black beard and a somewhat abstracted look. He was well clothed in flowing garments of an orange-yellow colour, and altogether looked very different from the Yogis with whom I had long been familiar.

When introduced to the audience, he stood up with his eyes shut and passed his hand over his face. After a long pause he began, in English, a prayer to God, addressing Him always as "Dear Lord," praising Him and asking His blessing for the chairman, the audience, and the speaker himself, in phrases that would not have been strange in the mouth of a very ordinary dissenting minister, or a free lance amongst Christian preachers of the less educated sort. Following the prayer came the lecture, also in English, delivered in slow, measured tones, and with an ample use of polysyllabic words, badly mispronounced.

Having made the allusions to John Stuart Mill and Herbert Spencer, which one must be prepared for on such occasions, the Swami warmed to his work. He told us his mission was to war with a destructive demon, a terrible devil who was in the midst of us, and was preying upon the life of our dear Mother India, adding with a mysterious intonation and appropriate gesture that the demon foe was in that very room even while he was speaking to us. "But," exclaimed Swami-ji emphatically, "I shall presently drag him before you, and you shall judge him for yourselves."

The Swami next narrated a story of the Mogul Emperor Akbar and his "legislative council." The famous monarch, said the lecturer, once asked his councillors whether they knew any way by which a dead man might be brought to life. One replied, "My Lord, I think this feat is not beyond the powers of the science of our great doctors at Constantinople. Let me go thither and learn the art and I will come back and answer your Majesty." Another councillor expressed the opinion that the secret of such wonderful power was known only to the Egyptians, adding that, if permitted to do so, he would go to the land of Egypt and learn what the great king wished to know. Akbar was too impatient to be satisfied with such answers, and sent off at once for his wise Hindu minister Rajah Birbul. When Birbul presented himself at the Imperial Durbar, the Emperor put the same question to him that he had addressed to the other councillors. But instead of replying, the astute Hindu begged for time till the next morning to give his answer. Birbul retired to his magnificent palace to think the matter over, and "the Emperor sought his *cosy couch*, or rather his hot and restless bed," for he could not sleep in his anxiety to learn what the wise Rajah Birbul's answer would be. "The cock, the herald of the morn, in due time awoke the whole world," and Akbar commanded Birbul to his presence. The sage Hindu appeared, and commenced by telling the king that there lived in his dominions a terrible demon, a malignant fiend, who destroyed great numbers of his subjects, and that if he could be controlled or driven away a great many dead people would become alive again. This information gave rise to the following dialogue:—

Akbar. Is it so? Can this be possible?

Birbul. Alas! it is too true.

Akbar. In what cave or forest does this demon live?

Birbul. Sire, he lives neither in a cave nor in a forest, but in a small, narrow, crystal palace of his own.

Akbar. In a crystal palace; and in my dominions?

Birbul. Yes, my Lord, in your own dominions and in this very city.

Akbar. What! here? and I not know about it. Who are his relatives, what is his name?

Birbul. His relatives, your Majesty, are many, such as Debility, Disease, Impotence, Insanity, Debauchery, and Crime. His name is one made up of only four letters.

Akbar. What four letters?

Birbul. W, I, N, E.

At which the audience cheered and laughed loudly, tickled at Akbar's famous minister spelling the demon's name in letters of the *English* alphabet to his august master.

In the midst of the hilarious applause the Swami produced from under his chaddar, I think, something wrapped in paper, and gradually removing the covering disclosed to view a bottle made of clear transparent glass, which seemed to contain some reddish-coloured *syrup*. With creditable dramatic power he exclaimed, "Here is the Demon in his crystal palace! Here is the enemy of our beloved mother India! I have dragged him before you! Behold the Monster!" Then changing his tone, "No," he said, cuddling the bottle, "this is Old Tom, who is the dear friend of so many of us," and then, regardless of the verities, went on excitedly to speak of it as whisky and brandy, using it as a symbol for strong drink. Holding up the bottle with its reddish-coloured contents, Swami-ji asked, "Has this no virtues?" and answering his own question said, "Oh yes, it has its virtues, as Rajah Birbul told the Emperor It has these virtues that he who takes it long is not visited by thieves, he never grows grey, and he is not likely to get hydrophobia, because he usually carries a stout stick to support his tottering limbs."

Leaving his figures of speech and turning to prosaic details, the lecturer told us how drink had been the curse of many of the best men in India, and particularly so in his beloved Bengal, where some of the leading men, whom he did not hesitate to name, had fallen victims to drink.[1]

The lecturer wound up his address with a story to which he requested our special attention, and which, whether original or not, is good enough to bear repetition. It was this:

An orthodox Hindu went on a round of travels—of course without a penny in his pocket—and one day resting under a tree saw in the distance what looked like a magnificent building. "Brother," he asked a passer-by, "what place is that?" "Mr. Traveller, go and see it," was the reply. "Can I enter it?" "Yes, surely." "And what is the charge for admission?" "Oh! nothing at all."

So "Mr. Traveller" girded up his loins, took his staff in his hand and proceeded towards the palace. When he approached it, he noticed that it had four splendid gates, each of which was guarded by an armed sentinel. He presented himself at the nearest gate and asked permission to enter. The door-keeper courteously assured him that he might do so, but only on one condition, and that an easy one indeed. "You see," continued the sentinel, "this platter in my hand. It contains a savoury dish of meat—the flesh of dogs—you have only to eat this and pass in."

"Oh, horror! what, I an orthodox Hindu and a vegetarian to eat the flesh of animals and worse still of dogs. That is abominable even to think of. I cannot do it. Is there no other way, Mr. Sentinel, of obtaining admission to the palace?" "Try the next gate," was the gruff response.

To the next gate went our orthodox vegetarian traveller. In reply to his inquiries, the sentinel on duty slyly pointed to a little boy who was playing not far off, well dressed, and covered with jewels, and told the traveller that if he

[1] At the conclusion of the lecture, Swami's statements in this respect were flatly contradicted by some Bengali gentlemen who were present.

would kill the child and help himself to his ornaments he might pass in to view the lovely palace.

"What! commit both murder and robbery? Never! Never!" said the horrified visitor, and passed on to the third gate. Here he found a beautiful woman sitting near the sentinel.

The modest lecturer felt that he could not utter before his "august audience" the shameful act which the traveller was invited to do. Suffice it to say that the orthodox Hindu hurried from the spot, and without looking back presented himself at the fourth and last gate. In a genial way the sentinel assured him that admittance could be easily obtained at his gate. He need only drink two *chhatánks*[1] of brandy out of the cup he held in his hand and might then pass in.

But Mr. Orthodox Hindu turned sadly away and went back to the shade of the tree. He pondered the matter, and still eagerly curious to see the inside of the magnificent pile which stood before him, combated the conscientious scruples which had been raised in his mind by the suggestions of the four sentinels. "After all," he concluded, "there is not so much difference between water and brandy, which latter is only grape-juice"; so he finally returned to the fourth gate, drank the brandy and obtained admittance to the palace.

When he came out he was singing merrily, and wanted *more* brandy; the sentinel at the gate declined to give him any more; but advised him to buy what he required at the public-house.

"I am a mere traveller," said the orthodox Hindu in surprise, "and have no money. How can I buy brandy?" "Very easily," was the reply. "Go to the second gate, murder the child you saw there, take his ornaments and purchase what you crave for."

Our orthodox, but now fallen, Hindu traveller, acting upon this suggestion, committed both murder and robbery, and satisfied his longing for more drink. Presently feeling hungry, he ate and enjoyed the dish of dogs' flesh he had previously declined, and after that filled up the measure

[1] *Chhatánk*—A two-ounce weight.

of his crimes by committing that other sin at the third gate which he had before resisted, and rolling on the ground in a disgraceful, insensible condition, found himself in the gutter.

It was an instructive parable we had heard that afternoon, and I need not point out that while battling in the good cause of temperance, as so many Westerns are doing to-day, the Yogi lecturer had a style and a method peculiarly his own, and yet very racy of the Indian soil.

Intemperance, as I have often been told by Indian gentlemen, has in recent years been on the increase amongst the better educated classes. As Indians of whatever social rank do not *associate* with Europeans, do not except on rare occasions eat and drink with them or even meet them on a friendly social footing, it is evident that the growth of habits of inebriety amongst the natives cannot well be attributed to the bad example of Europeans, and must be due to other causes; probably to the excitement and unrest which are undeniable results of contact with the strenuous ideals and modes of life and work in a hustling money-grubbing age like ours.

A rather curious encouragement to drink, in India at the present time, is the belief that ardent spirits act as a plague prophylactic. Perhaps alcohol in moderation is a preventive against this fell disease. I cannot say, but the belief amongst the natives is probably due to the immunity from plague generally enjoyed by the European community in India.

In every considerable town in the Punjab there are Temperance Associations, and I presume they would not exist if they were not needed. The Sikhs in the Native States have also taken up the question of Temperance very seriously.

In all the Provinces of India the same activity prevails. "Apostles of Temperance" from Europe, aided by Christian missionaries, have given a great impetus to the formation of Temperance Societies and Total Abstinence Associations, which, with local differences, are conducted upon the main lines adopted in Europe and America. These societies and associations hold meetings, have

THE SHAMEFUL RESULTS OF INTEMPERANCE—DEPICTED BY AN INDIAN ARTIST

lectures and addresses, encourage pledge-signing, organise processions with bands playing and banners flying, arrange for the public singing of temperance ballads in the vernacular, and the circulation of tracts illustrating the evils of drink. They further arrange for the performance of temperance plays, one of which I had the pleasure of witnessing in the native theatre at Amritsar, and a tolerably good play it was, setting forth in Hindu dramatic fashion the evils of alcoholism. Of course winged peris (angels or fairies) were amongst the *dramatis personæ,* and curiously enough some of the temperance hymns introduced into the play were set to once popular English airs, such as "Sweet Dreamland Faces" and "Wait till the Clouds roll by, Jenny."

Though equally demoralising in its results whether in the East or the West, drunkenness in India can, however, at times put on a complexion impossible in Europe; for Indian inebriates with the religious zeal of their race have actually been known to *worship the bottle.* A few years ago it came to my knowledge that an Indian clerk being suspected of certain fraudulent transactions, a sudden raid was made upon his residence by the police in order to secure, if possible, documentary evidence against him. His papers were seized, and amongst them were found an extraordinary collection of photographs, in which he and some of his friends appear worshipping the whisky bottle, or in all sorts of Bacchanalian attitudes with the bottle being drained, and so on. I am sorry to say that I never had the chance of seeing the photographs, nor have I had them properly described to me. But it is quite possible to imagine the young topers standing round a table, with garlands about their necks and bottles arranged before them. The host, high priest for the occasion, would be crowned with flowers and ornamented with patches of red lead or other such pigment. Standing in respectful attitudes before the bottles the worshippers would probably sing a *bhajan* or hymn appropriate to the occasion, and then go in for a real good carouse.

Without religion in *everything* the Hindu cannot apparently get on at all!

Like the rest of the world, the people of India have, unfortunately, their own drink difficulty, and must face it with all the weapons they can command. The Temperance movement in India of which I have been writing is by no means premature, and it has one very important feature which gives it more than ordinary significance, for in it are united, as a matter of course, all classes of the community—Hindus, Muhammadans, and Christians. It is a cause which can for a special purpose and a common object draw together into harmonious action all ranks and creeds, and so far is an instrument for bringing about *united effort*, the value of which from a *political point of view* is not, I am sure, undervalued by the local wire-pullers.

HINDU SOCIAL REFORMERS
—continued

SECTION III.—The reform of marriage customs the special aim of certain reformers.

AMONGST the subjects dealt with in the resolutions of the Social Conference already referred to, those relating to infant marriage and the remarriage of widows deserve serious attention, lying as they do at the very root of Indian family life.

In most countries and in all ages women have been looked upon by men as desirable possessions, and in the olden time, all the world over, wives had been obtained by capture at great personal risk, by purchase at varying prices according to circumstances, by service extending perhaps over many years, and sometimes—markedly so amongst certain European races—by open and honourable courtship. But in India for ages past a girl-child has been looked upon as so worthless that female infanticide was the commonest of crimes in that country. Even to-day in India a girl is so undesirable an addition to a family that no one would think of congratulating a parent on the birth of a female child, and her unhappy father has in due course to give the highest dowry he can possibly afford in order to find her a husband, *which he is bound to do under the most terrible social and religous penalties.* When he has done what the law requires of him, and has perhaps beggared himself in the doing of it, he may never, so it is enjoined, cross the threshold of his daughter's new home or partake of a morsel of food or a drop of water in her house.[1]

With such ideas pervading Hindu family life, the posi-

[1] Shib Chunder Bose, *The Hindoos as they are.*

tion of the woman has not been an enviable one, and it is not surprising that, under the influence of Western civilisation brought to their doors, efforts have been made from within to ameliorate the condition of these sufferers from long ages of unjust treatment.

Various questions of social reform have consequently been brought into public discussion rather prominently within recent years, giving rise to much controversy between the progressives inoculated with Western notions and the old school of orthodoxy; the discord being especially pronounced where the proposed departures from time-honoured customs affected the position and obligations of women in the Hindu social system.

Not many years ago a peculiar warmth was imported into these discussions, and a powerful impulse given to the movement for social reforms, by the intrusion into the arena of a non-Hindu native of India, who, well aware of the facts connected with the existing and widespread customs of infant marriage and enforced widowhood, urged the pressing necessity for reform on both these points. The outsider referred to, Mr. Behramji Malabari, a Parsee journalist of Bombay, devoted himself with rare energy and determination to the removal of what appeared to him to constitute palpable evils in Hindu social life.

Through the medium of the Press, also by means of lecturing tours and even by direct personal appeals to the highest British authorities, this gentleman created a great sensation, stirring up Hindu society to a remarkable degree, and, as might have been expected, exciting no inconsiderable amount of ill-will against himself. Not that Mr. Malabari was the pioneer in this cause. Many worthy Hindus of great ability and good social position had preceded him, and many were working contemporaneously towards the ends he had in view; but the burning, unresting zeal and public methods of the Parsee outsider attracted more general attention to the cause he had at heart than the more languid efforts of Hindu reformers, themselves hampered by dread of caste penalties and restrained by natural tenderness towards the feelings and prejudices of loved and venerated relatives and friends.

While many leading Hindus were brought by Mr. Malabari's crusade against infant marriage and enforced widowhood to a full realisation of the cruelty and manifold harmfulness of these customs, there were others so irritated by his attacks upon their ancient well-established social life as to resent his intermeddling in their affairs, and to vigorously deny both the accuracy of his facts and the validity of his conclusions.

The consideration of such matters, affecting as they do the happiness and reputation of Hindu households, could not be carried on without glancing for confirmation, or otherwise, at life outside the Indian zone. Contrasts between European and Indian modes of life were inevitably dragged into the discussions, accusations, and recriminations which arose out of these delicate questions. The real or sentimental status of women in the West and the East respectively were compared by angry scribes, who, as a rule, were ill-informed or wanting in judgment. Hindu conservatives, represented mostly by certain Bengali journals, used their ingenuity in this controversy to point out and to exaggerate the imperfections of European society in its treatment of women, and these critics were answered according to their lights by the advocates for reform amongst their own countrymen.

One result of this journalistically conducted warfare about social reforms has certainly been to bring before the world a large number of important facts, very welcome to European students of India, whether official or other, relating to Hindu home-life and the condition and treatment of Hindu women in our time, and it has also made clear the estimation in which the weaker sex is held by both educated and uneducated Indians at the present day.

Echoes of the strife soon penetrated even to the seclusion of the *zenanas*, and in many a quiet home the spirit of rebellion has thereby been stirred up in the hearts of women longing for the emancipation which is being promised to them by the prophets of this reforming age.

Interesting cases arising, without doubt, out of the dissemination of the new ideas have attracted public attention and evoked very conflicting sentiments and judgments. As an example of this I may allude to the case of the girl-wife Rukhmabai, which came into the law courts. The facts are simply: Rukhmabai, a Hinduani, had been married in infancy (and, of course, without her consent) to one Dadaji Bhikhaji; but the marriage had not been consummated. The husband, who is said to have been a worthless profligate, ruined in body and mind, was sensible enough, however, to be aware that his girl-wife, who had received some education and was also likely to inherit a little property from her grandmother, was an asset of some value. Such a wife, though hitherto neglected, was not to be lost sight of, so Dadaji called upon her to live with him under his uncle's roof. But the spirited girl's feelings revolted against the depraved fellow whom she did not know, and who had been no choice of hers, and she firmly refused to join him. Supported by his friends, Dadaji now resolved to invoke the assistance of the law to compel Rukhmabai to submit herself to his will. He therefore instituted proceedings against her, for the restitution or rather the enforcement of conjugal rights. The point at issue being the obligation involved in an unconsummated infant marriage, attracted in certain sections of Hindu society considerable attention at the time. Here were all the elements required to appeal on the one hand to the liberal sentiments of reformers generally, and on the other to excite the deep-rooted prejudices of an ancient and multitudinous community. The child-wife, whose consent had never been asked to the matrimonial alliance to which she had been made a party, discovered before the consummation of the wedding the utter worthlessness of the man to whom she had been linked. To become his wife in reality and share his home with him was hateful to her. Encouraged by the spirit of reform which was in the air, she resolved with rare courage to repudiate the alliance and to trust to the justice and liberal ideas of the alien rulers of her country to free her from the bonds in which she had been placed. Of course there were many to sympathise with the strong-minded girl in her revolt against the tyranny of custom, and when the English judge who first heard her case decided in favour of the girl-wife, her friends were elated with the victory thus scored against the system of infant marriage, while orthodoxy was shocked and alarmed. The matter was not allowed to end there. It was carried to the Appellate Court, when, to the disappointment of the reformers, the law was declared to be against Rukhmabai. No doubt this decision was correct and politic, but it was none the less deplorable.

I am not aware whether the assistance of the police was invoked to force the rebellious girl into the arms of her husband. But this course was certainly open to Dadaji, and is by no means a rare occurrence in India.

Because of the vastness of the country, hardly anything that can be affirmed about one part of India holds good, without ample qualification, for other parts of it, a point which should always be kept in mind in making general statements regarding the climate, the productions, or the people of the enormous territory under the sway of the Indian Viceroy. After making the necessary allowances on this account, the facts as regards infant marriage and enforced widowhood in India may be briefly summarised as follows :—

1. It is undeniably true that throughout India the marriage of very young girls from two to eight years of age, with equally young boys, or often with adults of any age, is a very common practice amongst Hindus.[1]
2. Equally true is it that (at least until recent legislative action by the Indian Government) even the consummation of the marriage has commonly taken place when the child-wife was perhaps no more than ten years of age.
3. Hindu widows, however young, and even if virgins at the time of the husband's demise, are, as a general rule, unable, on account of stringent religious and social regulations, to remarry,

[1] The practice also prevails in a lesser degree, amongst Parsees and Indian Muhammadans, but it cannot be repugnant to the religious sentiments of the latter, since the Prophet of Islam married Ayishah when she was only nine years old. She was his favourite wife, and lived to the age of sixty-seven.

although authorised to do so by British Indian law (Act XV. of 1856).

4. Hindu widows, as a rule, are a despised class, and under the recognised rules of Hindu society are systematically exposed to great personal indignities and hardships.
5. Despite reformers, there is an undoubted tendency at the present day amongst certain classes *to adopt the above practices, although these may not hitherto have been favoured by them.*

When we discover that the existence of such peculiar practices throughout the enormous area over which Hinduism holds sway is of very long standing, we are led irresistibly to the conclusion that they must have religious bases, and that the political and social conditions of the country must have favoured their prolonged continuance.

We may therefore profitably seek to ascertain and note such information as may be available to throw light upon these points.

For the better treatment of the subject we may deal separately with Infant Marriage and Enforced Widowhood, although, as we shall see, they are very intimately connected with each other.

HINDU SOCIAL REFORMERS

—continued

Section IV.—Infant marriage.

WE have it on the authority of Megasthenes that in his time (306–298 B.C.) early marriages prevailed in India in the case of girls, who might be wedded when seven years old; so that the contention that infant marriage is a comparatively modern institution in India is untenable.

What countenance the Hindu codes have given to the early marriage of girls will appear from the following texts cited by a learned Brahman, Dr. J. N. Bhattacharjee, in support of infant marriage:

1. "So many seasons of menstruation as overtake a maiden feeling the passion of love and sought in marriage by persons of suitable rank, even so many are the beings destroyed by both her father and mother: this is a maxim of law."—See *Dayabhaga*, chap. xi. sec. 11.

2. Paitinashi says: "A damsel should be given in marriage before her breasts swell. But if she have menstruated before marriage, both the giver and the taker fall into the abyss of hell: and her father, grandfather, and great-grandfather are born insects in ordure."[1]

Other unimpeachable authorities bear out the same views. In the *Angir-ásmriti*, which treats of ceremonial defilement and penances, it is said:

"There is no atonement for a man who has intercourse with a Vrishali," *i.e.* a woman who has her courses before marriage, and even contact through inadvertence with the

[1] Dayaram Gidumal, LL.B., C.S., *The Life and Life-work of Behramji M. Malabari*, p. 246.

husband of such a woman had to be atoned by ablution of both person and dress. It is also expressly stated in the same treatise that "the father, mother, and elder brother who tolerate a girl in her courses before marriage go to hell. A Brahman who will marry such a girl is not to be spoken of or admitted into society."[1]

If these texts are accepted as authoritative by orthodox Hindus, then the religious basis of the custom of infant marriage is undeniable, and in such a case the Hindu reformer's position seems hardly tenable, unless he is prepared to stand up against both Brahmanical law and the influential priesthood who uphold it. But as the decision of the question hinges upon authorities and upon Sanskrit texts with their interpretations, there is of course abundant room for differences of opinion amongst lawyers and exegetists.

I have before me a pamphlet by Professor Bhandarkar, C.I.E., entitled *A Note on the Age of Marriage and its Consummation according to Hindu Religious Law*, published in 1891, when the controversy on these subjects was at its height. In this pamphlet infant marriage, as we understand it, is not opposed, as indeed it could hardly be with this text of Manu to support it—"A man thirty years old should marry a girl pleasing to him of the age of twelve years." But the position taken by Professor Bhandarkar is that "the Hindu religious law allows the consummation of marriage being deferred for three years after a girl attains puberty," that the texts which prescribe the *Garbhâdhâna* ceremony which should immediately precede actual intercourse with the bride do not require that *this ceremony and intercourse* should come off on the occasion of the *first* monthly course, but leave the matter indefinite. Professor Bhandarkar's contention indeed seems to be that though infant marriage is unobjectionable, the consummation of marriage may lawfully be deferred till the wife is fully developed and capable of bearing a vigorous child.

Needless to say these views did not meet with general acceptance, and gave rise to much angry polemics. Opponents held strongly that according to the best authorities

[1] John Wilson, D.D., F.R.S., *Indian Caste*, vol. i. p. 365.

the *Garbhâdhâna* ceremony and intercourse with the bride should follow the very first proof of puberty, and could not be postponed to a later time without incurring unpardonable sin.

As opposed to the practice of infant marriage, the laws of Manu have been cited by the late Sir Monier Williams.

"A girl," says Manu, "having reached the age of puberty should wait three years, but at the end of that time she should herself choose a suitable husband."—Manu, Book ix. verse 90.

But Sir Monier Williams himself admits that "it is true that modern commentators maintain that this self-choice is only legal when there are no parents to give a daughter away,"—an admission which deprives the text of much of its seeming importance.

The late Professor Max Müller, to whom we were accustomed to look for enlightenment on most matters relating to ancient India, maintained "that infant marriage has no sanction from either Sruti or Smriti." "Manu," he adds, "wishes a young man to marry when he may become a *grihasta* (householder), *i.e.* when he is about twenty-four years of age. As to the girl, she is to marry when she is fit for it, and that may vary in different climates."[1] Obviously the interpretation of fitness for marriage in the case of the girl is just the very point at issue, and Professor Max Müller, with all his Sanskrit learning, was of course not able to help us to a solution of the matter.

When the subject we have been considering was before the Indian Legislature in 1871, and religious feeling was greatly excited especially in Bengal, the well-known Babu Keshub Chunder Sen, of the Brahma sect, issued a circular letter to a number of European and a few Native medical men, asking for an expression of opinion on the matter, from a scientific point of view. The opinions elicited, which were naturally in favour of adult marriage, are given *in extenso* in a volume on *Indian Social Reform*, published by Messrs. Thompson & Co., Madras. Physiological considerations necessarily dominated the views of the physicians, but there was some ill-considered writing indulged in about racial

[1] *Life of Behramji M. Malabari*, p. 202.

deterioration and national decay resulting from the custom of infant marriage. As, however, the opinions on this special point were not based on any actual data whatsoever, their scientific value was not very high, and some of the writers, more especially Dr. D. B. Smith, were conscious of this fact. The Brahmans on their part thought, as they have long done, that in the Indian climate, and under the usual joint-family system obtaining in their country, the fit time for a girl's marriage is the attainment of puberty.

Whatever room there may be for discussion upon this delicate point between reformers and Pandits, we may take it that general agreement, as a result of any such controversy, is neither likely nor possible.

Meanwhile the weight of immemorial custom is on the side of infant marriage, and it is a curious fact that the fashion has a tendency now to become even more widespread than heretofore, owing partly to a spirit of revolt against innovations backed by non-Hindus, partly to a desire of the lower castes to imitate their betters, but more than all to the increasing stringency of the matrimonial market. Exceptions, however, are not unknown amongst certain castes, the Kulin Brahmans of Bengal for example; it having been ruled amongst them that "if the daughters of the first and second subdivisional classes of Bhanga Kulinas cannot be given in marriage to husbands of their own classes, they must remain unmarried." [1]

Infant marriage in India, be it remembered, is an altogether different thing from what infant marriage if practised in Europe would be. For the comprehension of this very real distinction it has to be borne in mind that in India after the wedding ceremony has been duly performed the infant bride may still dwell with her parents for a while. It is true that she is actually transferred to the husband's home at a *very early age*; but then the husband is usually a boy, and the husband's home is more often than not in a joint-family establishment consisting of a large number of persons or groups ruled and managed by an elderly female. Into this large household the child comes as a stranger, yet heartily welcomed by the inmates, and if not cursed with

[1] Dr. John Wilson, *Indian Caste*, vol. ii. p. 207.

unamiable qualities, she is likely enough to be happy. Unfortunately, it often happens that girls being destined, under the infant-marriage customs, to leave the shelter of the paternal roof at a tender age, their fond but foolish mothers spoil them by over-indulgence while still at home, with the result that they pass to the care of the mother-in-law to be trained and broken into habits of usefulness, a process which may be, and no doubt often is, attended with bitter tears and many hardships. But if the picture which Miss Noble gives us, of the affectionate reception and tender treatment of the child-bride in a Hindu household, be a fairly accurate one, and Miss Noble speaks from personal observation, we may in ordinary cases reserve our compassion, and unconcernedly leave the child-wife to find her proper place in the household to which her husband belongs.[1]

The premature consummation of the marriage of Hindu girls under the system we are considering is undoubtedly a very real objection to it, causing personal suffering and permanent injury in too many instances. That the Hindu lawgivers desired to place some restraint upon the too early consummation of infant marriage may be inferred from the fact that in the *Angirasmriti* it is laid down that "the chandrayana[2] penance ought to be performed by all who eat in the house of a woman who had become pregnant before she is ten years of age." But disapproval so expressed could not have much effect in restraining brutal passions, and it is gratifying to know that since Mr. Malabari's agitation, and the public controversies already referred to, the British Government in India has found itself in a position to afford a certain amount of protection to child-brides by an Act (passed on the 19th March 1891) in which it was laid down that *the age of consent* should at the lowest be twelve years,—an age which, the climate of the country and the habits of the people being kept in view, seems an adequate minimum at present. The passing of this measure was productive of very sore feelings on the part of the Hindus generally and especially in Bengal, as being an unnecessary interference with their customs and

[1] *The Web of Indian Life*, pp. 34–36.

[2] Vide *supra*, p. 48.

their religion, and I know that even Europeans have regarded it as a piece of unwise legislation. However, its educative effect will, I have no doubt, be good in the long-run, and if it prevents needless suffering to innocent children it is certainly deserving of commendation.

In connection with the subject of early marriages in India, the following extracts relative to Western Europe, particularly Italy and France, at the time of the Renaissance, will not, I think, be without interest:—

> "Very frequently the 'best' marriages were negotiated by intermediaries more or less obliging, relatives or friends. Princes and princesses were married through the good offices of diplomatists. Indeed, ladies and gentlemen of the Court did quite a respectable trade in match-making, for a consideration.
>
> "But after all the task of marrying his daughter was essentially and especially one for the father.
>
> "For the most part, the father would be only too glad to wash his hands of the business. In every case he was in a hurry to bring matters to a head, and believed that in losing no time he was acting in the interest of his child. She was to belong wholly to another household, since it was a woman's lot to belong to her husband, and so it was well for her to enter upon her new life as early as possible, before she had formed ideas of her own, and at an age when the paternal household would not yet have set its stamp indelibly upon her.
>
> . . . .
>
> "In distinguished families, betrothal was by no means unusual at the age of two or three. At this tender age Vittoria Colonna was betrothed to the Marquis of Pescara.
>
> "Consummation usually took place at the age of twelve. That was a favourite age with the husbands; though, according to the best judges, fifteen was the age when the physical charms were at their best, and the soul was most malleable—a view dating as far back as Hesiod and Aristotle. . . .
>
> "In vain did the French physicians implore the men in mercy to have a little patience, beseech them to wait at least until the fourteenth year: they demurred, for it was humiliating for a father to have a fifteen-year-

old daughter on his hands: at sixteen they would have called it a catastrophe. Champier, one of the gravest of writers, proposed that after the age of sixteen young women should be provided with husbands by the State, on the lines of Plato's system. Some parents betrayed such haste to get their girls off their hands that they anticipated the ceremony, handing them over to their husbands-elect on the strength of a mere promise of fidelity."[1]

Infant marriage amongst Hindus invites further investigation. To say that it rests on the Hindu religious law is neither sufficient nor satisfactory. We desire to know more of its origin and of the advantages it offers, for without some inherent recommendations, it would not have been so widely adopted as it has been in India. Leaving then the Hindu law out of sight for the moment in order to view the matter on its own merits, we find it stated by its advocates that infant marriage has done an incalculable amount of good, inasmuch as it has prevented the immorality which admittedly prevailed when in some remote age adult marriage was the custom in India. They also deny that in practice it is attended with the sufferings and hardships which outsiders naturally attribute to it, although there is no denying that instances of such suffering and hardship do occasionally occur and even come to public knowledge in various ways, sometimes through the police courts. Both these pleas may be just, and I have no wish to controvert them; but they are certainly not exhaustive, and though I am an outsider I take the liberty of offering the following suggestions as to the circumstances and considerations which have favoured the establishment of the practice of infant marriage in India, and have even specially stimulated it within more recent years.

To my mind, then, after a study of the controversies which have raged round the question, infant marriages are and have been encouraged by the following causes:—

1. *Priestly greed.*—Life, especially infant life, being very uncertain, the earlier the ceremony of marriage is performed

[1] R. de Maulde la Clavière, *The Women of the Renaissance*, translated by George Herbert Ely, pp. 25–28.

the surer is the Brahman of his fees, and the same applies to the Garbhâdhâna ceremony.

2. *Alleged female frailty.*—The deeply engrained belief in India that women are by nature utterly depraved naturally suggests a very early marriage, as that alone could ensure the bride reaching her husband in a state of physical purity.

3. *The constant splitting up of castes into sections between whom marriage is not allowed.*—This ever-increasing subdivision of the castes has an obvious tendency to narrow the marriage market and to stimulate the competition of parents seeking suitable alliances for their girls, who, as explained already, *must be provided with husbands before attaining puberty.* In support of this contention I may state that I have been informed by the best authorities that it is not an uncommon thing for a desirable man to have overtures of marriage made to him (or his guardians, if he be a minor) while *his wife is breathing her last*, and certainly before her body has been cremated. One such instance I learned direct from the lips of the eligible youth concerned.

4. *Poverty and rapacity.*—In those castes, and there are a few such, wherein fathers or guardians are permitted to receive money—really purchase money—from the bridegroom's family, the desire to obtain the price would be a direct inducement to hasten the wedding.

5. *The marriage brokers.*—The professional matchmakers whose business it is to discover suitable husbands for girls, may be trusted to exert all their persuasive powers to effect early marriages, for life being uncertain the sooner the ceremonies are performed the more certain the brokers' fees.

6. *Fashion and rivalry.*—Fashion, that terrible taskmistress, having decided that early marriages are *proper*, what woman would not uphold the custom?[1] When any postponement of the marriage of a daughter beyond the age of puberty is *orthodoxly impossible*, and when an *approach* to that

[1] The force of fashion has made child marriage common even amongst some Muhammadans in India, although there is no difficulty under Islam about the remarriage of widows.

critical period would seem to imply a difficulty in obtaining a bridegroom, involving a reflection upon the status of the girl's family, what wonder that early marriages are so common.

7. *Feminine love of excitement.*—This weakness, universal and very imperious too, finds lively gratification in the ceremonies, reunions, processions, and displays of the elaborate and often costly Hindu betrothal and marriage ceremonies, and the festivities which occupy not one but many days, weeks perhaps, and permit of a degree of freedom of intercourse not known at other times.

8. *Feminine yearning for power within the domestic circle.*—Mothers-in-law, aunts-in-law, and sisters-in-law dwelling in a joint-family home are all equally desirous that the brides who are to come and share the home with them should be children, indeed young children amenable to discipline and motherly handling. Probably this handling is at times more severe than absolutely necessary.

9. *Carnality.*—By no means the least important or least powerful of the influences which make for child marriage is the lust of men, for be it remembered that the Hindu widower may remarry over and over again, and at *any* age can have a child-bride. Moreover, if one wife fails to bring him issue he may marry a second one, while the joint-family system relieves him from the inconveniences which might have been his lot under other circumstances, since the young wife is not necessarily called upon to order and manage the household. Her elders do that and also help the inexperienced child-wife to rear her offspring.

10. The fairly successful suppression by the British Government of the once very common practice of female infanticide is also a fact, perhaps in some cases an important one, in the encouragement of early marriages. The number of girls in the matrimonial market has thus increased, and as a husband has to be found for *every* girl, the competition for desirable bridegrooms has become more keen, with the result of lowering the age of matrimony.

No one who has lived in India and kept his eyes and ears open, no one who, without visiting India, has read anything of what I may call zenana literature, can have failed to become aware of many cases illustrative of the extreme cruelty, evil effects, and lifelong suffering resulting from the infant-marriage system, involving, as it does, in the eyes of Western peoples, a gross wrong, since the infants given in marriage are far too young to be really *parties* to the contract.

Moreover, there are reformers who, while making the most of these facts, insist further that over and above the wrongs and sufferings of individuals, under the infant-marriage system, is the far larger and more important question of the deterioration of the race. It is held by these reformers that where child marriage prevails, the offspring of such unions must necessarily be puny and degenerate. This *may* be true, but nevertheless nature does to a great degree neutralise the evil by killing off the degenerate early issue of immature parents. It cannot be denied, I think, that Hindus of all classes throughout India are, as a whole, well formed and well grown, and, *given sufficient food,* are capable of enduring quite as much prolonged physical exertion as the peoples of most other countries.

In view of the Hindu scriptural basis of infant marriage, and with so many other causes to bolster it up, it does not appear to me that the practice in question is likely to undergo any change in the near future. And the Legislature cannot wisely do much more than it has already done for the discouragement of the custom.

It is true that infant marriage, when the bridegroom may be of any age, is directly responsible for a large proportion of widowhoods; but the custom at least gives *every girl* a husband, which is far from being the case in the "catch-as-catch-can" system of the West. If we weep over the Hindu widows condemned to perpetual widowhood, we should not forget the old maids of the West, equally *condemned*, by the stress and strain of an age of economic conflict, to a life of single unblessedness.

HINDU SOCIAL REFORMERS

—continued

SECTION V.—**Enforced widowhood.**

ACCORDING to a custom which we know existed in India at least as far back as the fourth century B.C., the Hindu widow was required to mount the funeral pyre of her dead husband and be cremated along with his corpse. If the husband died, at a distant place, the widow was, none the less, to be burned alive on a pyre by herself.

For this practice, known as *Suttee* or *Sati*, the reason assigned by Strabo (*circa* B.C. 31–A.D. 21) was the necessity of protecting Indian husbands against their wicked wives, Indian women being much addicted to poisoning their lords with a view to other alliances.

Sati would certainly be a very effective protection for husbands against such murderous practices, because the death of the husband would mean that of the wife also.

Referring in another book[1] to this explanation by the Roman geographer of the origin of *sati*, I felt constrained to remark that it was, no doubt, an unmerited calumny upon Indian women; but I find, not without surprise, that the same accusation is levelled at them by their own countrymen even at the present day.[2]

Under many easily conceivable circumstances it would not be either desirable or possible to enforce the cruel law of *sati*, and as an alternative it was ruled, probably from the earliest times, that the woman who did not undergo cremation with her dead husband should be compelled to lead a

[1] *Indian Life Religious and Social*, p. 165.

[2] *The Life and Life-work of Behramji M. Malabari*, pp. 63, 64.

life of rigid self-denial and suffer social humiliations almost intolerable.

To the *sati*, " the virtuous wife," *i.e.* the wife who elected to perish in the flames which were to consume her husband's body, great honour was paid; and high-born, high-spirited women did not hesitate to face the fire rather than the degrading alternative of the widow's miserable life. Consequently until the practice of widow burning was made a punishable offence by a British-Indian enactment passed by Lord William Bentinck in 1829, numerous *satis* occurred every year all over India.[1] And long after the date of the ordinance in question the rite was freely practised in Hindu States outside the jurisdiction of the British power. One instance of this kind is the *sati* which accompanied the cremation of the body of Maharajah Ranjit Singh of the Punjab in 1839, when four of his wives and seven female slaves were burnt to death on the funeral pyre with the corpse of their lord and master.

Aiding and abetting the performance of *sati* having, under British law, been declared a criminal offence, it has now become very rare. A few cases of *sati* do, however, still occur, and some have been reported within quite recent years. One, for example, was carried out in Behar in October 1904, and resulted in six men being sentenced to various terms of rigorous imprisonment, varying from nine months to five years. In March 1905, at a village some thirty miles from Ajmere, a Hindu woman followed her husband's corpse to the place of cremation, and when the funeral pile was ready and the dead body laid upon it she threw herself upon the corpse. Some one, amidst the great confusion and uproar which this act occasioned, ignited the pyre, and the woman, who made no attempt to escape, was burnt to death. Another *sati* took place towards the latter part of 1905 at Maypur, a village in the Punjab. A Hindu woman whose husband had died two or three years before,

[1] *Sati* "would also fall under the definition of culpable homicide given in the Indian Penal Code, sec. 299, though by the 5th exception appended to sec. 300 it would not amount to murder."—"Legislation under Lord Mayo," by Sir James Fitzjames Stephen, being chap. viii. vol. ii. of Sir W. W. Hunter's *Life of the Earl of Mayo.*

made a funeral pyre, set fire to it, and committing herself to the flames, died in the presence of a number of persons.

In 1906 a *sati* occurred in Cawnpore and another in Calcutta. In both cases the widows, quite young women, set their own clothes on fire and so committed suicide.

Although the rite of *sati* has been practically suppressed, the alternative, enforced widowhood, with its degrading accompaniments, still remains in force notwithstanding the legislative permission accorded, by Act XV. of 1856, to the remarriage of Hindu widows.

However young she may be, the Hindu widow has from the moment her husband dies, not only to deplore the loss of a companion, perhaps a beloved companion and supporter, but she has also to take a position of utter degradation in the household where formerly she had an honoured place.

In many parts of India it is customary a few days after the cremation of the husband to perform what may be called the ceremony of formally degrading the widow, when she has her head shaved by the barber and is deprived of the use of all her personal ornaments. Ever after that she is condemned to sleep, not on a bed, but upon a mat spread on the floor; to have but one meal a day; and to be excluded very strictly from all festivities and family gatherings. Not only is the widow degraded and set aside, but her very presence on joyful occasions becomes an actual offence, and her mere shadow is in certain cases unpropitious.

Without doubt the lot of the Hindu widow thus stated is extremely hard, and it has afforded European women writers material for some very natural displays of feeling and sentiment over the sufferings of their unfortunate Indian sisters. But we must be cautious neither to wholly judge Indian institutions by European standards nor to gauge the feelings of Indian women in particular situations by those of European women if they could now be placed in similar circumstances. Women reared in the semi-religious atmosphere of Hindu society are in all probability able to accept the widow's position *as the decree of fate*, and to bear with equanimity the tyranny of an immemorial custom, particularly when it allows of no exceptions and is most onerous in the case of the best-born. The calamity of widowhood is no doubt received by the Hinduani just as the infliction of an incurable disease might be. There is no way out of it, and this fact almost compels patient endurance. Besides, there must be a large proportion of cases in which the widow is too strong in character, or too well placed, to allow of her humiliation being anything more than nominal, especially so when she is the mother of sons devoted to her, or when she is the possessor of wealth of her own. Then again, there must at all times be instances innumerable in which the natural tenderness of relations and intimate friends greatly mitigate or even mollify the cruelty of the widow's situation. Often it is not so, and then the wretched sufferers, according to age and the circumstances of each case, take refuge in religion; are driven to suicide, or, when very young, fall into immoral courses involving perhaps repeated infanticides and other heinous crimes.

In this connection I may cite the following painful and characteristic instances reported in the *Indian Spectator*, a paper edited and managed by natives:—

> "*The Hindu Widow and her Woes.*—'The Gujarati' reports a case of infanticide at Jetpur in Kattywar. A 'high-caste' widow, long suspected by the police and closely watched gives birth to a child. The new-comer's mouth is immediately stuffed with hot kitchen ashes. Thus 'religiously disposed of' and thrust into a basket of rubbish, its loving grandmother deposits the child into the nearest river. The village police *then* come to know about it.
>
> "A very similar case is reported to us from Viramgaum; high-caste widow, new-born baby, and hot ashes, though no mention is made of the loving grand-mother or the basket of rubbish. Three persons are implicated in the former case. It must be remembered that the mother is very seldom a party to the 'act of merit.' After all it is her child, flesh of her flesh. In the Jetpur widow's case, we may say she is no more a murderer than is the head of the local police. The father of her unclaimed child, whom your humane English law never thinks of calling to account, is the prime mover with the widow's parents and caste-people as his accomplices. So cleverly is the affair managed, that hardly one case out of twenty can be detected.

In most cases the child dies before birth. The patient is removed far from her home, on a visit to a friend, or on a pilgrimage, and there she is absolved of the burden of sin. She is lucky if she escapes with permanent injury to the system, for the village surgeon is but a clumsy operator. If less lucky, she succumbs under the operation. But least lucky is the widow whose case does not yield to the manipulations of the *Dái*. And woe be to her if she belongs to a respectable family. Then they get up a ceremony in her honour, what they call a *cold Suttee*, they serve her with the best viands, they ply her with sweet intoxicants, and they cap her last supper on earth with something that will settle their business. The widow is soon a *cold Suttee*, and is forthwith carried off to the burning ground,—the pious Hindoo cannot keep a corpse in his house ten minutes. This *cold Suttee* means a double murder. Let us hope it is a very rare practice. But a case is known where the widow suspected foul play in the midst of the nocturnal festivities in her honour. She turned piteously to her mother and asked to be saved, but she was thus urged in reply:

"'Drink, drink, my child, drink to cover thy mother's shame and to keep thy father's *abru* (honour); drink it, dear daughter, see, I am doing likewise!'"[1]

Infanticides committed in order to escape disgrace are unfortunately not unknown in the West; but nothing analogous to the ceremony of the *cold Suttee* could be possible outside India.

In strange contrast with the austere severity of sentiments which could culminate in the tragic rite of a "*cold Suttee*," it may be mentioned that sometimes widows are actually *encouraged*, as amongst the Tulava Brahmans of Southern India, to take to "prostitution in the name of religion."[2]

Regarded from any point of view, the cremation of Hindu widows with the bodies of their dead husbands was a decidedly barbarous practice, and the same may be said of the formal degradation of Hindu widows and their perpetual

[1] Dayaram Gidumal, LL.B., C.S., *The Life and Life-work of Behramji M. Malabari*, pp. cii and ciii.

[2] Dr. John Wilson, *Caste in India*, vol. ii. p. 70.

exclusion from the ordinary pleasures of life. Either practice, if justifiable at all, can be so only on the plea which has actually been put forward, that as a rule Hindu wives desirous of forming new alliances would not hesitate to poison their husbands, and as a matter of fact commonly did so in the days before the *sati* and its alternative were enforced.

This charge of old standing, dating back at least to the beginning of our era, and unhappily not yet withdrawn, would, if true, reflect so seriously upon the virtue and moral character of Indian women, and at the same time point so unmistakably to gross tyranny on the part of the men driving their wives to deliberate murder, that I prefer to regard the accusation in question as at least *not proven.* We are therefore constrained to look for other causes.

The roots of the custom known as the *sati* are to be sought in a barbarous age at a time when it was considered —as indeed it is at the present day amongst certain West African and other tribes—that the spirit of a departed chief or other prominent personage should be attended and ministered to by the spirits of his wives and slaves.

Human sacrifices being once established as part of the funeral rites of chiefs and kings would, in ordinary course, be regarded as a mark or proof of rank, power, position, or influence. Every family which claimed to be of any importance would desire to include human sacrifices amongst the funeral ceremonies adopted by it; and if it were fit that some near and dear to him in life should attend the deceased in spirit-land, who more necessary or acceptable to him than his wives and female slaves.

Fashion and the rivalry of tribes, clans, and families would tend to make the practice of widow burning a comparatively common one, though at no time could it have been *general.*

Thus established in the old-time and hallowed by hoary custom as an indication of superior respectability, widow burning would, in later and less barbarous times, be duly encouraged and justified by convenient religious texts, extolling the virtue of the willing victim and exalting the rewards of her self-sacrifice. Common-sense reasons would also be given in support of an obviously inhuman custom, and the poisoning propensities of Hindu wives, which *may* have had some foundation of truth, would be one of these, appealing very strongly to the cowardly selfishness of men.

Certainly *sati* relieves the dead man's family from the burden of maintaining his widow or widows, a fact to which that famous jurist Sir Henry Maine attached special importance, as having tended greatly to perpetuate the cruel custom.

After having been practised in India for over two thousand years, widow burning has been suppressed by the strong hand of a foreign Government; but there is every reason to believe that even now it would be revived in many parts of the country if the laws against it were abrogated or suspended, and it is evident that while such feelings on this point continue to exist amongst Hindus generally, any considerable amelioration of the condition of the widows is yet afar off.

However, it cannot be denied that at least some Hindus are beginning to realise sympathetically, in a way hitherto unknown, the unmerited tribulations and sorrows of the widows of their community. As the outcome of this sentiment a movement to countenance widow remarriage has come into existence; but it meets with strenuous opposition from the orthodox priesthood and from the great body of women, who look to the priests for guidance. Consequently, although there have been and are many individual advocates for widow remarriage throughout India, although there are many *Widow Remarriage Associations* in the country, and matrimonial advertisers in the interest of the same cause are not wanting, yet the conservative opposition to the movement is so strong that the results up to the present time are small, though as a *beginning* they may be considered encouraging. For example, one Widow Remarriage Association of Upper India was recently able to report that under its auspices forty-seven marriages of widows had taken place in one year, most of these amongst respectable Brahman families. But even in small sects like that of the

Brahmas which have cut themselves off from orthodox Hinduism, the cause of the widows has had little if any success.

As already stated, the remarriage of a Hindu widow is permitted by British Indian law, so that no legal objection to such a step exists; but the religious sentiment or prejudice of the Hindu community unfortunately renders the law almost a dead letter.

Actuated by motives not always meritorious, some few persons, defying the public opinion of their society, do, however, under the ægis of British law, venture to act up to their professions in respect to the propriety of widow remarriage, and such marriages are duly chronicled by the Indian Press, as in the following cases, for the encouragement of others:—

> "A widow remarriage of an advanced type took place in the City under the auspices of some Arya gentlemen on Tuesday evening. Both bridegroom and 'bride' are of a mature age, and the latter has a child by a previous husband."—*Tribune* (Lahore), 17th February 1894.
>
> "A widow marriage took place at Bhera on the 19th January 1894 between Bhai Hira Singh Bohra, aged about 35, and Raj Devi, a Khatri widow, aged 20. It was also a case of intermarriage. It was chiefly owing to the efforts of Malak Hans Raj Anand, who, as secretary of the Anand Sabba, takes a deep interest in social reform questions. That he was successful in persuading even the Sanatan Pandita to take part in the marriage is a sign of the times."—*Tribune* (Lahore), 21st February 1894.
>
> "Under the auspices of the local Arya Samaj, a widow marriage of considerable public interest has been performed in Amritsar. The bride is the widowed daughter of a zealous Arya, and the bridegroom a respectable young man of Kaithal. A large number of guests were present at the marriage."—*Pioneer Mail*, (Allahabad), January 1906.

If I am not misinformed, parties contracting these marriages usually suffer such serious persecution of many kinds that their fate has been a warning, instead of an encouragement, to others disposed to disregard the strongly maintained views of the caste to which they belong. Some fifteen years ago it came to my knowledge that an influential and very learned Bengali gentleman had been instrumental in effecting some fifty widow marriages, with the result that he had the pleasure of supporting all the happy couples, for it was only to secure this kind support, and on condition of receiving it, that bridegrooms could be found for the widows. There is no denying that caste persecution in such cases has ample justification in the precepts of the Hindu law-books, for Manu has laid down that amongst the persons to be carefully shunned are "the husband of a twice-married woman and the remover of dead bodies." Yet some instances, very rare ones it is true, are known in which the remarriage of widows is actually permitted, for example amongst the Audichya, Barada, and the Sinduvala Brahmans of Gujarat; while the Tage Brahmans of the Punjab take widows of their own caste as concubines, and so do the Brahmans of Nepal. Brahman widows are also known to find husbands outside their caste, and even outside their creed. On this point the Rev. J. Vans Taylor writes in connection with certain Gujarati Brahmans: "Widows are at once a loss to the population and their own castes. But Brahmanis sometimes become feeders to other castes. Many Rajputs, Kolis, Kulambis, and Musalmans (I know of one case even of a Bhangi) get Brahmanic widows as either their second or secondary wives."[1]

To sum up the present situation. Under British law the Hindu widow may not be sacrificed or sacrifice herself on the funeral pyre; she may, if she can find a partner, marry again. But in obedience to the rules of immemorial custom, her second husband, herself, and any children born to them would in such a case in all probability be outcasted, an outlook which few care to face.

As far as legislation goes, the British Government seems to have done what it could for the Hindu widow, but outside the law much may reasonably be done by the State for these unfortunates, as I shall point out later on.

[1] Dr. J. Wilson, *Indian Caste*, vol. ii. p. 122.

HINDU SOCIAL REFORMERS —*continued*

SECTION VI.—Temple women.

CERTAIN Hindu reformers have recently invoked the interference of the authorities to abolish the custom, common in some parts of India, of marrying young girls to Hindu gods—such marriages being merely the prelude to a state of licensed prostitution in the service of religion. A memorial on this subject was, a few months ago, addressed to the Government of Bombay by Dr. Bhandarkar, C.I.E., of Poona, and about one hundred other influential natives of Western India, setting forth the notorious frequency of this evil practice, and praying that it may in future be officially regarded as an offence punishable under the Indian Penal Code. The memorialists also petitioned that the minors wedded to idols should be "placed in the care of proper guardians or in mission orphanages," a very significant and flattering testimony to the high esteem in which these establishments are held by some liberal-minded Hindus.

With the caution which, as a rule, characterises the action of the British authorities in India where matters affecting the religious sentiments of the subject peoples are concerned, the Governor of Bombay gave orders for a preliminary series of inquiries to be carried out by certain Government officers, with the view of obtaining competent opinion in regard to the law as applicable to such cases, and of ascertaining the state of Hindu public opinion on the points raised by the memorialists. We may patiently await the result, confident that if a fair proportion of the better class of Hindu society declare against the practice, the weight of the British Government will be thrown on the same side.

It is hardly necessary to state that religious prostitution is not an institution of yesterday, nor peculiar to India. It was very common in ancient times amongst the Lydians; and in Syria, Armenia, Chaldæa, and Egypt, a similar, or even more shameless cultus of unchastity was known. "Devoted women" attached to the great sanctuaries were familiar even to the Hebrews. "Religious prostitution was not confined to the temples of Astarte, nor to the worship of female divinities. Numbers xxv. 1–5 connects it with Baal-peor; Amos ii. 7, Deuteronomy xxiii. 17, 18, etc., show that in Israel similar practices infected even the worship of Yahwe (Jehovah). There is no doubt, however, that the cultus of Astarte was saturated with these abominations."[1]

In India the religious prostitutes (*dēvidasis*) are consecrated to the deity to whose temple they are attached. They are carefully trained in the Terpsichorean art and in music, and are taught how to make themselves agreeable and attractive. Their public duty is to dance daily before the idol of the god and to sing hymns, often erotic in character, in his honour. Certain allowances are made to them from the temple treasury to which their earnings belong.

> "Their ranks are recruited by the purchase of female children of any caste, and also by members of certain Hindu castes vowing to present daughters to the temple on recovering from illness or relief from other misfortune. The female children of dancing-women are always brought up to their mother's profession, and so are the children purchased by them, or assigned to the temple service by the free-will of their parents."—Sherring, *Hindu Tribes and Castes.*

The existence of the custom of devoting girls to the service of Hindu temples, and all that is involved in such dedication

[1] *Encyclopædia Biblica*, vol. i. c. 338.

is, of course, well known to the Christian missionaries in India, who naturally condemn the shocking institution and bewail the fate of the girl-victims of this horrid practice.[1]

Unfortunately, prostitution seems to be a permanent institution all the world over, and especially rampant in the most civilised countries. It is an evil over which Christianity has apparently been unable to exercise any effective check, and the restless Hindu reformer and the ardent Christian missionary may well bethink them whether, after all, prostitution sanctified by religion and under recognised control is not morally less harmful to all concerned than the prostitution which, in defiance of religion and law, not only pervades the slums but makes its flaunting presence unpleasantly conspicuous in the most fashionable thoroughfares of the populous cities of Europe and America. This view of the matter, though certainly very unconventional, may still deserve a moment's consideration from thinking men and responsible legislators.

[1] Amy Wilson-Carmichael, *Things as they are: Mission Work in Southern India*, chap. xxiv.

HINDU SOCIAL REFORMERS
—continued

SECTION VII.—The old and the new woman.

Life behind the Purdah.—

NO one interested in India can be unfamiliar with the words *purdah* (screen) and *zenana* (women's apartment), both associated with the seclusion of women in that country, a subject on which much has been written.

The visitor to India sees Hindu women of the lower orders everywhere; but women of the higher castes or of moderately good social position do not generally appear in public unveiled, and as long as they are virtuous or reputable, hold no social intercourse whatever with any men outside the family circle. Even within the family circle there are many male members with whom they may not so much as speak, and before whom they must not appear unveiled.

Amongst the Muslims, also, women are kept in seclusion, in the harem.

Now, however *we* may regard the matter, this seclusion is amongst both Hindus and Muslims a coveted mark of social superiority, and is accordingly highly appreciated by Indian women. It is by no means distasteful to them, as European women, reared under quite other social conditions, are prone to think. But it cannot be denied that within recent years the seeds of discontent have been introduced by foreign agencies into many Indian homes, and may be expected to bring forth fruit in due season.

From those who have seen the inside of Indian home-life, we obtain accounts and opinions diverse indeed and, as might have been expected, both highly appreciative and entirely the reverse. Some Europeans writing on the condition of the female sex in India, cannot find words strong enough in which to denounce the degraded state of Indian women, while others find an almost ideal beauty in the life behind *the purdah.*

A few quotations from the works of writers on the subject will suffice to make this point clear.

> "It may be said with truth," wrote the Abbé Dubois eighty years ago, "that so far are the Hindu females from being held in that low state of contempt and degradation in which the Rev. —— repeatedly describes them in his letter, that, on the contrary, they are under much less restraint, enjoy more real freedom, and are in possession of more enviable privileges than the persons of their sex in any other Asiatic country. In fact, to them belong the entire management of their household, the care of their children, the superintendence of the menial servants, the distribution of alms and charities. To their charge are generally intrusted the money, jewels, and other valuables. To them belongs the care of procuring provisions and providing for all expenses. It is they also who are charged, almost to the exclusion of their husbands, with the most important affair of procuring wives for their sons and husbands for their daughters; and, in doing this, they evince a niceness, an attention, and foresight, which are not certainly surpassed in any country; while, in the management of their domestic business, they in general show a shrewdness, a savingness, and an intelligence which would do honour to the best housewives in Europe.
>
> "In the meanwhile, the austerity and roughness with which they are outwardly treated in public, by their husbands, is rather a matter of form, and entirely ceases when the husband and his wife are in private. It is there that the Hindoo females assume all that empire which is everywhere exercised, in civilised countries, by the persons of their sex over the male part of creation; find means to bring them under subjection, and rule over them, in several instances, with a despotic sway. In short, although outwardly exposed in public to the forbidding and repulsive power of an austere husband, they can be considered in no

other light than as perfectly the mistresses within the house.

. . . .

"The authority of married women within their houses is chiefly exerted in preserving good order and peace among the persons who compose their families; and a great many among them discharge this important duty with a prudence and a discretion which have scarcely a parallel in Europe. I have known families composed of between thirty and forty persons, or more, consisting of grown sons and daughters, all married and all having children, living together under the superintendence of an old matron—their mother or mother-in-law. The latter, by good management, and by accommodating herself to the temper of her daughters-in-law; by using, according to circumstances, firmness or forbearance, succeeds in preserving peace and harmony during many years amongst so many females, who had all jarring interests, and still more jarring tempers. I ask you whether it would be possible to attain the same end, in the same circumstances, in our countries, where it is scarcely possible to make two women living under the same roof to agree together."[1]

Very different from the good Abbé's picture of Indian home-life is the following, from the pen of Dr. Emma Ryder of Bombay, who, in a paper entitled "The Little Wives of India," said:

"In coming to India I expected to find women and girls that would much resemble those I had seen in other tropical countries—in Mexico, Central America, and on the Isthmus of Panama—healthy, with dark faces and laughing bright eyes. I can never express the sadness of heart that I experienced when I met these half-developed women, with their look of hopeless endurance, their skeleton-like arms and legs, and saw them walking the prescribed number of paces behind their husbands, with never a smile on their faces. I expected the little girls in India would be the same precocious, strong, fully developed girls that I found in other tropical countries; and how great was my

[1] The Abbé J. A. Dubois, missionary in Mysore, *Letters on the State of Christianity in India*, pp. 182–185. (London, 1823.)

astonishment to behold the little dwarf-like, quarter-developed beings, and to be told that they were wives, and serving not only their lords and masters, but the mothers-in-law, and often a community or family of ten, twelve, fourteen, or twenty. Talk of maturity for these little creatures! They can never come to full maturity, for they were robbed before they were born, as were their ancestors. If they could have proper exercise, with all the food they need, and above all, if they could be made happy until they were twenty-five years old, it might not be a sin for them to give birth to an immortal soul."

Referring to the Hindu husband, the same lady says:

"If I could take my readers with me on my round of visits for one week, and let them behold the condition of the little wives, it would need no words of mine to send you forth crying into this wilderness of sin. If you could see the suffering faces of the little girls, who are drawn nearly double with contractions, caused by the brutality of their husbands, and who will never be able to stand erect; if you could see the paralysed limbs that will not again move in obedience to the will; if you could hear the plaintive wail of the little sufferers as, with their tiny hands clasped, they beg you to 'make them die,' and then turn and listen to the brutal remarks of the legal owner with regard to the condition of his property; if you could stand with me by the side of the little deformed dead body, and, turning from the sickening sight, could be shown the new victim to whom the brute was already betrothed, do you think it would require long arguments to convince you that there was a deadly wrong somewhere, and that someone was responsible for it? After one such scene a Hindu husband said to me, 'You look like you feel bad' (meaning sad). 'Doctors ought not to care what see. I don't care what see, nothing trouble me, only when self sick; I don't like to have pain self.'"

To the sympathetic eyes of Miss Margaret Noble, the Hindu household is almost ideal.

"All the sons of a Hindu household," says this lady, "bring their wives home to their mother's care, and she, having married her own daughters into other women's families, takes these in their place. There is thus a constant bubbling of young life about the elderly woman, and her own position becomes a mixture of the mother-suzeraine and lady abbess. She is well aware of the gossip and laughter of the girls amongst themselves, though they become so demure at her entrance. Whispering goes on in corners, and merriment waxes high even in her presence; but she ignores it discreetly, and devotes her attention to persons of her own age. In the early summer mornings she smiles indulgently to find that one and another slipped away last night from her proper sleeping-place and betook herself to the roof, half for the coolness and half for the mysterious joys of girls' midnight gossip.

"The relationship, however, is as far from familiarity as that of any kind and trusted prioress with her novices. The element of banter and freedom has another outlet, in the grandmother or whatever aged woman may take that place in the community house. Just as at home the little one had coaxed and appealed against the decisions of father or mother to the ever-ready granddam, so, now that she is a bride, she finds some old woman in her husband's home who has given up her cares into younger hands, and is ready to forego all responsibility in the sweetness of becoming a *confidante*. One can imagine the rest. There must be many a difficulty, many a perplexity, in the new surroundings, but to them all old age can find some parallel. Looking back into her own memories, the grandmother tells of the questions that troubled her when she was a bride, of the mistakes that she made, and the solutions that offered. Young and old take counsel together, and there is even the possibility that when a mother-in-law is unsympathetic, her own mother-in-law may intervene on behalf of a grandson's wife.

. . . .

"Long ago, when a child's solemn betrothal often took place at seven or eight years of age, it was to gratify the old people's desire to have more children about them that the tiny maidens were brought into the house. It was on the grandmother's lap that the little ones were made acquainted; it was she and her husband who watched anxiously to see that they took to each other; and it was they again who petted and comforted the minute granddaughter-in-law in her hours of home-sickness. Marriage has grown later nowadays, in answer amongst other things to the pressure of an increasing poverty, and it does not happen so often that an old man is seen in the bazaar buying consoling gifts for the baby brides at home. But the same instinct still obtains, of making the new home a place of choice, when between her twelfth and fourteenth year—the girl's age at her first and second marriages—the young couple visit alternately in each other's families."[1]

The above somewhat lengthy extracts refer to the domestic life of the people of the territories of Madras, Bombay, and Bengal respectively, and at different periods. If we grant their substantial correctness, they would show how unwise it would be to draw general conclusions about the whole of India from any statements made by persons acquainted with only limited portions of that vast country. If the more favourable of these impressions of Indian home-life, recorded by Europeans of both sexes, reveal pleasant glimpses of amenities which we may reasonably hope are by no means rare, we are yet unable to forget the less satisfactory pictures of *zenana* life which missionary ladies have given to the world, and the more so in face of the multitudinous facts illustrative of domestic tyranny which Indians themselves, in their zeal for reform, have made public within the past few years.

With such knowledge of the matter as is now common property, one cannot but feel that at the very least there is ample reason to desire the admission of more intellectual light into the Indian *zenana*, and the concession of more personal freedom to its inmates. But let us see what the Indian reformers are themselves thinking about.

Female education.—When social reforms are in the air we may rest assured that men become keenly alive to the desirability of many improvements in the character, behaviour, and customs of their women-folk; and since in recent years education has come to be regarded as the

[1] The Sister Nivedita (Margaret E. Noble), *The Web of Indian Life*, London, 1904, pp. 34, 35.

panacea for nearly all human ills and shortcomings, female education occupies, as we have seen already, a foremost place in the Indian reformer's programme. But the difficulties in the way of female education in India are immense, and little progress has yet been made in attracting girls and women to such schools as have been provided for them.

According to the census of 1901–2, the number of girls in the secondary stage of instruction among one hundred thousand of school-going age was only about twenty-seven in the case of Hindus and about five in the case of Muhammadans—*i.e.*, not three in *ten* thousand amongst Hindus, and only *one* in *twenty thousand* amongst Muslims.

Hindu Scriptures are opposed to female education, not permitting women even to take part in the worship of Saraswati, the Goddess of Learning.[1] Immemorial custom is equally unfavourable to female education in India. From Megasthenes we learn that the Brahmans did not permit their wives to attend their philosophical discussions, fearing they would divulge their secret doctrines, and also because instructed females would be prone to assert their independence and desert their husbands. Early marriage is another difficulty and a serious one too, as Christian missionaries have often pointed out with regret, drawing painful pictures of bright child-wives longing for instruction, being removed from their happy mission schools to be immured in dull *zenanas*.

Yet notwithstanding the immense disabilities under which they labour, many Indian women have already qualified themselves for and received the degrees in arts, science, law, and medicine of the Indian Universities. I have myself met some educated Indian ladies, mostly, I must admit, Christians or Parsees, and have been struck by the extreme modesty of their bearing.

In respect to home education, European ladies who, as teachers, nurses, or physicians, gain access to the secluded homes of the better classes of the Indian community do not, as a rule, give encouraging reports with respect to a desire for education amongst the inmates of the zenanas,

[1] Shib Chunder Bose, *The Hindoos as they are.*

and they deplore the disinclination of the *purdah nasheens* to adopt modern Western habits, which in the eyes of European ladies generally constitute an absolutely indispensable factor of true civilisation.

Indian gentlemen who write on the same topic are often not more hopeful. One great obstacle to zenana teaching by European ladies is the wide gulf which lies between Oriental and Occidental ideas upon most matters, and even upon essential points. For example, to quote an educated Punjabi gentleman: "The ladies (*i.e.* Hindu ladies) know and believe it, as a maxim, that to remain dirty is a religious duty, a Bahu Bati should never be dressed neat and clean like a *Kanchan-mangan*"; and yet, "women who have the dirtiest possible *dhoti* as their dress keep telling their clean and respectable European teacher at every minute to be careful not to touch them."[1]

What female education is expected to do for India is set forth in the following speech made by the Gaekwar of Baroda at the Alexandra Girls' School, Bombay, on the 30th March 1904. His Highness said:

> "The greatest difference in Eastern and Western conditions is our lack of real social life. This is both the cause and effect of defective education, for education is not a reality without some interchange of ideas. On the other hand, until our women are more educated we shall not break through their splendid isolation—isolation which we cannot too strongly condemn if we find it retarding the mental and physical development of our women and men. While our lack of social life is a great deficiency, it robs us of some of the strongest bonds of national union, for it accentuates all petty caste restrictions. It is also intensely narrowing, for we meet our neighbours too much on a business or official footing, while, on the other hand, our home interests are too purely domestic. It is this gap between the details of the household and our work which our women can help us to bridge over. It is this widening of the interests at which we have to aim —the broadening of woman's views on life in every

[1] From a letter to an Indian newspaper on "Teaching in the Zenana," by Piyare Lal, B.A., teacher, Central Model School, Lahore.

respect—so that she may be better fitted to order her own household, to look after her children, to make her home more beautiful and attractive, to widen out the interests which surround the home, until they can include her neighbours, so that social life may become a reality and so stretch out to national life, and so enable the woman to bear her full share in the development of the race and the future of India. I would even allow the new woman, however shocking the heresy may sound, to find her own level, and to prove for herself the reality of the claims she has made for equality. We need women to play a stronger part in our national life for many reasons, and I would venture to remind you that under the more strenuous conditions of Indian social life which prevailed not so very long ago, our women took a larger and more active part in our national life. In the disintegrating conditions of our present society they are not playing that part. And there is another point to which I wish just to call your attention. I do not think our present society exerts sufficient influence on public and private morality. I fear that we judge a man too much by his adherence to customs and forms, and too little by his real character. It is women's influence which we need to help us to build up strong public opinion on these matters, an opinion which will work towards a higher standard of social purity. I do not think we shall be able to insist on one method to attain these ends, nor do I recommend that we should hastily adopt European methods because they are successful in Europe. I do not believe that all our old customs can be entirely valueless, nor, on the other hand, are they valuable merely because they are old. But we need some touchstone to apply to them, to show us which is the gold and which is the dross of ignorant superstition which has gathered round them. Such a touchstone education must supply."

The Gaekwar's address shows how much is expected from female education in India. It is to promote social intercourse, break down caste prejudices, widen life's interests, improve public and private morality, and create or strengthen bonds of nationality.

We may be permitted at least *to hope* that *some* of these sanguine anticipations may be realised at a future time.

Women advocates of women's rights.—As I have pointed out in a previous page, the demand for even elementary education on the part of females has, as yet, been very slight indeed, although a few women have actually graduated with credit at the Indian Universities. Yet it is a remarkable fact that, in spite of old-time ideas and prejudices, Indian women are themselves coming forward publicly to advocate their own cause and that of their neglected sisters.

Some years ago it was my good fortune to listen to one of these advocates of women's rights. It was on the occasion of a public meeting at the Deva Dharma Mandir, Lahore.

For me the attraction of the evening was an address by a native lady on "Home Life." The hall was a newly built one about 50 feet by 25 feet in the clear. At one end the room was double-storeyed, both ground floor and gallery being screened off by *chicks* (reed screens), from behind which a number of women watched the proceedings under great difficulties. A large company had assembled by the time I arrived. Comfortable chairs had been provided for the audience, and were occupied mostly by native gentlemen of the better educated classes. On an open space in front of the first row of chairs sat about fifty members of the Deva Dharma Society with their friends, all unostentatiously squatted on a white cloth which served as a carpet. Some arm-chairs were placed against the *chicks* facing the audience, and a small table provided with a lamp and ornamented with a vase occupied the middle part of the same end. The arm-chairs were soon occupied by seven unveiled native ladies, who commenced the proceedings of the evening by singing a hymn in Urdu. When this was over the lady lecturer, Premdevi, neatly attired in skirt, bodice and chaddar, kid shoes and white stockings, with an orange-coloured kerchief pinned over her head, came forward, and taking her stand in a modest attitude at a little table, read her lecture with the greatest composure, in a clear musical voice of considerable compass. She commenced by laying special stress upon the great importance of a mother's influence upon the character of her offspring, illustrating her point by reference exclusively to the biographies of Europeans, and especially of Englishmen. Having dwelt sufficiently on this subject, the lecturer proceeded to contrast Indian with English home-life, much to the disadvantage of the former. She told us that Indian homes were a hotbed of tyranny and contention, and she upbraided the highly educated classes — the University graduates, lawyers, and others—with keeping their women virtually in a state of slavery and imprisonment, while they themselves posed before the public as liberal-minded reformers of a quite radical type. Passing to other matters, the lady said a word for the Devi Dharma Mission, to which she had dedicated her life, and she warmly defended the domestic life of the founder of the new sect from certain criticisms which had been levelled against it.

Within the hall the lady's address was listened to by her audience in complete and chilling silence. But outside, loud angry shouting and vigorous knocking at the gates made it evident that there was at least a section of the Lahore public to whom Premdevi, or more probably the party she had joined, was anything but acceptable. Regarding the lecturer's antecedents, a word may not be out of place. As far as I could ascertain, she had been a student in the local medical college, had completed a four years' course there, and had left the institution with honours. Amongst her friends she was known and spoken of as Doctor Premdevi.

The lecture to which I have just referred was given on the 16th February 1891. Some years previously I had had the pleasure of listening to another Hindu lady lecturing in the hall of the Arya Samaj on the woes of the inmates of the zenana, and I have given the substance of her complaint in another book.[1]

Some years earlier other Indian women had taken up the battle for their own emancipation. One prominent instance was that of Pandita Ramabai.[2]

This Brahman lady, a Mahratta by birth, was the daughter of a learned man, who, renouncing secular life,

[1] *Indian Life, Religious and Social*, pp. 117–119.

[2] *Pandita Ramabai Sarasvati, the High-caste Hindu Woman* (Fleming H. Revell Company, New York, 1901).

retired into the jungle with his family, there to pass in devotion and study the remainder of his days. Under his instructions Ramabai acquired a knowledge of the Sanskrit language and of the sacred Vedas and Puranas of her religion. Strange to relate, she does not seem to have been married during her father's lifetime, and after his death she made a tour of India accompanied by her brother. Putting aside the prejudices of caste and disregarding the customs of her people, she made her own choice of a husband, not a Mahratta Brahman but a Bengali Babu, a graduate of the Calcutta University. A union like this between members of two widely distinct Indian nationalities was a most unorthodox and daring proceeding; which, however, has been imitated many times since amongst the more highly educated classes. Only the other day the papers announced a marriage between a Bengali lady graduate of the Calcutta University and a Punjabi medical man educated in England.

Within a few months of Ramabai's marriage she became a widow, but with her natural recalcitrance she declined to accept the degraded position or to undergo any of the humiliations of Hindu widowhood. Her utter contempt for the cherished conventions of Hindu religious and social life shocked and scandalised the orthodox, but with characteristic self-reliance she determined to devote herself to the ambitious task of raising the intellectual, social, and moral condition of her countrywomen. With this object Pandita Ramabai set about delivering public lectures on the education and emancipation of Hindu women.

For a time this Brahman lady attracted a good deal of *public* attention, and was the subject of many eulogistic addresses and notices, but her social position was a cruelly isolated one, and she readily fell under the spell of certain kind Christian missionaries, who easily induced the clever and impulsive young wanderer from the fold of orthodox Hinduism to accept their sympathetic hospitality and help. Influenced by her new friends, the Pandita went to England, taking her little daughter with her. On her arrival in England, Ramabai received a cordial welcome from the Sisters of St. Mary at Wantage, and shortly afterwards embraced the Christian religion, she and her little girl being baptized there in 1883.

The convert learned English at Wantage, and was appointed Professor of Sanskrit at the Ladies' College, Cheltenham, where she studied mathematics, natural science, and English literature. However, before completing the usual course at that institution, she went to America to be present at Philadelphia on the occasion of her cousin, Mrs. Anandabai Joshee, receiving a medical degree. In America, Ramabai formed various schemes for the education and elevation of her sisters in India; but her projects finally took shape in the determination to found a purely secular home for Hindu widows, where they might be trained in such work as would enable them to earn an independent living. By 1889 she got together by means of subscriptions a sum of £4000 for the establishment of a Home for Hindu Widows at Poona, and started it, in accordance with her original idea, as a purely secular institution; but later on, yielding against her own judgment to the persuasion of Christian friends, she made the teaching of Christianity an essential feature of the place, and, as might have been anticipated, the venture, under these conditions, proved a complete failure.

Pandita Ramabai's original idea was a good one, but even if strictly adhered to, would not, in all probability, have been attended with success, on account of her position as a convert to Christianity. It would have been very different had the Pandita remained a Hindu, even an unorthodox one. But her scheme, as it first took shape in her mind, has very much to recommend it, and in any and every part of India there is room, indeed a crying demand, for the establishment of Industrial Homes for destitute widows. Hindu philanthropists could hardly find worthier objects for their liberality than such homes. And the State, on its part, might also afford legitimate and inexpensive assistance to the peculiarly deplorable cause of Indian widows, by founding *training* schools in which widows, and widows only, would receive such instruction as would enable them to carry the torch of elementary knowledge into the twilight of the zenanas. Such training schools as I have in my mind would be strictly secular, conducted by women only, *and would neither attempt nor suggest any interference with the manners and customs of Hindu society*. Widows trained in these schools, having in no essentials departed from their religion or the social habits of their own people, would be freely received in the zenanas without that prejudice which necessarily and invariably attaches to the Christian zenana teacher.

Their superior education, counteracting in a great measure the sense of their unworthiness as widows, would give them considerable influence for good, and in time spread a certain degree of education through the households of all the better classes of the Hindu world. Gradually widows would cease to be regarded as objects of contempt, the old-world prejudice against them would, in time, die out, and a large number of them, by securing honourable and remunerative employment, would cease to be unwilling and unwelcome burdens on the family and the community to which they belong by right of birth or of matrimonial alliance.

A yearly increasing number of educated widows working regularly as teachers behind the *purdah* would, as already stated, gradually dispel much of the ignorance which at the present time is entrenched in the almost inaccessible zenanas of the land. And when ignorance is diminished, the spontaneous adoption of reforms and improvements in social life may be confidently looked for.

Possibly my suggestion in regard to *secular training schools for Hindu widows destined for zenana work* has been anticipated, but as I am not aware of such being the case, I commend it to the Indian Educational authorities, in the belief that it contains the potential germ of a gradual, wholly unobjectionable, and far-reaching internal revolution in Hindu social life, entirely free from the irritation inevitably associated with interference from the outside.

The attitude of men towards female education.—In spite of much affected earnestness on their part, I do not fancy that even educated Indians generally, whether Hindus or Muhammadans, take a specially keen interest in the intellectual improvement of the inmates of the zenana, and

I am sure they do not relish being lectured by Hindu women on their own shortcomings. With the *Parsees* who are not Hindus at all, but followers of Zarathushtra, and in the case of certain Brahmas of Bengal who have practically cut themselves off from Hinduism, the question of the education of women and of their intercourse in society with the opposite sex, is, of course, on a different footing.

That some educated young men devote attention to the instruction of their girl-wives in reading and writing, and often encourage their pupils by means of rewards in the shape of jewellery for proficiency in the tasks set them, I am well aware. But a large majority of the men, while recognising, in an academic fashion, the great importance of female education, are by no means anxious for any special advance in this direction, at least during their own lifetime; for the subjection of women has always been a cardinal doctrine in the East, apparent even in its folk-lore. For example, Professor Max Müller in his interesting essay "On the Migration of Fables" establishes the Indian origin of the idea or motif of the charming fable of the silly little castle-building milk-maid, so familiar in different forms to European children. He gives two or three versions of the fable as known in Western nurseries, and as related by Eastern fabulists; but the learned philologist does not notice what has a special interest of its own, that the Eastern fable has always a *man* for its hero, whose imagination seems to picture as the highest possible pitch of pride to kick and beat his wife. In the West the subject of the story is a woman, whose misfortune results from feminine vanity or childish delight, finding expression in a toss of the head or a frolicsome caper. The contrast is instructive!

Immodest bathing.—There are, however, other directions than education in which many men find congenial scope for their energies in the advertising of themselves and the reforming of the sex; one of these is immodest bathing.

One April morning I drove down to the river Ravi on the occasion of a Hindu fair. I was on the road by a quarter after seven, but already a host of people in *ekkas* and ordinary four-wheeled carriages, on horseback and on foot, were returning from the river; while another somewhat smaller stream of behind-time persons of both sexes was hurrying towards the river. It was an animated and picturesque crowd, displaying a good deal of bright colour and no little amount of good looks.

From near a spot where some Yogis had encamped, the moving crowd left the main road, and crossing a track over the fields made for the bathing-place. I passed on to the bridge of boats, and had a good view up and down stream. The water was low, and the bathers were able to go right out into the shallow stream, which in some places was little more than knee-deep. The most frequented part was about five or six hundred yards below the bridge, so I turned off and took a pathway along the riverside, protected from the sun by a forest of trees.

The bathers were, for the most part, congregated upon a low sandbank, separated from the riverside by a shallow channel, and here I noticed a long screen made of *daris* (cotton carpets) in the usual Indian fashion, set up, as I soon learned, for the special object of concealing the women bathers from the prying eyes of their countrymen.

This was an innovation probably acceptable to neither sex, the outcome, in fact, of the recent teaching of Hindu *social reformers* of the modern school.

It has for ages been the practice as it is to-day for Hindu women in the Punjab to bathe in the same streams and tanks as the men use, to frequent the bathing-places at the same hours as the men do, and to bathe stark naked, for when they are seen thus their sins are forgiven. But the old custom has become *shocking* to the modern reformers, and they have been raising an outcry about it which had borne fruit in the very prominent screen which had attracted my attention. However, the men who chose to bathe in advance of the screen were not cut off from witnessing the aquatic performances of the fair ladies, and if I may judge from what I saw, there was quite a large number of men not indisposed to avail themselves of this vantage-ground. These were evidently the unregenerate. But a party of "*reformers*," nothing loath to do likewise, stole round to a favourable point of view and set up a camera for the purpose of having a "study from the nude," with the laudable object of exposing the scandal and refuting the denials of the orthodox by a sun-picture that could not lie. However, the orthodox party raised an outcry against these well-meant proceedings, and the police, never too discriminating, hustled the zealous reformers with their camera away out of eye-shot of the naked damsels.

Of nude women I myself saw none *on this occasion.* Only one stood outside the screen with nothing but a skirt on to arrange her toilet, and some few waded through the ankle-deep water, keeping their skirts nearly up to their hips. But, alas! only a fraction of their sins could be *thus* expiated.

On the bank of the river, a hundred yards or so behind the sandbank where the screen had been put up, there was a *Shāmiyana* (pavilion) closed on three sides, but open towards the river face, carpeted with daris and a clean white cloth, which invited the passer-by to sit down and listen to the words of wisdom from the lips of a learned Brahman, a man acquainted with the Vedas. This pavilion had been pitched by the *Sanathan Dharma Sabha, i.e.,* the Orthodox Hindu Society. The learned Brahman sat, to my mild surprise, at a table in an arm-chair. Neither table nor arm-chair were worth a second thought except in connection with that orthodox Brahman, who exhibited quite an *advanced* tendency by using such articles of furniture, surely never heard of in Vedic times.

The Pandit at the table, a grey-bearded man wearing a *pugri* (turban), was reading Sanskrit texts and expounding them to those who cared to listen, the burden of his teaching being that the Vedas *did* inculcate the necessity of bathing in the Ganges, the Jumna, the Saraswati and the other rivers, and declared the religious merit of such bathing. These harangues were meant to counteract the unorthodox teachings of certain recent reforming sects, to the effect that such *bathing ceremonies* were useless if not worse.

While witnessing the above noted efforts at screening the Hindu women from the gaze of the public, I recalled to mind that a couple of years previously a great outcry had been made by certain persons against a police officer in the Punjab, because in his district a woman had been, so it was stated, disrobed for the purposes of a police inquiry. A great deal of *political* capital it was hoped would be made out of this "outrage," but though that expectation was not realised, the outcry led to the police officer's partisans directing special attention to the bathing habits of the people, and to their practical indifference to the disrobing of their women in public places; and it struck me that probably this counter-move may have to some extent hastened the reforming movement and led to the practical result embodied in the *kanat* on the Ravi sandbank.

The sentiment against nude bathing had certainly been growing for some years past. In the English supplement, dated 21st February 1881, of the paper published by the Society known as the Anjuman-i-Punjab, a correspondent writing from Multan stated that a private association was being formed amongst the native gentlemen of the place for the prevention of the custom which obtains in the Punjab of women bathing naked in the public baths. He stated that at a *Suraj-Kanth* festival, held at a distance of four miles from Multan, thousands of women bathed naked in the sacred reservoir in sight of the men, many of whom, *badmashes* (profligates) he calls them, went amongst the women, while others, less bold, stood farther off stealing sly glances at the charms of the fair bathers.

How curious and contradictory are the habits of female seclusion and women bathing naked, and how strange that nowhere, so far as I am aware, do *men* bathe in an absolutely nude state in any part of India.

The inimitable "Ali Baba" speaks of "the privileges of nakedness conferred by a brown skin," and there really is something in this. I remember well an educated native gentleman being quite shocked at the flesh-coloured tights of an English ballet-girl, whose coloured photograph he saw in my album; quite forgetful that the women of his own race went about in a costume which left exposed to view, bare and naked, far more of the person than was covered by the silk tights of the ballet-dancer.

Although, as far as I know, it is not the usual practice in India, outside the Punjab, for women to bathe naked, yet mixed bathing is common and may be witnessed everywhere along the banks of the great rivers, and that it has attractions, other than religious ones, for the ordinary Hindu, will be evident from the following quaintly expressed views of a Bengali gentleman:—

> "The ghauts at Benares are by far the most striking of all its architecture;—and the ghauts of a Hindoo city are always its best lounges. Upon them are passed the happiest hours of a Hindoo's day. There, in the mornings, the greater part of the population turns out to bathe, to dress, and to pray. In the evenings, the people retire thither from the toils of the day, to sit on the open steps and gulp the fresh river-air. The devout congregate to see a *Sunyasi* practise austerities, or hear a *Purumhunso* pass judgment upon Vedantism. The idler lounges there, and has a hawk's eye after a pretty wench. There do the Hindoo females see the world out of their zenanas, cultivate friendship, acquire taste, pick up fashion, talk scandal, discuss the politics of petticoat government, learn the prices current of eatables, and propose matches for their sons and daughters. Half their flirting and half their romancing go on at the ghauts. There have the young widows opportunity to exchange glances, to know that there are admirers of their obsolete beauties, and to enjoy the highest good humour they can harmlessly indulge in.
>
> "Being the headquarters of religion, the centre of wealth, the focus of fashion, and the seat of polite society, Benares is the great point of convergence to which is attracted the beauty of all Hindoostan. To have a peep at that beauty, the best opportunity is when the women sport themselves like merry Naiads in the waters of the Ganges. Then do you see realised the mythic story of the apple of discord between goddesses personified by the Khottanee, the Mahrattanee, and the Lucknowallee — each contending to carry off the prize. The Hindoostanee women have a prestige from the days of Sacoontola and Seeta. But it is to be questioned whether a youthful Bengalinee cannot fairly stand the rivalry of these charms. The dress and costume of the Khottanee

> certainly kick the beam in their favour. But we would fain raise the point on behalf of the women of Bengal, whether 'beauty unadorned is not adorned the most'—whether in the nudity of their muslin-saree they are not as naked as 'the statue that enchants the world.'"[1]

Curiously enough mixed bathing is every year becoming more and more popular in Europe, notwithstanding that certain persons are scandalised, and the susceptibilities of some good folks outraged thereby. What is it a sign of?

Immoral songs at weddings.—When the social pathologist casts his critical eye about, he usually lights before long upon some evil or other which he longs to remove. This is true everywhere, but especially so in Hindu India.

As is well known, it has been a custom amongst the Hindus for grossly immoral songs to be sung, even by respectable women of good social position, on the occasion of weddings, when also a licence of speech is permitted which is nothing short of astonishing. Now young India, realising that these practices are such as Europeans can reasonably take exception to, raises what protest he can against them, and the new social purity associations also seriously denounce such "degrading practices." If, say some reformers, we have none but obscene songs to sing at a marriage feast, let us sing hymns (*bhajans*) on such occasions; not Vedic hymns, but the hymns which have been recently composed for the purposes of the new religious Samajes.

To have the joyous, sensuous licence of the marriage festivities thus curtailed, revolutionised, destroyed, must be intolerable to women to whom these social gatherings are a welcome relief from the monotony of seclusion, and a much appreciated opportunity for a little, perhaps too excessive, freedom of speech in the hearing at least of the opposite sex.

However, in some cases that I have heard of, *bhajans* have been substituted by reforming zealots for the usual marriage songs, not always with happy results. An Indian friend of mine once related to me the ludicrous results

[1] Bholanath Chunder, *Travels of a Hindoo*, vol. i. pp. 252, 253.

of this decision, at any rate on one occasion. He was at the wedding of some respectable people who had been inoculated with the social reform fever, and consequently patronised hymns; so hymns were being sung, to the great discontent and almost open revolt of the ladies. My friend gave attention to the words of one of the hymns, which did not seem particularly lively, and lo! to his astonishment, he discovered it was a funeral dirge which the not too discriminating singers were providing as an epithalamium.

Women's dress.—Wherever under the sun civilised men and women are to be found, women's dress is one of those subjects on which the mere man holds strong convictions when the tendency of fashion is towards unnecessary exposure of the person. On this important subject I may be permitted to quote the following quaint passage from a book written by an educated Bengali:—

> "It would not be out of place to notice here that it would be a very desirable improvement in the way of decency to introduce among the Hindoo females of Bengal a stouter fabric for their garment in place of the present thin, flimsy, loose *sari*, without any other covering over it. In this respect, their sisters of the North-Western and Central Provinces, as well as those of the South, are decidedly more decent and respectable. A few respectable Hindoo ladies have of late years begun to put an *unghia* or corset over their bodies, but still the under vestment is shamefully indelicate. Why do not the Baboos of Bengal strive to introduce a salutary change in the dress of their mothers, wives, sisters, and daughters, which private decency and public morality most urgently demand? These social reforms must go hand in hand with religious, moral, and intellectual improvement. The one is as essential to the elevation and dignity of female character as the other is to the advancement of the nation in the scale of civilisation."[1]

The new woman.—Strange as it may seem, we already hear in India complaints of the new woman, and from many quarters too. I have frequently heard men say that

[1] Shib Chunder Bose, *The Hindoos as they are*, p. 194.

their women who had learned to read and write made use of these arts only to indite love-letters or make assignations. Possibly there may be some truth in this statement, also in the very curious accusation against educated Indian husbands contained in the following passage from a book written by a great *zamindar* (landowner) of Bengal:—

> "Many of the wives of the educated people in the towns and suburbs know how to read and write a little. But how does this little knowledge serve them? It is not utilised to help them to higher education, but is used to pander to the vicious tastes of their husbands, who derive an unearthly pleasure from an unholy epistolary correspondence with their wives, the diction and sentiments of which will put many an abandoned woman to the blush.
>
> "If young men educate their wives so as to be able only to write filthy letters or to read erotic novels that should never be allowed to cross the threshold of any man of good taste, and train them so to disregard their parents and superiors and to utterly neglect their household duties, then I say the sooner we get rid of such education and training the better it will be for our country."[1]

In the face of such statements it may reasonably be doubted whether the importation of education, and a strong infusion of Western ideas regarding liberty, into Indian home-life will be quite as beneficial as some well-meaning persons think. In this connection the following indictment of the new woman in India, contributed to an Anglo-Indian newspaper by one of her own countrymen, will not be out of place or uninteresting:—

> "In some instances the little learning of our girls is producing very unwholesome results. Girls that can read or write are still in a great minority as compared with their unlettered sisters; hence their attainments, however insignificant these may be, are not a little apt to be overrated. This in some cases turns the heads of the poor girls, and they consider themselves as belonging to a higher and nobler order of existence.

[1] B. C. Mahtab (Maharajah of Burdwan), *Studies*, pp. 44, 45.

> They are thus puffed up with pride and are unfitted to take their share in household duties. They think it beneath them to cook, to cleanse dishes and cups, to scrub the floor, or to fetch water from rivers or tanks. If married to poor people they look upon themselves as thrown away, and have been known on slight provocation to put an end to their existence by swallowing opium or by hanging or drowning themselves. Sometimes when they are allowed to take the upper hand in the management of the household affairs they grow lazy, domineering, extravagant, and selfish. The toilet is their great scene of business, and the proper adjusting of the hair the chief occupation of their lives. This I say is the state of ordinary women, though I know there are multitudes of these of a more elevated life and conversation that move in an exalted sphere of culture and virtue and are imbued with religious fervour and piety that fill their male beholders with awe and fear!"

The above is certainly not an encouraging picture, and we have moreover native Indian newspapers already bewailing the demoralisation of the so-called educated ladies of Bengal, who frequent theatres and indulge in cigarette-smoking and wine-drinking.

The future.—Although very little indeed has yet been achieved in respect to female education in India, it is certain that under British rule means for the intellectual advancement of the women will not be lost sight of, and that progress will be made. Gradually, in the course of time, education will get a firm footing behind the purdah, and, as an unavoidable consequence, the zenana system will be weakened. Greater liberty of movement and action, more personal independence, will be conceded to Indian women, or be assumed by them as in the many cases already familiar to us in the very infancy of the movement, and, under the new conditions, Hindu society will be entirely transformed. The instructive spectacle presented to us to-day in the breaking down, with deplorable consequences, of the old family system in Japan as the result of the extension of female education in that country, ought to be a warning to the more sanguine advocates for the admission of women in India to the educational privileges of the other sex.[1]

With an irresistible desire to peer, as far as may be possible, into the future, we naturally pause to ask ourselves, What the effect of such a radical change in Hindu society would be?

Education is, in these days, a magic word, a word to conjure with; but stripped of fictitious glamour, what does it mean for the great mass of females of all classes even in advanced Western countries? For the vast majority of Indian women, well trained as they are in the arts and requirements of Indian domestic life, it would, if not actually prejudicial to this domestic training, simply mean a superadded knowledge of reading, writing, and ciphering, to be used most likely, as we have already learned, in poring over unedifying fiction, writing passionate love-letters, communicating gossip to friends at a distance, and perhaps in casting up accounts occasionally.

After much careful consideration of the subject, I yet cannot help feeling that in India female education, which to a very great extent involves female emancipation from control, will not be an altogether unmixed blessing, and that the great benefits expected from it will never be realised. Of one thing we need have no doubt that Indian women, of whatever class, when they have been educated will assert themselves and claim a social freedom denied to their sex at any and every period of Indian history of which we have any knowledge. If the time ever comes when this great emancipation of Indian women is an accomplished fact, then, by their inevitable rivalry a much higher and more expensive standard of living will become general and a much more strenuous life will be imposed upon bread-winners than any of which the Indian people have as yet had experience. As a result of extravagant living, coupled with an increased desire for *freedom* on the part of both men and women, *marriages will become less frequent and less permanent.* Existing caste barriers will inevitably be carried away, because superior "up-to-date"

[1] See "Education in the New Japan," by Mrs. Mary Crawford Fraser, in *The World's Work*, November 1906.

men and women would naturally rise above such *old-world prejudices*, while quite as inevitably a new order of castes, based most probably on wealth, would come into existence.

The strenuous life, with its concomitant discouragement of marriage, once inaugurated, *competition between the sexes for employment* will become as unavoidable, as keen, and as deplorable as it is in Europe and America, and in this strife of interests and individuals the unsuccessful of both sexes will as elsewhere go down to the abyss and be submerged.

Amongst the voluptuous races of India a freedom of intercourse between the sexes, such as is permitted in European social life, would, *under existing conditions*, be morally disastrous, but whether, with the spread of education amongst all classes and both sexes, such social intercourse would be productive of good or evil is a question which must be left to the decision of time.

HINDU SOCIAL REFORMERS—*continued*

SECTION VIII.—Social intercourse between Europeans and Natives.

THE desirability of promoting social intercourse in India between Europeans and natives, or between the rulers and the ruled in that great dependency, is a subject often on the lips of English men and women, who have not given so much as a thought to the thousands of years of history, legends, and dreams, of religious systems and social institutions which lie between the two nationalities, and will lie between them for ever. With the sunshine and warmth of millenniums in their veins can the Indian races ever really relinquish their traditions, their hereditary feelings, ideas, and customs in order to consort with their frigid masters from the fog-bound islands of the West? Can they do all this? for no soul ever imagines, even for a moment, that the dominant race will ever willingly consent to abate one jot or tittle of its intellectual pretensions or alter its insular manners and customs in the minutest degree to further social intercourse between themselves and the natives. Therefore all the concessions, all the modifications, and all the sacrifices must come from the Indians, if they are to come at all.

On the other hand, if with the hope of gaining political or personal advantages the upper ranks of the subject races were induced, in the course of time, to abandon their religious exclusiveness and to recast their social systems so as to fit in with those of their European masters in order to bring about free social intercourse between the men and women of the two races, does any well-informed person really believe that such changes would be welcomed by the rulers or by English society *in India*?

However, the introduction of such changes as I have just contemplated is contingent upon so many very improbable circumstances, in the case of Hindus and Muslims alike, that the question does not at the present time call for serious consideration. But it may, nevertheless, be profitable to survey the extent of the intercourse between the two races which exists at the present time as the result of ordinary administrative and business requirements, and the deliberate action of social reformers.

In the upper strata of Indian society, European and native, some half-hearted attempts to bring about social intercourse are not wanting; but in the lower ranks of life there is nothing of the sort, no drawing together either real or feigned. Ambitious and pushing natives naturally desire to keep themselves as much as possible before the eyes of the higher English officials—dispensers of Government favours, rewards, and honours — and these well-paid officials on their part, posing as liberal-minded administrators devoted disinterestedly, heart and soul, to the welfare of the country, are constrained to encourage any movement that may reasonably be thought conducive to the welfare and improvement of what, with fine humility, they style their native fellow-subjects. Under the promptings of such motives as I have just mentioned, associations have been formed for the especial object of promoting social intercourse between Europeans and natives; but their influence has been infinitesimal. Associations of this sort generally arrange for one or two formal reunions of Europeans and natives each year; conversaziones perhaps, or more likely garden-parties. A few prominent European officials attend these functions, and lay themselves out to repay with pleasant but condescending civility the attentions of the native gentlemen present. No Hindu or Muslim ladies grace such assemblies with their presence, and though it may be taken as all but certain that every native gentleman present has a wife at home, it would be a gross breach of Hindu or Muslim etiquette to ask about even the health of the ladies behind the purdah or make any allusion whatever to them.

Only a very few native Christian ladies may be seen at these mixed assemblies in Northern India. But a fair attendance of English ladies may be counted upon, all of them, with extremely rare exceptions, quite unacquainted with the native gentlemen amongst whom they move about with unconcealed indifference during a brief hour or two.

Amidst the evident boredom of all parties concerned, the suggestion of refreshments comes as a relief to Europeans and natives alike, and now the striking hollowness of the attempt to bring about social intercourse between Europeans and natives is still further accentuated; for at this juncture, a marked, if gradual, separation of the three communities, European, Hindu, and Muhammadan, becomes apparent as they respectively gravitate towards three widely separated refreshment buffets provided with viands of very distinctive kinds. One of the essential barriers between the three communities thus stands revealed in an inability to eat or drink together. I well remember at one such garden-party trying to persuade a native gentleman to join me at the buffet where Europeans were partaking of refreshments; but he politely excused himself and hurried off smiling but none the less dismayed, though he had been in England, had been called to the Bar there, and had of necessity lived with Europeans for about three years. At home in India he was another man, and eating and drinking with non-Hindus in the sight of his own countrymen could not possibly be indulged in without the gravest consequences.

A few native gentlemen of high position, Rajahs and Maharajahs for example, make it a practice to extend magnificent hospitality to European gentlemen and ladies for perhaps a week at a time once or twice a year. Nothing that money can provide or courtesy dictate is wanting on such occasions for the entertainment and comfort of the guests. The host and the male members of the family take a lively personal interest in the arrangement and management of everything, organising shooting-parties, races, and sports of all kinds. The Maharajah himself and some of his relatives and high officers may even dance with the English ladies; but no native ladies are present, and these neglected ones may, at most, obtain from behind the jalousies of the zenana an envious glimpse of the doings of their gay lords.

Sometimes we hear of an Indian Muslim feudatory and two or three of his sirdars sitting down to dinner on a State, or very special, occasion with high Anglo-Indian officials and European ladies, but needless to add that not a single Muhammadan lady is present at these *social* gatherings.

Wealthy Babus who have official or business relations with Europeans do now and again invite them to their houses to witness a *nautch* or perhaps the tricks of Indian jugglers, and on such occasions provide their guests with a sumptuous repast and champagne *ad libitum*; but native ladies are conspicuous by their absence at these entertainments, which are generally a mere incident in the prolonged festivities connected with a wedding in the host's family.

In official, professional, and commercial life, that is in business generally, a certain degree of perhaps daily intercourse takes place between the men of the different races. In the Council Chamber, on the Bench, at the Bar, in all the administrative departments of the State, in the Universities and Colleges, in Government, railway and commercial offices, in banks, markets and business places of every kind, Europeans and natives meet regularly as fellow-workers. Under such circumstances they come to know a great deal of each other *as workers in the sphere to which they belong*, and on the whole there can be no doubt that such contact tends to mutual respect and kindly sympathy and even personal regard and affection, and yet does not encourage social intercourse.

Sports in which both Europeans and natives meet in friendly rivalry also afford opportunities, not very numerous it is true, for the men of the two races to understand and appreciate each other; for tiger-hunting; and such games as polo, football, and cricket have a tendency to draw out certain good points of men's characters, whether the players be white or brown.

Freemasonry has admitted to a knowledge of its secrets a handful of Indian deists, and these gentlemen partake, along with their white "brethren of the mystic tie," of those refreshing banquets that usually reward the exhausting labours of the craftsmen. Perhaps in this fraternal association some real friendships may possibly be formed and cemented; but then the ladies on both sides are by the masonic code rigorously excluded from all strictly masonic gatherings.

Intercourse between Europeans and natives in the ordinary business of life and in sports of all kinds will probably increase as time goes on, with the inevitable result of a certain *levelling up from below and lowering from above*, fraught with momentous political consequences.

Here and there an Indian prince may be found whose wife accompanies him into European society, but on inquiry the prince would probably prove to be a man of *inferior caste*, probably not a professing Hindu at all, or a very unorthodox one.

Amongst the minor non-Hindu and non-Muslim communities of India there are some, the well-known Parsees of Bombay for example, whose customs permit of freer intercourse between their women and Europeans in society than is admissible in the case of Hindus and Muhammadans; but though very prominent in Western India, these clever and amiable followers of Zarathushtra form but a very inconsiderable fraction of the vast population of India.

Mixed marriages, by which I here mean marriages between Indian men and European women, almost unknown formerly, have not been quite so rare in recent years, and being indicative of an appreciable *levelling up*, may possibly help to create a certain amount of social intercourse between the sexes and also between Europeans and natives, though I am doubtful that the latter result would follow unless the husband happened to be a Christian, cut off from his own kith and kin.

Mr. Oscar Browning certainly tells us how he dined at the house of an English lady, brought up at Girton, and married to a distinguished Hindu, and there met six Indian ladies attired in graceful native dress; but he omits to record whether these six ladies were Christians, Brahmas, Parsees, or Hindus, and whether they really ate at the same table with himself and his English hostess. He admits, however, that at the after-dinner reception, "the male and female elements did not seem to mix. The ladies sat huddled up on a sofa together, while their lords and masters wandered about entirely careless of their existence," adding the significant remark, "Still they seemed happy enough."[1]

I have known English married ladies to visit, now and again, the wives and families of native gentlemen with whom their own husbands were associated in business, and to have been very interested in all they saw and heard in the zenana. They have been catechised by their hostess and her companions as to the value of their jewellery and the amount of their husband's earnings. They have had to submit to the close and curious inspection of all the details of their dress and attire generally; and have called forth expressions of astonishment and horror on being led to admit that they had unmarried daughters at home of eighteen or even twenty years of age. The visitors have had to admire the scantily clothed baby-boy carrying on his tiny person a valuable assortment of pure gold ornaments; they have had to partake of confections to which they had not been used, and which at the conclusion of the visit were all packed up and sent with the visitors, a kindly meant but still doubtful compliment, when it is remembered those sweets had become impure and unfit for home consumption, owing to the presence and contaminating touch of the visitors themselves.

If we indulge our fancies we may imagine that while the English ladies driving to the residence of their hostess had perhaps been discussing certain details of a recent station ball or a new book by a popular novelist, their Hindu friends may have been arranging about a proposed pilgrimage to Hardwar or bewailing the misfortunes of an accursed child-widow of ten or twelve years of age. If the hostess belonged to a Muslim family she might have been talking about the approaching fast of Ramazan, or the expected return of a Haji from Mecca.

But *after* the visit was over we may be *sure*, conjecture being quite unnecessary, that both the European and

[1] *Impressions of Indian Travel*, pp. 57, 58.

native ladies were busy commenting, with more pungent criticism than kindly appreciation, upon each other's strange ideas, quaint manners, and odd peculiarities of dress and behaviour.

Lady doctors and zenana teachers, on different grounds, and for their own purposes, obtain admission into the houses of the natives, and no doubt help the secluded inmates of Indian homes to realise to some extent the position, the freedom, and the aspirations of European women.

European ladies of the very highest position have held receptions for native ladies from which all men have been scrupulously excluded, and the outside world has been duly assured that these functions were very successful indeed.

No doubt the company must have very greatly interested the English hostess and her English countrywomen, and the meeting given both hostess and guests much to talk about afterwards; but whether these receptions really tend to promote social intercourse between Europeans and natives may well be doubted. A few Indian ladies have come with their husbands to Europe, and some have been presented at Court; but they have none the less been unable to obtain or maintain a footing in Anglo-Indian society.

Affectation and hypocrisy aside, English men and women in India have no desire to mix on intimate terms, or on a footing of social equality, with natives of even the best class; while natives on their part have not the least inclination or the remotest intention of admitting Westerns to the intimacy of their own home-life. As already explained, there are doubtless some natives who desire the acquaintance or formal friendship of well-placed Europeans, but merely because they hope that such friendship, maintained strictly *outside* their family circle, may be an honour or a worldly advantage to themselves. There are also a few Englishmen of the commoner sort who for pecuniary gain are not ashamed to be hangers-on to the native princes and aristocrats. But the modes of life, habits of thought, religious beliefs and prejudices, ethical standards, manners, and etiquette of the two races have so little in common that *a strong desire for each other's companionship,* which, after all, is the true basis of friendship, would be extraordinary indeed, and would be more extraordinary still in the existing relative positions of the two races as dominant and subject members respectively of the body politic; a fact which finds expression in the natural if offensive racial pride of the ruling class, and has its complement in the deep-rooted objection of many upper class natives to accept even the semblance of patronage from members of the present dominant *caste.*

Racial antipathies, accentuated by political inequalities and religious exclusiveness, are amongst the fundamental difficulties in the way of social intercourse between Europeans and natives in India, and will probably prove insurmountable.

Some of the ways in which the assumption of race-superiority on the part of official or unofficial Europeans is made objectionably manifest in the disdainful treatment of natives, are set forth in a recent pamphlet written by a Parsee barrister-at-law.[1] The writer alludes to incidents which are common in railway travelling, on railway platforms, in the law courts and elsewhere, and his statements are both true and temperate; but I fear there is no remedy for the evil such as it is.

Other more obvious causes which hinder social intercourse between Europeans and natives are so well known that it may be sufficient to merely mention them here. One of these is that native ladies may not appear in society along with men. Under such circumstances Europeans naturally object to their own wives and daughters having social intercourse, however formal, with native gentlemen, and as the presence of women is an indispensable feature of European society, all natives are in consequence excluded from it, except in such rare cases as those already referred to.

Then there is the previously stated difficulty about eating and drinking together.

Again, the requirements of administrative efficiency compel every European official occupying a responsible

[1] K. E. Ghamat, Barrister-at-law, *The Present State of India: An Appeal to Anglo-Indians* (Bombay, 1905), pp. 10–27.

position—whatever his goodwill towards the natives may be—to hold himself aloof from friendly intercourse with them, because, beside the risk of compromising his dignity, he is well aware that in most cases his friendship is sought by natives, even of high rank, from interested motives not always unobjectionable. And, in any case, the evidence of friendship between any European official and a native would surely give rise to jealousies and suspicions amongst the less favoured Indian gentry.

Superior European officials being thus wisely shy of forming any but the most nominal friendships with natives, their juniors, as well as Europeans of other classes, take the cue from them. Subordinate European officials and non-officials have no need whatever to be particularly stand-offish; but, on the other hand, their friendship is not courted by native gentlemen, for the simple reason that it would not *pay*.

I hope I have now made it quite clear that there is no natural drawing together of Europeans and natives in any stratum of society from the highest to the lowest, but rather the reverse, and that, though much friendly feeling may exist between individual members of the different communities, the only encouragement which exists to social intercourse between them is purely artificial, being due mainly to an affectation of liberality and large-mindedness on the part of a few officials, desirous of posing as men above the narrow prejudices of race, colour, and creed; interested motives in the case of natives anxious to secure useful friends and patrons amongst the white ruling class; and desire on the part of certain Indians who have enjoyed and appreciated the hospitality and friendship of people in England to retain the same privileges in India.

When one hears Sir Civilian Administrator, K.C.I.E., or General Sir Indian Army, K.C.S.I., speaking of his dear friends the Rajah of Racepore or Sirdar Polo Singh, we need not take their expressions literally but discount them freely, as being evidently tainted with that *official insincerity* (become second nature) which is engendered by and inseparable from the high position he holds or has held in his day. Also when the Rajah or the Sirdar alludes to his old and valued friend Sir Civilian Administrator, K.C.I.E., or the General Sahib, be sure he feels that by this claim he is conferring an honour upon himself.

Where such antipathic communities as the English in India on the one hand and the natives of that ancient land on the other are concerned, unreserved personal intimacies between individuals and families belonging to the intrusive and the native stocks respectively, are and must continue to be very rare indeed, while a forced and unnatural social intercourse between nationalities in every way so dissimilar can only have the undesirable result of aggravating the mutual contempt and dislike already existing as consequences of ethnic, climatic, historic, religious, and political causes which will and must continue to operate in spite of all the present-day social reformers, however amiable and well intentioned they may be.

PART II

CERTAIN HINDU FESTIVALS AND CEREMONIES

THE HOLI FESTIVAL IN UPPER INDIA

A LUNAR ECLIPSE IN INDIA

ASHES TO ASHES

THE HOLI FESTIVAL

THE · PROCESSION · IN · LAHORE ·

CHAPTER I

THE HOLI FESTIVAL IN UPPER INDIA

SECTION I.—Procession through the streets—Obscene exhibitions—Rites and practices—Legends.

IT was the season of the vernal equinox. Since early morning all the streets of Lahore had been astir, presenting a peculiarly bacchanalian appearance. Hundreds and hundreds of men and women were moving about in garments besmirched with wet daubs of pink or yellow colour; their faces often disfigured with patches of red or purple powder. Rude fun, a sort of dishevelled gaiety, prevailed on all sides, accompanied with laughter and foul words not seriously meant to hurt, nor apparently giving much offence, though couched in terms of quite primitive indecency. And this had been the prevailing condition of the streets and lanes of the city for several consecutive days.

All along the principal thoroughfares the crowd kept gradually increasing, and through the idle throngs of men, women, and children, of lean oxen, sacred bulls, and mangy street dogs, I threaded my devious way as well as I could, being bound for a house in the street known as the Machhwa Bazaar, or Fish Market. As I went along, every flat house-top, every window, every balcony was crowded with both sexes, all ranks, all classes, and all ages.

Presently having reached my destination, I was provided with a seat in the elevated balcony of a Hindu merchant's house, and there, at leisure, surveyed with interest the striking scene before me, which was certainly not without quaint picturesqueness, a characteristic rarely absent from the streets of Lahore with their tall houses and highly artistic carved balconies.

The thousands who occupied every coign of vantage, basking in the warm atmosphere of the bright sunny day, seemed drowsy with a sort of amorous languor. Though with Oriental patience, which tires not, they waited and waited undemonstratively, there were indications enough that something was expected, from a certain direction. Presently these indications became more pronounced, as down the long narrow street, fringed on either side by three or four-storeyed houses, there came rollicking along a noisy band of excited revellers, dripping wet and bespattered all over with glaring daubs of red, for this was the crowning day of the Hindu saturnalia, misnamed the festival of Holi. One glance, and it was evident that some at least of the usually sedate and orderly Hindu people were indulging in unrestrained licence, while the rest were looking on appreciatively under the influence of a strange, almost incomprehensible blending of religious mysticism and exuberant voluptuousness, born of the warm breath of spring in this Eastern land.

Three loud instruments, discoursing from their brazen

throats an excruciating travesty of European music, led the way. Immediately behind the musicians was a young fellow on horseback, dressed up as a bridegroom, attended by rowdy companions, who sang, or rather shouted lustily, rhymes of flagrant indecency. As they sang and gesticulated in corybantic style, they addressed themselves pointedly to the occupants of the windows and balconies, aiming at them their ribald shafts of buffoonery and coarse indecencies, too gross for reproduction or description.

In the wake of the bridegroom followed a small litter, behind whose flapping screens the bride was supposed to be concealed. Next came, lumbering along, a big springless cart, drawn by a sturdy humped bull, mild-eyed and docile. In this jolting vehicle stood two or three tubs of blood-red water out of which four or five men and boys were throwing the crimson liquid about promiscuously to right and left with metal bowls, or else squirting it through long tin syringes to the upper windows, where the spectators of the better classes were huddled together, habited in their most homely garments in anticipation of these rude attentions.

Presently there came another huge cart freighted with that incarnation of amorous passion Krishna himself and four or five of the *gopis* (milkmaids or rather herdswomen), who shared his wandering affections. The god and his favourites were personated by a handsome young man and some frail if fair women of the town.

For a moment the steady if very slow movement of the procession was interrupted by what looked like a scuffle in the mud of the street, but on closer inspection it turned out to be a gross exhibition of indecency perpetrated by mimes under the approving eyes, and, I believe, at the suggestion of two native policemen.

The crowd surged on in a sort of intoxicated fanaticism of licentiousness. As hundreds passed along, other hundreds followed, equally bent on diffusing the immoral contagion.

From the streets and street-doors, from the windows, the balconies, and the flat housetops, eager onlookers watched the mean and tawdry procession, and listened with open ears to the libidinous songs or catches which, from time to time, filled the air, as one party after another passed along the road, halting here and there, under native police direction, to give the preceding parties time to move on.

Nearly all the women spectators had their faces unveiled, and with the girls and boys listened eagerly to the licentious rhymes shouted by the bands of revellers who passed along. Here and there a woman, a trifle more modest or more affected than the others, would draw her chaddar partially over her face to conceal it from view. One of them I particularly remember on her picturesque carved balcony close by, as she displayed the whole of a lovely bare arm in the act of slightly adjusting her veil to half hide a pretty face from the too ardent eyes of some rude fellow in the crowd below.

But other bridegrooms appeared, other gods took part in the procession. Even the chief of the gods, Mahadeva, was personated by a whitened man in a yellow flowing flax wig, a necklace of immense beads, and a trident in his hand. Beside him sat his mountain bride Parvati.

A group of youths, carried away by the excitement of the occasion, insulted, or more correctly amused, the spectators by perpetrating the grossest indecencies, aided by coarsely fashioned mechanical toys of naked simplicity, and their proceedings were not resented except by banter and abusive words.

Again, cartloads of crimson water came lumbering by, casting their contents about; again, excruciating music filled the outraged air, and erotic songs or rhymes stirred up the passions of the multitude. Once more the gods of India countenanced the uncouth revelry by their august presence. This time it was the elephant-headed Ganesa, God of Wisdom, in attendance on another Mahadeva and his consort, and then another amorous Krishna added sanctity to the scene.

Near the gods of Mount Meru was an open carriage occupied by a couple of courtezans and their attendant musicians. Not far behind, on a sort of litter borne on the shoulders of four men, appeared a singing-girl who delighted the bystanders in a soft soprano voice with a song, apparently quite to their taste, which she emphasised with not ungraceful movements of her small hands. As she sang, she showed her pretty French shoes and fine stockings beyond the edges of her silken skirt, and looked, I must own it, really attractive in her jewels and fine raiment and her neatly arranged coiffure, plainly visible under her gauzy chaddar.

A comical element, or rather buffoonery of the crudest type, was now supplied by a *Sadhu* (ascetic), a *real* one I was told, who was seated on a rickety cart which swayed like a boat in a storm. He was attended by five or six persons, his *chelas* (disciples) perhaps, who shared the cart with him, and he had at hand his indispensable iron pan of fire and his *chillum* (pipe) for smoking *churrus.* As he passed before us he rose up on the shaky vehicle to make a silly and degrading exhibition of himself. After performing an absurd little dance of his own at some personal risk, he suddenly snatched off and flung about the road the turbans of his fellow-riders, just as a mischievous monkey might have done.

For two hours, for three hours, for four hours, the procession, a tossing stream of humanity, flowed slowly along, with little if any interruption, and very limited variety, down the narrow road. And for these slowly moving hours all classes of the Hindu community had been pleased spectators of the show, and presumably enjoyed its gross extravagances. The pompous native official was there, a little shyly it may be, and the native editors of the local Akhbars and Patrikas, no doubt just for the sake of "copy," with dangerous political agitators in their train. Native barristers, hailing from the Temple or the Inns of Court, and University graduates, did not disdain the show; while merchants, tradesfolk, artisans, labourers, and beggars crowded to it with zest. All the Hindu world and only the Hindu world, in its various grades was here, wife and family included. Muhammadans were conspicuous by their absence. Not even one European police officer was present, and, unless they were in disguise, no English or American people attended to enjoy the treat provided for the benefit of all who cared to partake of it.

At last the tail of the interminable procession disappeared down the street, taking with it the noisy discords, the crimson water, the erotic songs, the complaisant gods and goddesses, and the frail sopranos who had claimed our attention and admiration; but leaving behind in the minds and hearts of many a one the seeds of an immoral harvest in the coming year.

"Did you observe," I said to my companion, "how that girl at the window opposite was listening to the obscene songs, and beating time with her fingers?"

He nodded assent.

"Did you also," I went on, "note how the lad carried upon the arms of his companions indulged in a deliberate and shameless exposure of his person as he looked eagerly towards her window?"

"I did," said the Hindu, with a bland approving smile. "I think she is an educated woman, for I saw a book in her hand."

"A moral reader, no doubt!" I ventured to suggest.

"Perhaps so," assented my friend with Eastern imperturbability, and a mind so steeped since childhood in the atmosphere of the Holi and similar joyous nature-festivals, as to be able to regard with vague, undefined *religious* approval the words we had heard, and the sights we had that day witnessed together from the pretty balcony in which we were seated.

The uncouth tragi-comedy of life we had seen was no doubt only a very expurgated edition of the displays of realistic licentiousness which were openly indulged in before the advent of British rule, and which are probably still not unknown in places more remote from European influence and supervision than the capital of the Punjab.

It is difficult for a non-Hindu to enter into the feelings and ideas of a people who call all things by their real names without euphemistic disguises, who use naked words to describe natural processes and functions, who while dreaming warm dreams of sexual gratification, love to speculate about the soul and the All-soul, till steeped in the mysticism and occultism of pantheistic philosophy, they revel in the orgies of the Holi festival, and make their gods partakers of their happiness, dwelling, while the licence of the Holi is still in their ears, "on the devotional purity the grand festival of spring awakens in Hindu hearts."[1]

In all parts of the world are known, or have been known, joyous festivals—saturnalia, carnivals, and what not—coincident annually with seed-time and harvest, or perhaps, more correctly, with the equinoxes and solstices; and whatever myth these festivals may be associated with, they are none the less the natural outcome of the effect of the seasons on the emotions and passions of men. Everywhere men have experienced annually the quickening effects of the spring renew within themselves the mysterious wonder of creation and the joy of reproduction, and under this spell the more emotional races have given way to unrestrained mirth and debauchery, casting aside for the moment all the ordinary conventions, often even the decencies and moralities of life. The Holi is such a festival, being a true expression of the emotions of the Hindu East at spring-time, when the warm sun which bronzes the cheek of beauty, also subtly penetrates each living fibre of the yielding frame, awakening with his mellowing touch sensuous dreams, soft desires, and wayward passions, which brook no restraint, which dread no danger, and over which this metaphysical people readily throw the mantle of their most comprehensive and accommodating creed.

Has one lived in the East and does one still ask why the zenana system prevails there, why early marriages are there the rule, why *burquas* and *yashmaks* are imposed, why the harem is protected by high walls and grated windows. If so, he knows not the people of the East, and will never comprehend them.

Does one ask, "When will these things all cease to be?" I hardly dare venture a reply. Change of form there certainly will be, and ancient rites and customs will put on decorous disguises. That at least may be confidently predicted, for as I shall presently show there are signs of it even now, in the *Hola* of the Sikhs and the *Pawitra* (pure) *Holi* of certain well-meaning reformers.

But the Holi as it annually rages—for rage it does—

[1] *The Tribune* (a Lahore newspaper conducted by Hindus), 6th April 1899.

is in the blood of the Hindu, fermenting in his veins under the sun's rays of his native land, and must find a vent for its energies, if not on the streets, then elsewhere.

However, there are in India so many forces, mostly extraneous, now at work tending to the discouragement of indulgence in public of indecencies of any sort, whether in connection with the Holi or any other festival, that we may trust that the authorities will, at no distant future, feel able to put down with a strong hand such objectionable outrages of propriety as I have referred to; and towards the attainment of this desirable end the support of the better educated classes of the Hindu community may be confidently depended upon.

Certain rites connected with the Holi and their legendary explanations are, I think, of sufficient interest to be noticed even in this brief account of a very characteristic Hindu festival.

"We find in almost all the Hindu literature, that a spring saturnalia called Basantotsava was very reverentially observed by the Hindus of the old day. On that occasion even princesses and ladies of the noblest classes used to dance in public places and the god Madana (Cupid) was worshipped." Thus wrote a Hindu, Pandit Rishi Kesh, a few years ago.[1] His statements may, or may not, be wholly correct; but the Holi or a festival corresponding with it, in point of time and resembling it in its joyous extravagances, is known throughout the northern parts of India, including Bengal, Orissa, and the Central Provinces, and, as might have been expected, the procedure or ritual is not the same everywhere. Wide divergences in practice may be noted, but there are certain resemblances too. Every village in Bengal and Upper India gathers its own pile of wood and other combustibles for the occasion, and, in keeping with the hilarious season, a good deal of rough liberty is sometimes taken with other people's property in providing the fuel for the annual blaze. In the cities too, wherever possible, each several ward has its own bonfire and, at any rate, every householder is able to burn before his entrance door two or three logs of wood.

[1] Pandit Rishi Kesh, *Journal of the Anjuman-i-Punjab*, 26th April 1881.

Ceremonies of some sort, but by no means identical in their details, precede the lighting of the Holi fire, and these ceremonies afford some indication of the ideas underlying the institution of this festival. In some places it is the custom to circumambulate the bonfire seven times with ears of barley corn in the hands and then to throw them into the fire, and is connected with a belief that in the Holi fire is destroyed a monster inimical to the ripening crops.

Elsewhere, as in Bengal, is burnt "the effigy of an uncouth straw image of a giant named Maydhasoor," who was destroyed by the God Krishna.

But a more elaborate ceremonial is said to be observed in the United Provinces where the Holi is celebrated with the greatest enthusiasm.

> "On Basant Panchami"—I quote from an unsigned article which appeared in the *Pioneer* of the 2nd April 1883—"a pile of wood is erected outside the limits of the village or Mahalla. Here by a vivid imagination are supposed to be gathered together all the sicknesses and misfortunes which threaten the inhabitants.
>
> "Next, a stalk of the castor-oil plant, together with a pice and some betel-nut is planted at the spot by the hand of the ever-essential Brahman, who by his wondrous power causes it to become a living person. At the full moon of the month of Phalgun, the Hindu (man, woman, and child) smears his body with a paste of flour and perfumes (called *whatan*), and consigns the scrapings of his body to the pyre. By this act he succeeds in removing also all future evils from his person. Then each one throws a thread, the exact length of his own height, into the heap. The moment the moon becomes full the living castor-oil individual gives up the ghost—the pile of wood with its accumulation of future disasters, and the thread substitutes, is set fire to, and all possible evil removed for at least a year."

Of course there are superstitions connected with the *Holi* and many legends to account for them.

The origin and details of the above rites is thus explained in a Sanskrit book named *Nirnayamrita*, cited by the anonymous writer referred to above. Long ages ago when Yudhisthira reigned in Hastinapur, a dreadful plague visited the country, and caused the destruction of vast numbers of the king's subjects. In his trouble Yudhisthira consulted Krishna, at that time incarnate on earth, as the King of Dwarka. Krishna assured his kinsman that the direful plague was the work of a terrible she-demon named Holika, who destroyed the people in their sleep. He prescribed the rites connected with the annual Holi fire as an effectual means of driving the monster away, and, whether at the god's suggestion or on their own initiative, is not quite clear, the people indulged in foul and indecent speech and abuse to hasten the demon's departure, for after all Holika, although cruel, was at least modest and sensitive. By this crude, inartistic legend, the annual bonfires of the Holi, are justified by the Brahmas, on what we would call sanitary grounds, and is so far interesting, though it does not really appreciate or apprehend the *vera causa* of this great springtide festival.

Another legend explanatory of Holi is this:

> "Holika or Holi was, they say, sister of Sambat or Sanvat, the Hindu year. Once at the beginning of all things, Sambat died, and Holi in her excessive love for her brother insisted on being burnt on his pyre, and by her devotion he was restored to life. The Holi fire is now burnt every year to commemorate this tragedy." [1]

According to Punjabi expositors of the spring festival and its attendant ceremonies, there once lived a king who acquired by austerities and magic rites so much power that he waged successful war with the very gods themselves. Puffed up with pride, he desired to be made greater even than the god Vishnu, and his claim to this superiority, though generally recognised, was boldly repudiated by his own son Prahlad a devoted worshipper of that deity. Prahlad's royal father, irritated beyond measure by his son's preference for the god, and carried away by an overweening conceit, resolved to put an end to his own son, but somehow, through the intervention of Vishnu, all his attempts to kill him failed signally. As the king's wrath was not appeased, it was

[1] W. Crooke, *The Popular Religion and Folk-lore of Northern India*, vol. ii. p. 315.

decided to effect Prahlad's destruction in another way. The king's sister Holi, who had reason to believe herself proof against the effect of fire, proposed to sit upon a blazing pyre with her obnoxious nephew in her lap—in full expectation that while she herself would come out scathless from the ordeal, the recalcitrant boy would perish in the flames. But the result of this cruel attempt was quite the reverse of what had been anticipated, for, by the will and power of Vishnu, it was Holi who was destroyed, while Prahlad came forth uninjured. The multitude, overjoyed at the result, rushed in and in wild delight flung about the ashes of the pyre of unkind Holi, and the event has ever since been celebrated by a great annual festival.

It is evident that this primitive legend affords no justification for the lewd excesses of the Holi. Possibly a festival based on the Puranic legend of Prahlad and his wicked aunt may have synchronised with a joyous festival in honour of the advent of spring, and got mixed up with it in the popular mind. If so, the incongruity I have alluded to is at least explicable.

THE HOLI FESTIVAL IN UPPER INDIA

—continued

Section II.—The Hola of the Sikhs—A new departure—The presumption of certain women reproved.

THOSE well-known Hindu sectarians, the Sikhs, have their own peculiar way of celebrating the *Holi* festival, which, however, they name *Hola*, apparently to discriminate it from the orthodox saturnalia with which it synchronises.

I learnt that the best spot from which to view the *Hola* procession—a good deal of Indian religion is manifest in processions and *melas* (fairs)—was near the Sonari Musjid, so thither I directed my steps. On the way I met an orderly party of school children singing *bhajans* (hymns), and ascertained that they belonged to the new *Sanathan Dharm Sabha.* They were, I fancy, supposed to be engaged in pure devotional exercises, and to have had no eyes or ears for licentious words and obscene gestures, which could be heard and seen everywhere in the streets along which they had passed. Most of the shops were shut, for the owners were not disposed to risk the horse-play or endure the insulting chaff of the unruly man-in-the-street.

Through the courtesy of the custodians of the Sonari Musjid (the golden mosque), I was accommodated with a seat in the window of a sort of anteroom of the sacred edifice, overlooking the road, and, as I sat there, successive parties of men and boys passed by, some singing songs of the loves of the old time, and some songs or rhymes of gross obscenity which were pointedly addressed to the women and children in the upper windows and balconies or on the flat roofs of the houses.

Although I had a carpet to sit upon, and a long pillow, or bolster, to rest against, I was glad to leave my seat in the window and go out upon the steps of the Musjid to watch the Sikh procession as it surged down the street. The position at the meeting of two streets was an advantageous one, as it faced and commanded a long stretch of the road along which the crowd was approaching.

A band of musicians, armed with two cornets, a bassoon, a clarionet, a big drum, cymbals, and kettle-drum, was drawn up at the foot of the steps of the mosque to welcome the advancing crowd. It struck up the once popular tune of "Just before the Battle, Mother," as the head of the procession came within two or three hundred yards of us, while another, and equally noisy band, which had accompanied the Sikhs, played another English air with ear-splitting energy. The advancing multitude divided off at the foot of the stairs into two streams, passing on the two sides of the mosque. When the main body of the processionists, with banners flying and singing *bhajans*, arrived, a halt was made, and gave me an opportunity of observing that there were many leading Sikh gentlemen in the throng, although almost disguised out of recognition by the coloured paint with which their faces had been daubed over. Some had taken the wise precaution of protecting their eyes with goggles, against the showers of coloured powders to which they were exposed along the route.

Flag-staffs surmounted by spear-heads were borne, in some cases at least, by *Akalis*, conspicuous by their warlike headgear. Any halt was a signal for quantities of red and purple powder (for both kinds were used) to be flung at the crowd from the sides of the road, or any position of advantage, such as an upper window or balcony. This was a reversal of the procedure followed when the Hindu procession passed along. In that case it was the processionists who flung the coloured water on the bystanders and onlookers. I noticed some women casting upon the Sikhs below, handfuls of powder from the low housetop of a neighbouring dwelling, where many of the fair sex with a number of children were gathered together. Against this behaviour a loud and angry protest was made from below, and the police interfered, it being too indecorous for women, even on an occasion like this, to presume to throw the powder on *men.* I kept an eye on the offenders, and was amused to discover that they did not discontinue their audacious practices, although they indulged in them a little more circumspectly or surreptitiously.

All was not fun and ribaldry in the streets; for the prevailing licence of speech and act occasionally provoked a fight, and hard blows were then freely exchanged; for Punjabis are tough, and though usually good-tempered or more properly imperturbable, can lay about them right vigorously when excited to anger. And the meekest might well be roused at some of the tricks practised, especially on the country bumpkins who visit the town on this occasion. Spotting one of these, a fat *bunneah* might come up to him hastily, and ask if he was disposed to earn a trifle by just helping to carry a pot of *ghee,* urgently wanted a couple of streets away.

"Why not!" says the strong countryman, and accompanying the *bunneah* to a place where the jar is supposed to have been left by another fellow, he cheerfully lifts it up and places it on his head. Before he has walked many paces, the pot is broken on his head by a blow from a stick or a stone, and its contents—not *ghee* certainly—flows over the unsuspecting yokel, to the huge delight of the jeering rabble. A practical joke not unlikely to provoke a row.

These breaches of the peace, however, had nothing to do with the hymning Sikh procession, which was, as indeed it was intended to be, a dignified public advertisement, partly for official edification, of the disapproval of the Sikhs of the usual licence and freedom of the Holi, and it was at the same time a suggestion carried into practice, but ludicrously inappropriate, for the celebration in future of the great joyous spring festival of their ancestors.

What legend we are to have in support and justification of the *new* Hola, remains to be seen.

That this Hola, organised by a certain advanced section of the Sikh community has not displaced the Holi even in the sacred places of the sect, will be apparent from the following extract taken from a Sikh newspaper:—

> "A correspondent writes from Amritsar: 'The Holi festival in Amritsar was a very ugly affair. Even in the Golden Temple people lost all sense of shame. Obscene language was freely used in the presence of *Grunth Sahib*.[1] Formerly no one was allowed to put off the turban of a Sikh; but this time no authority appeared to be exercised on the lawless mob. This insult to Sikh susceptibilities in the most sacred shrine of the Sikhs is deeply to be regretted.'"[2]

[1] The Sacred Book of the Sikhs.

[2] *The Khalsa*, 12th April 1899.

THE HOLI FESTIVAL IN UPPER INDIA
—continued

SECTION III.—Pawitra Holi—A *pure* Holi introduced recently by some Indian reformers, backed by Christian missionaries.

AS an example of the retention of the name of a festival, while entirely ignoring its *raison d'être*, and discarding all its traditional peculiarities, nothing could well be better than the *Pawitra* (pure) Holi inaugurated in recent years by well-intentioned Hindu reformers in conjunction with certain Christian missionaries.

Let the following notice from which I have struck out the names, speak for itself:—

"PAWITRA HOLI

"will be celebrated this year as usual for three days, viz., 26th, 27th, and 28th February 1896, in *the gardens between the Lohari and Mori Gates.* The following programme will be observed:—

"WEDNESDAY, 27th February, 5 to 8 p.m.	Bhajans by Rababis and Latifas. Lectures by— Lala —— on "Nauches." Babu —— on "Temperance." Bhai —— on "Holi."
"FRIDAY, 29th February, 8 to 10 a.m.	Bhajans. Exposition from Grunth Sahib. Recitation of Veda Mantras, by the boys of the Dayanand High School.
3 to 4 p.m.	Bhajans by Rababis and Latifas.

"FRIDAY, 28th February,	Lecture by Rev. ——[1]
4 to 5 p.m.	on "Personal Purity."
5 to 8 p.m.	Dr. ——[1] will preside.
	Brief Report of the Punjab Purity Association will be read.
	Lala —— will move a Resolution expressing regret at the unworkableness of the clause provided in the Municipal Act regarding brothels.
	Lala —— } Lala —— } will address the meeting. Lala —— }
	Members of the Temperance Society, Amritsar, will entertain the public with temperance songs.

"*All are cordially invited.*"

[1] American missionary.

A LUNAR ECLIPSE

·THE·GOLDEN·TEMPLE·
·AND·SACRED·TANK·AMRITSAR·

CHAPTER II

A LUNAR ECLIPSE IN INDIA

Scene at the Pool of Immortality—Hindu legend of the cause of eclipses—Almsgiving — Progress of obscuration — Legends of the Pool.

IT was in the small hours of a December night. The atmosphere was crystal clear, the air keenly cold. In the blue sky sailed the full moon, and with the attendant stars, brightly beautiful, made a truly glorious spectacle.

At my feet lay the *Pool of Immortality* (Amritsar) mirroring softly in its glassy surface the Golden Temple of the Sikhs and the tranquil stars above.

Standing in

the middle of the pool, a spacious sheet of artificial water, the temple is only accessible on one side by means of a stone causeway built on arches.

The sacred pool, which is rectangular in shape, is surrounded on all sides by wide stone and marble pavements and many trees, beyond which rise moderately lofty buildings of Oriental character with one unfortunate exception, a tall clock tower of modern European design, quite out of harmony with its surroundings. Notwithstanding the incongruous bastard-Gothic clock tower, and the many undeniably rough and mean features about the precincts of the fane, the whole scene was, under the spell of the soft moonlight, mellowed into a picture of dreamlike and captivating beauty.

With some Sikh companions, I sauntered slowly round the pool.

Under the dark shadows of the fig trees many men and women were moving about noiselessly with unshod feet upon the marble pavements, and so was I with only velvet moccasins on my feet.

Presently, in the hush of the still night, a faint shadow began creeping, like the mysterious hand of destiny, on to the edge of the moon's disc, and then, suppressed voices repeating the words, "Dan poon ka valâ" (This is the time to bestow alms), were heard on all sides, as an army of beggars suggested their claims upon the assembling people with many alluring hints in respect to the great merit and special advantages of liberality at this momentous hour, when the bright moon-god was in the grasp of the evil demon Râhu; for was it not said by them of old that it was this disappointed demon who through the ages had been pursuing sun and moon to devour them. For the cause of his malice we must go back to that remote age when the gods and the Asuras at the suggestion of Narayana (Vishnu) churned the ocean to obtain *Amrita* —the water of life. What wonders occurred on that momentous occasion are they not recorded in the Mahabharata; but here it will suffice to recall to memory that when at length Dhanvantari arose out of the seething ocean, bearing in his hands a vessel containing the precious nectar which had been churned out of the deep, the Asuras claimed the prize and prepared to dispute its possession with the gods. It was an extremely critical moment! What if the Asuras should drink the *Amrita* and enjoy immortality!

Immediate action was necessary, and Narayana was equal to the emergency. Assuming the bewitching female form of Maya (illusion), the god easily persuaded the Asuras to part with the vessel of nectar. When they discovered the trick of which they had been the deluded victims, the Asuras pursued the gods, who had been hurriedly taking draughts of the elixir. In the company of the celestials, a demon named Râhu disguised as a god partook of some of the precious liquid, but before it could pass beyond his throat, he was discovered and denounced by those ever watchful celestials, the sun and the moon.

Instantly Narayana severed Râhu's head from his body; but the head having partaken of the Amrita was, of course, immortal, and, bent on vengeance, has ever since that remote time persistently pursued the great luminaries through space, swallowing them up periodically, only to find them escape through his severed throat.

And now, before our very eyes, the terrible monster was once again gratifying his desire for vengeance, as he had done on countless occasions in the æons of the past.

Indeed, this critical moment afforded an opportunity not to be lightly lost; for, as the Brahman mendicants declared,

> "Yaha ka dân
> Ganga ka ashnân"

(a gift here is equal to a dip in the Ganges), and

> "Dâta ka dân
> Gareeb ka ashnân"

(the rich man who gives is like the poor man who bathes). And yet I noticed that the liberality of the visitors was on the poorest of possible scales, usually extending to nothing more than a handful of grain, doled out to the more importunate of the priestly mendicants. Nevertheless, on these all-important occasions, there are always some Hindus who are generous, and perhaps even lavish in their gifts to the poor—but in such cases the element of self-interest is often too apparent, as when from prudential considerations *ghee* (clarified butter) is given to the Brahmans. When this is done, the donors first melt the *ghee* in a pot, and then view their own countenances in the liquid butter. After which they hand it over to the beggars, *together with their own earthly troubles*; a shrewd, if selfish, act of liberality, which the hereditary priests of India are good enough to encourage.

An eclipse is a favourable time for securing other benefits besides the very desirable one of parting with one's own immediate griefs, vexations, and difficulties; for it is well known that *mantras* (charms and spells) written during an eclipse, especially during the period of total obscuration, are fifty thousand times more efficacious than those written at other times, and, consequently, the fleeting minutes are diligently utilised by many a sagacious Brahman scribe, with a keen eye to his own future gain.

While men were busy in these very mundane affairs, the mysterious shadow crept onwards over the face of the moon, and, as the obscurity increased, the fulgent stars and planets grew even brighter than they were before, till they literally blazed out of a cloudless sky. Over the darkening earth the gloom was slowly spreading, and the umbrage of the banyan trees which sheltered the shrine of Siva at one corner of the tank, looked impenetrably black.

But now, one by one, tiny lamps, lit by Brahman worshippers, appeared around the noble sheet of water, lending a new beauty to the strange scene. Devout Hindus of both sexes entered the sacred water uttering prayers, while accommodating Brahmans took charge of their clothes and lighted charcoal braziers to afford them warmth after their cold immersion.

There were hundreds present who had learnt in the schools how European science accounted for the lunar eclipse; but in the increasing obscurity the old gods of India crept silently out and once more asserted their ascendancy over the hearts of even such as, under rationalistic or other influences, had become alienated from or forgetful of the national faith and its obligations.

In the mysterious awe-inspiring gloom, hereditary

feelings, early impressions, and the teachings of the ancient religion, recovered their potency, with the result that discarded beliefs were almost unconsciously readopted for the present occasion at least.

The twinkling lights kindled by the Brahmans multiplied in number as the darkness blotted out the celestial moonlight, and, in the murk, enlightened Hindu reformers, and cultured graduates of the University, oblivious of consistency or Western science, took a stealthy dip into the chill *water of immortality* and surreptitiously responded to the appeal " Dan poon ka valâ."

I watched it all in the weird gloom of that chill December night, and realised the charm of the hoary myth of Râhu and the *Amrita* churned from the deep by gods and demons, as I recalled it again to mind here by *Amritsar*, the Pool of Immortality, associating, through the local legendary, the old titanic story with the water at my feet.

Tradition has it that as far back as those now remote days when the gods lived in the fair " land of the five rivers," there was at this very spot a sacred pool, and on its banks ascetics and sages of the old-time lived and worshipped. This pool was known as the Amrit Kund, because a portion of the *Amrita*, or nectar of immortality, had been somehow spilt or collected there. For Sikhs, however, wishing to sever themselves from the past of Hinduism, the claim of the pool to consideration depends upon a very much more modern event connected with the history of the fourth guru of their sect, Guru Ram Das (A.D. 1574–1581).

The story runs thus: In the time of the guru just named there lived a man who had a beautiful daughter, devoted heart and soul to religion. Being for some reason or other angry with the girl, the father gave her in marriage to a man with maimed hands and feet, some say a leper, and the heartless parent scoffingly bid his daughter support herself and her helpless husband upon the bounty of God.

In Indian fashion, the young wife performed her duty to herself and her crippled husband, by collecting alms from the people around, and in her begging tours she usually carried her lord in a basket on her head. One day she left her burden in the shade of some trees near

Photo by W. Campbell Oman

BATHERS IN THE RIVER RAVI DURING AN ECLIPSE OF THE SUN

a weed-covered pond, and went off to a neighbouring village to beg for food. While she was away, her husband noticed with astonishment that a lame crow came and dipped its injured legs into the water, and by doing so, not only recovered the use of those limbs, but had its plumage miraculously bleached to a perfectly white colour. The healing power of the water so strikingly manifested might, thought the cripple, benefit himself too, and so he crept to the edge of the pond, and entered the water, with the result that, to his infinite joy, he became whole again.

When the dutiful wife returned to the spot she could not recognise her transformed husband, and did not believe that the sound man before her was the cripple she had left in the basket under the trees; but her very natural doubts were dispelled when the Guru Ram Das himself assured her that the man was indeed her own husband.

Here then at the site, no doubt, of the ancient Amrit Kund of the fore-time, was a fit place for a temple to the living God, and Ram Das therefore had a beautiful tank excavated, and also laid the foundations of a place of worship where the present building—which is of considerably later date—now stands.

Such is the Sikh legend connected with the famous "Pool of Immortality"—Amritsar—which gives its name to a considerable and important city. The legend, strained and artificial in its association with old Hindu mythological conceptions, and uncouth in its details, is neither impressive nor poetical; but is, it seems to me, fairly characteristic of Sikh culture.

Discussing with my Sikh companions at the temple, Guru Ram Das and his doings, the time slipped quickly by till dawn began to appear in the east.

With the dawn the number of idle spectators, bathers, and beggars increased considerably. The wet marble pavements, now thickly covered with a mass of trampled grain of various kinds, presented an unsightly appearance; my velvet moccasins—leather shoes were not allowed within the temple enclosure—were soppy, and I was glad to escape from the motley and unpicturesque crowd which looked both silly and tawdry in the searching daylight.

ASHES TO ASHES

·BURNING·GHAT·BENARES·

CHAPTER III

ASHES TO ASHES

Hindu funeral rites and their underlying sentiments.

WITH rare exceptions, the Hindus of Northern India cremate their dead.[1] I had often chanced to get a distant view of

[1] "In the south the ascetic followers of both Siva and Vishnu bury the dead (Dubois, 56); so do the Vaishnava, Vairagis, and Sannyasis in the north of India, and the Saiva Jogis. The class of Hindu weavers called Yogis have adopted a similar practice (Ward, i. 201); all the castes in the south, that wear the *Linga*, do the same (Birch, i. 27)."—Professor H. H. Wilson, *Essays on the Religion of the Hindus*, p. 196.

a Hindu cremation, and had gruesome recollections of a few I had seen on the banks of the Ganges, at Benares, and elsewhere; but never having witnessed at close quarters the ritual actually followed on such occasions, I went one warm autumn morning to the crematorium of Lahore, in company with a Hindu friend, on the mere chance of being present at a funeral there. And I did see one, a most quaint and touching, though not unbarbarous old-world ceremonial, amply repaying the curiosity which had led me to pry into the customs of my neighbours, and the teachings of a religion hoary with age, but not yet, by any means, in decrepitude.

The place set apart for the cremation of the Hindus of Lahore is reached by a narrow road alongside a broad surface drain and through some ill-kept gardens. It is a large space enclosed by a high brick wall, and is entered through a narrow doorway. Splendid wide-spreading banyans with opulent foliage and fine pipal trees afford ample shade, and lend agreeable picturesqueness to the quiet spot, where I noticed, with a sort of uncomfortable eerie feeling, the enormous stacks of firewood provided for the crematory requirements of a populous city. Just outside the gate is a low platform, about ten feet by seven and not more than fifteen inches high, built of bricks and mortar, at the foot of one of those sacred fig trees which grace so many a quiet scene in India. This platform is known as the *Adhmarag* or half-way place. Close at hand, also overshadowed by trees, is a small well, furnished with a wheel and axle, and twenty or thirty yards farther off, near a temple of Mahadeva, is a masonry tank of stagnant water, which I found covered with a thick emerald-green scum.

When I entered the crematorium some men were busily engaged sweeping the grounds, which were more neatly kept than I had expected. No cremation was in progress, so I had time to look about me. Here and there were *Samadhs*, or cenotaphs, if they may be called so, erected over the ashes of cremated Hindus of a past generation; but they bore neither date nor inscription. These very Eastern structures of plastered brickwork naturally attracted my attention, but I was more impressed by four quite new tombs,[1] two of them in marble, so European in style and finish as to suggest the idea that they had been recently transplanted to their present site from the neighbouring Christian cemetery. They were *Samadhs* like the rest, and, though bearing tablets, had nothing to do with any actual interments, but were none the less interesting as visible signs of the imitative spirit of the educated Hindu in his present transitional state. I would not like to affirm that these tombs do not represent something more than that, for their durable material and clear-cut English inscriptions may possibly be the outcome of a new craving in the Hindu heart for an abiding place in human memory. I hope, indeed, it may be so; since it seems to me that the cremating races who happen also to believe in metempsychosis must only too easily forget their ancestors, and lose, as the Hindus have done, all real hold of the genuine history of preceding times.

While I waited in expectancy in the grounds of the crematorium, my companion was telling me that a Hindu, whatever be his rank or station in life, must not, on any account, be allowed to die in his bed, but on the ample bosom of mother-earth, nor should he be permitted to expire under a roof, however magnificent, but beneath the free and open expanse of heaven. When he has breathed his last, his son, or other near relation, should place in the palm of his now pulseless right hand, a lighted lamp (known as *Diwa-wattee*) to guide his faltering footsteps through the great unknown and untrodden darkness beyond. I had read of these things before, and as I listened now I felt that the *Diwa-wattee* in the dead hand appealed to one's feelings with a pretty sentimentality not to be denied; but as to the other practices, those connected with mother-earth or the boundless vault of heaven, what possible defence could be offered for them, when it is too evident that, with quite unnecessary cruelty, they must inevitably extinguish the last lingering ray of hope in the heart of the dying? And, sentiment apart, it is well known that these practices, in conjunction with customs which grew out of them, have been productive of no little evil and many a tragic event in the Hindu household.

[1] Illustrated in the tailpiece, p. 276.

Finding that no funeral arrived, my companion and I, having nothing better to do just then, proceeded together, on foot, towards the city. After passing through the Taxali gate, we came upon a funeral party.

The corpse, which lay upon a light bier, was covered with a red cloth and was borne, feet forward, by four men. An *Acharaja*[1] (a low-caste Brahman priest, whose special function it is to conduct funeral rites) was in close attendance near the head of the corpse, which the bearers were hurrying along at a brisk pace. As the funeral party wended its way through the narrow and crowded lane where we met it, the *Acharaja* kept crying out at short intervals "*Ram, bol Ram*" (Ram, say Ram), to which the corpse-bearers' responded regularly and loudly "*Ram, Bhai, Ram*" (Ram, brother, Ram) as they scurried on their way with little ceremony. Occasionally the bier on which a Hindu is carried for cremation is shaped like a ship fitted with sails, perhaps of coloured silk, and adorned with flaunting pennons; but the funeral I am describing was a very ordinary one, and there was not even the usual band of noisy musical instruments in attendance.

Amongst the followers was one, the chief mourner, who carried in his hand an earthen vessel like a Grecian amphora, and also a leaf-cone containing some barley meal, wherewith to make *pindas*, which, although only pellets of dough, are of extreme importance in Hindu funeral rites.

While we followed the quickly moving procession, my companion explained to me, with reference to these *pindas*, that after death they have to be placed near the corpse, also at the threshold of the home of the deceased, near the gate of the city, on the *Admarag*, or half-way place, and beside the pyre. For thirteen consecutive days after death, and thereafter at intervals, *pindas* are made and offered for the express, if somewhat naïve purpose, of supplying materials for the formation of a new body for the freed soul, an operation which takes place very gradually, commencing with the most important member of all, the head, and is not completed in less than nine months.

[1] In the United Provinces of Agra and Oudh, the *Acharaja* is usually termed Maha-Brahman or Maha-Patra (the great vessel).

Christians and Muslims commit their dead to the safe keeping of the earth, which is our home, in the sure and certain hope of an eventual resurrection, but they who, like the Hindus, stand by and witness the complete destruction by fire of the human form divine, who see it disappear amidst the devouring flames, feel, as the *pinda* ceremony sufficiently proves, the necessity for some material, some tangible *substance* wherewith to *reclothe the disembodied soul*, if it is to have a *real* existence after death, for, say what we may, it is certain that a purely spiritual, immaterial existence is for the bulk of mankind, may I not say for *all* of us, an utterly unimaginable state, and one that most assuredly fails to satisfy the imperious cravings of human nature for a substantial, sensuous existence *in continuation of this earthly life.*

As the funeral procession passed through the gate of the city, the *Acharaja* changed his loud monotonous chant of "*Ram, bol Ram*" to "*Har bâse so Bindraban*[1] *hai*" (where God is present that place is Bindraban), to which the corpse-bearers now responded: "*Yihi to Bindraban hai*" (this is Bindraban). These cries were repeated alternately, without intermission, till the body arrived near the entrance of the crematory and was placed on the *Admarag.*

I found on inquiry that the deceased was a physician by caste, and of the sect of the Gusains. Some thirty men accompanied the bier, and in default of a son the adopted son of the dead man was the chief mourner already referred to. Very soon about forty or fifty women came up, some wailing, though not ostentatiously. While the body with its head towards the gate of the crematorium lay upon the platform, the *Acharaja* in attendance repeated some appropriate, or at any rate some duly prescribed, sacred Sanskrit texts, or *mantras.* Then the adopted son, with head hairless save for one scalp-lock, and face clean-shaven, even to the eyebrows, came forward to perform his duty. He was a young man, slight and spare, with a look of mild anxiety in his somewhat sunken eyes. He went round the body

[1] Bindraban. A learned Pandit explained to me that *Bindra* means a company, an assembly, especially of *Davetas* or gods, and *ban* means a wood, a grove. So Bindraban may be rendered the grove of the gods.

once, pouring water on the ground out of the earthen vessel which he had brought from home. At the completion of his circumambulation he lifted up, above his head, the same vessel, which was probably half full of water, and then broke it to pieces on the platform with a sudden and startling crash, quite close to the head of the corpse. As he did so he uttered a cry; only the monosyllable "Ah," but delivered with such depth of feeling and perfection of pathetic intonation that it filled the air with a sense of mourning and sorrow. It came into my mind, naturally enough, that the breaking of the clay vase was symbolic of man's frailty; his body, like the waterpot, being destined to eventual and inevitable destruction. However, my companion interrupted my reflections by informing me, in a whisper, that at the crash of the shattered vase, shivered to fragments on the *Admarag* the soul of the dead man had become dimly aware that *some member* of the family was dead, that some one, or other, had deserted the hearth, but that its confused consciousness did not go beyond this vague, if painful impression.

This part of the ceremony being completed, the *Acharaja* made a few *pindas* of barley meal and placed them near the head of the corpse; then followed sundry sprinklings of water with tufts of the sacred *Kusha* grass by the adopted son, under the instructions of the same priest. After that, the body was removed from the platform to the neighbourhood of the well, where the red shawl was taken off. The corpse, which was completely swathed in cotton wraps, had water poured over it freely. This done, the shawl was replaced, and the deceased was carried towards the gate of the crematorium feet foremost, the men exclaiming "*Yihi to Bindraban hai,*" while some of the women raised a subdued wail.

The platform had hardly been vacated when down dropped four watchful crows from the leafy branches above, and hopping on to the *Admarag* quietly swallowed up the *pindas* of barley meal, after a little friendly tussle amongst themselves. No one interfered; no one resented their apparently rude officiousness; so I presume the crows were quite in order, and probably only doing their duty.

In the ample grounds of the crematory, the body still lying on its bier was laid in an open space. The men now retired while the women gathered round it and, this being the appointed time for the demonstration, wailed aloud, beating their breasts and crying "*Háe*!" (Alas!). One woman I noticed let her *chaddar*, or veil, slip off. Indeed she tied it under her arms, leaving her shapely head and shoulders exposed, and then, beat her chest and forehead vigorously, while uttering exclamations of sorrow and tender regret. She was, perhaps, the deceased physician's daughter, or his adopted daughter-in-law, and I trust I am not doing the good lady any injustice in thinking that, even in her grief, she was not unmindful of effect, not indifferent to the impression she made upon the living who are ever more present than the dead.

Meanwhile some male members of the family went off to arrange for fuel. Presently a large quantity of firewood, in logs of about five to seven inches in diameter, was brought up in a hand-barrow, and as much as was needed for the cremation was soon on the spot.

When a part of the fuel had been piled up by an attendant attached to the crematorium and some straw had been laid upon it, the corpse was placed upon the pyre, face upwards, with a small earthen pot near the head, to mark or indicate its position later on. The *Acharaja* now repeated some texts; the wailing was redoubled, and the women claimed the right of seeing the dear face for the last time. To gratify them, presumably in accordance with immemorial custom, the red covering was removed, and the white cloth beneath it also lifted, so as to expose the dead man's face to view. Sorrow was genuinely expressed on the countenances of many bystanders. Tears fell from many eyes, and the manifestations of grief on the part of the women were, if not in all cases quite sincere, at least sufficiently dramatic. After a minute or two some men interfered to end the painful scene. The women were gently requested to stand back; the cold, set features of the corpse were veiled once more, and the body was turned over face *downwards* on its uneven bed. It had had its last glimpse of our sun and sky. Who that has stood by the unfilled grave of a loved one has not *felt* the cruel thud of the clods as, spadeful after spadeful, they fell upon the coffin and gradually, but effectually, shut it out of view for ever; but the *inversion* of the corpse, which was somewhat roughly done, seemed to me still more distressing, and to savour strongly of primitive barbarism, though I dare say the idea underlying it is that the man should enter the new life as he entered this, face downwards. Many of the spectators, although of course prepared for this uncouth proceeding, were visibly affected by its apparently purposeless inhumanity.

The coloured shawl was now replaced finally, a few small bits of sandal-wood were put upon the body, more for show than anything else, and then heavy pieces of wood were rudely piled upon it, eliciting from the women many exclamations of pitying sorrow, a sort of parting valediction. In this fashion was the pyre built up, with alternate layers of grass and wood, the corpse being in the centre of the pile.

For fire to light the fuel, application was made to a young *yogi*, Goraknath Ka Padri (priest of Goraknath) he designated himself, officially installed within the walled enclosure of the crematorium in a hut of his own. This holy man seemed to have nothing more important to attend to than smoking *churrus*, receiving small gifts, and supplying the fire required for kindling funeral pyres.

With the lighted torch the adopted son set fire to the pile on which the corpse lay, and in a few minutes both grass and wood were kindled into a fierce blaze, from which every one willingly retired to a distance. The women now left the grounds to bathe themselves and wash their clothes in some convenient tank on the way, or at some well-side in the city, prior to re-entering their homes. Gathered in small groups, the men conversed in subdued tones while they watched the roaring fire do its work of destruction.

A few minutes after the pyre had been kindled the *Acharaja* instructed the chief mourner to walk round it six times. Each time he circled about the blazing pile he carried a piece of grass or reed in his hand, given to him by the officiating priest, and having made a complete circuit, threw it on the fire, as his special contribution in the shape of fuel. The first and second time the adopted son walked round bareheaded, but after that he was only too glad to cover both head and face with a wet cloth to protect them from the fierceness of the heat, which would have been bad enough at any time, but was intolerable on that bright sultry autumn morning. He was a strange and weird object that gaunt young man, with sharp features and sunken eyes, as he appeared sometimes boldly defined against the ruddy flames, at other times in uncertain outline, like a phantom dimly visible, through the fire and the clouds of white smoke which rose rapidly upwards in the quivering air.

After he had circled round six times, the other male relations of the deceased were summoned by the officiating priest to take part in the ceremony. They responded to the invitation immediately, and, led by the adopted son, went round the pyre once only. The attendant attached to the crematorium, a ghoul-like creature who had built up the pile on which the physician's body was being consumed, took the chief mourner by the arm and began pointing out to him with his skinny finger something apparently of special interest amidst the flickering flames.

Ungainly indeed was his attitude, as, bending from the waist to get his eyes upon a lower level, he tried to make his companion see where the deceased's skull was still visible in the centre of the mass of red-hot fuel.

Handing him a pole, the attendant directed the chief mourner to break the glowing skull. He accordingly made a thrust at it, and the almost calcined bone readily gave way under the impact.

. This was a supreme moment, for now, at last, the spirit of the deceased was finally released from the trammels of his body, which, no doubt, had been reduced to ashes with the express object of effecting this ultimate and happy liberation.

Each man present picking up a dry twig or chip of wood, of some kind or other, went out of the crematory.

The wandering soul, freed from its prison-house, but still bound by earthly ties of affection, accompanied them. All

Photo by J. Campbell Oman

FUNERAL PYRE REFERRED TO IN THE TEXT

To face page [illegible]

present, not excepting even the liberated spirit, assembled together a few feet away from the platform outside the gate. Here the *Acharaja*[1] repeated some more texts, ending with these words: "*Yatra Agata Tatra Gata*" (Whence he came thither has he gone). As soon as the final syllables were uttered all the men broke their twigs, or chips of wood, simultaneously, and rose to their feet with a prolonged "Ah!"

Such was the conclusion of that morning's ceremony. The living departed to attend to the duties of life, but the soul of the dead man, homeless and alone, and now for the first time fully conscious of the severance of all its earthly ties, was left to find its own way to the realm of Yama, God of Death, on the way to the regions, happy or otherwise, appointed for its sojourn until the time of its next re-incarnation. Hindu imagination has created for the wandering spirit just released from the bondage of the flesh, many dire difficulties and troubles, including the passage of an abominable flood, the dread Vaitarani River. The Egyptians of the old time held somewhat similar ideas. According to Buddhistic belief, the disembodied spirit, the poor errant solitary soul, has to face the Powers of Darkness arrayed in monstrous shapes to terrify it; and Christianity, too, has not been free from notions of terrible beings who, under the command of the "Prince of the Power of the Air," oppose the upward flight of the liberated soul, as indeed St. Anthony, "carried away in spirit," knew from actual experience.[2] Perhaps the latest reminder we have of this belief is in the impotent scorn hurled by the demons at the disembodied soul of the Christian, as pictured in "The Dream of Gerontius," so familiar to lovers of music.

The rite of cremation, well known in many countries of the ancient world, has a special justification in the case of the Hindu because of his belief in the reincarnation of the soul in a *new* body, human or other, a belief which excludes

[1] The story of the origin of the Brahman caste of the Acharajas, or funeral priests, is related in Dr. John Wilson's *Indian Caste*, vol. ii. p. 175.

[2] St. Athanasius cited in *The Monastic Life from the Fathers of the Desert to Charlemagne*, by Thomas W. Allies, pp. 36, 37.

the idea of the *resurrection of the body* as held by Christians[1] and Muslims, who ordinarily look forward to the miraculous reanimation of the corpse by divine decree at the Day of Judgment. From the Hindu point of view, it is evident that when the soul quits its mortal tenement, that tenement is of no further use or value, and its destruction by the purifying element of fire is for him a reasonable and convenient mode of disposing of the dead. This seems to me a natural result of the doctrine of the transmigration of souls, yet some scholars are known to maintain, rather oddly I think, that the embalming of dead animals amongst the Egyptians in the old time was due to this very doctrine.[2]

A few days later I went again to the crematorium for a further inspection and to clear up a few points. Two or three diminutive toy-tents only a few inches high, made of white or coloured cloth, had been pitched amidst the grey ashes which marked the sites of some previous cremations. They looked odd, indeed ridiculous, did these little toy-tents, but they were nevertheless touching evidences of human affection and sympathy, having been put up by loving hands in the fond, if fatuous, hope, of affording a refuge from the inclemencies of the weather to dear, disembodied spirits, believed to be still lingering disconsolately near their earthly homes. In connection with these tiny tents I was told that they were in each case erected on the fourth day after the lighting of the funeral pyre, as on that day the nearest relatives of the deceased pay their last visit to the crematorium to search amongst the ashes for such fragments of bone as may have escaped total incineration, with the object not of preserving them (for urn-burial is not a Hindu practice) but of committing them to the sanctifying waters of the sacred Ganges, or of some other running stream more accessible if less renowned.[3]

At Hardwar, I had myself seen under the clear water

[1] For some quaint observations on this subject, *vide* Sir Thomas Browne, *Hydriotaphia, Urne-Buriall*, at the end of chapter iii.

[2] Dr. Lortet in *Revue des Deux Mondes*, 15 Mai 1905.

[3] It seems hardly necessary to remark that the idea which directs the placing of a lighted lamp (the *Diwa-wattee* already referred to) in the hand of the corpse as soon as life is extinct, is not in harmony with these later ceremonies and their underlying sentiments.

which laves the sacred ghat, white fragments of the bones of departed Hindus which had been conveyed thither by considerate kinsfolk from probably long distances, and dutifully consigned to the Ganges at one of the most holy places on its banks.[1]

While I talked with the attendants, my attention was directed to a number of small owls staring wonderingly at us with queer round eyes, from amidst the leafy recesses of the beautiful banyan tree near which I was standing. A handful or two of grey ashes, representing the remains of a fellow-creature and of the fuel which had been used in his cremation, were strewn at my feet, mixed with the tawny dust of the soil on which they lay. The human body had practically vanished into thin air, and these ashes now commingled with the dust of the earth were all the visible relics of it. The grey fluffy little birds overhead became uneasy and restless, apparently at my too long confabulation in their neighbourhood. I could not help turning my eyes in their direction, and the sapient looks with which the owlets met my gaze suggested the mournful reflection that, after all, these staid inhabitants of the place probably knew quite as much, or quite as little, about a life beyond the veil, as any one who had ever visited or would ever set foot in the Lahore crematorium.

On my homeward way I stopped at the pretty Christian cemetery hard by, attracted to its peaceful silence by fond if painful memories. As I wandered amongst the quiet tombs which testified by their neat appearance and the floral tributes which adorned them, that the long-buried dead were still affectionately remembered, I felt that the trim graveyard with its pretty marble and sandstone monuments, slumbering in the hot sunshine, was far more conducive to tender and elevating sentiments, far more humanising than any crematorium could ever be. And I pondered with deep regret, that "God's acre" might some day be a thing of the past; for sanitarians, with their

[1] Readers who desire ampler details of the post-cremation rites connected with Hindu exequies in Upper India are referred to *Religion and Folk-lore of Northern India*, by W. W. Crooke, vol. ii. pp. 55–59, and *Brief Review of the Caste System*, by Mr. J. C. Nesfield, pp. 69, 70.

microbes and bacilli, will probably so work upon the timidity of a neurotic society that in the interests of Mammon and pleasure, Christian burial will gradually be replaced by pagan cremation. I appreciate the arguments put forward in support of cremation, and the sentiments which prompt men like Mr. Herbert Spencer and Mr. W. E. H. Lecky to have their remains incinerated, yet I cannot help believing that should this practice become general, the world would assuredly be the poorer for the change, paying a heavy moral price for, at best, a doubtful physical advantage.[1] Besides, is it a small matter that the practice of inhumation has given us those relics of pride and affection, the stately tombs of bygone generations, from the Pyramids of Egypt and the Mausoleum at Halicarnassus to the Taj of Agra and the royal sepulchre at Frogmore, as well as the humbler, but perhaps more touching memorials of domestic affection scattered through the graveyards and churches of Christendom?

[1] *Quarterly Review*, July 1900.

PART III

ISLAM IN INDIA

THE MUHARRAM

FAQUIRS

THE MUHARRAM

THE·TA'ZIAH·PROCESSION·

CHAPTER I

THE MUHARRAM

SECTION I.—The historical basis of the great celebration.

YOUNGEST of the great world-religions, and still possessed of much of that vigorous vitality which ensured the wonderful triumphs of its adolescence, Islam, from every point of view, affords a subject well worthy of study.

The Muharram celebration, inspired as it is by gory tragedies of the earliest days of Islam, and still, after thirteen hundred years, capable of stirring to passionate grief the hearts of millions of Muhammadans in many countries, is an annual event which, even if little understood or appreciated by the European resident in India, cannot have quite escaped his perhaps unwilling notice.

Of Islam itself it may be well to recall to memory that though it originated in the early days of the seventh century of the Christian era, it has lost little of the fervour and fanaticism which, after ensuring its initial triumphs, enabled it to practically displace Christianity in Western Asia, to conquer Constantinople, and hold with a masterful hand considerable European and African provinces of the Roman Empire, to retain its grip upon Jerusalem against the enthusiastic valour of the Crusaders, to inspire at the present time the loyal devotion of over two hundred millions of the human race, and still to win daily new adherents to the faith in both Asia and Africa.

In the British Empire there are *ninety-four* millions of persons who profess the Muhammadan religion, and of these over *sixty-two* millions belong to India, being *four* millions in excess of the entire Christian population to be found, according to the latest census, throughout the dominions of H.M. King Edward VII., a striking fact well worth pondering in this twentieth century of the Christian era. The Indian Muslims are divided very unequally into two principal sects, the *Sunnis* or traditionists, and the *Shiahs* or dissenters, the latter being very much in the minority; and between these two sects the bitterest enmity often prevails, leading sometimes to armed antagonism and the spilling of much blood. Even now, after over 1200 years since the date of the events which occasioned the schism, the *Sunnis* and the *Shiahs* are only too ready to fly at each other's throats. So lately as July 1903 we had a Sunni faquir in Tirah on the British Indian frontier getting up a crusade against the Shiahs in the border-land, with the result that some sharp fighting took place in the Mani Khel country, with not inconsiderable casualties amongst the fanatical tribesmen on either side.

Besides the *Sunnis* and *Shiahs* there are also to be found in the ranks of Indian Muslims the reforming *Wahabis*, the mystics known as *Sufis*, and many other sectarians whom

I need not name here. Besides these, there are a few fanatics known as *Ghazis*, burning with religious zeal against all *infidels*, amongst whom European Christians probably hold the foremost place.

Of the Muhammadans of India very few are of the stock of the Muslim conquerors of the country, and still fewer can lay claim to purity of descent. Nevertheless, in many families linger traditions and written evidences of dominion and power enjoyed only a few generations back. However, the vast majority of the Muhammadans of British India are converted Hindus or the descendants of such converts, by far the greatest number, no less than 25,265,342, being *Bengalis*, a most important fact, which is quite lost sight of by most newspaper and magazine writers, who, when speculating about the future of India, *in the event of its abandonment by the British*, assert quite confidently that the dominion of the countries south of the Himalayas would inevitably fall into the hands of the Indian Muhammadans. Such predictions are ill-advised; but as they are often made, I would suggest to the political seers just referred to, a careful study of the geographical distribution of the Indian Muhammadans, and the *nationalities to which they belong*, as a preliminary to these vaticinations.

Stated broadly, the religious practice of Indian Muhammadans consists largely in pilgrimages to the tombs of saints. It is true that the regular call (*azán*) to prayers rises five times each day from the proud minarets of the mosques in every city of the land, but, as in Christian Europe, only a small minority observe strictly the obligations of their faith. The great majority are heedless of the azans and the services in the Masjid, neglect all private devotions, and do not go beyond an attendance at the mosque twice a year on the occasions of the two principal Islamic festivals, Idu'l-Azha[1] and the Idu'l-Fitr.[2]

The religious observances of Indian Muslims have little

[1] *Idu'l-Azha* or *Id'-i-Zuha*, "the feast of sacrifice," is a part of the rites of the annual pilgrimage to Mecca, and it is also observed throughout the Muhammadan world as a great festival.

[2] *Idu'l-Fitr*, "the festival of the breaking of the fast," which follows the great fast of the Ramazān, is especially one of almsgiving.

of the noise and bustle which are associated with so many of the Hindu religious festivals. But once every year in the month of Muharram, which is the first month of the Muslim year, the Muhammadans of the Shiah sect appear in a new and impetuously demonstrative aspect, filling the streets of the principal Indian cities with a certain regulated uproar, of which the keynote is fanatical, yet well-disciplined lamentation. At such seasons noisy drums disturb the air with their throbbing dissonance, and cries not of joy but of sorrow are heard above the beating of the drums. After nightfall torches flash in the thoroughfares, and expert performers do honour to the occasion by weaving flame-figures in the air with the aid of long poles having a lighted torch fixed at each extremity. This annual orgie of mingled sorrow, bustle, and unhealthy emotionalism is the public and therefore prominent feature of the imposing ceremonial known as "the Muharram."

I have witnessed the Muharram in different parts of Northern India and also in the Madras Presidency, and have noticed that the celebration has in each place its local peculiarities. There are, however, certain features fairly common to all.

The Muharram is held by the Shiah sect, and extends over ten consecutive days. The more orthodox sect of the Sunnis refrain from participation in these doings; but it happens that on the 10th of the Muharram falls the *Ashuraá*, the day on which, according to the traditions, God created our first parents, Adam and Eve, and this the Sunnis piously observe. However, in India, at any rate, many more Muslims participate in the Muharram than would care to be ranged under the exclusive banner of the Shiah sect.

Of the ten days of the Muharram celebrations, nine are devoted to *mátam* or lamentation on account of the assassination of Ali, the Prophet's son-in-law, in the mosque at Kufa, of the untimely death of Hasan, the Prophet's grandson, who was poisoned by his wife Jadah, and more especially of the tragic fate of Imam[1] Husain, who was killed at Karbala fighting desperately under circumstances both touching and dramatic.

[1] Imam means Sovereign-Pontiff.

For the comprehension of the purpose and origin of the celebration of the Muharram, it is desirable to take note of certain events which occurred subsequent to the death of the Prophet-founder of Islam. As is usual in such cases, there are certain discrepancies in the narratives and traditions which have come down to us; but the historicity of the more important features of the case may be depended upon and freely accepted.

The immediate successors of the Prophet Muhammad, as heads of both Church and State were:

1. *Abubakr* (A.D. 632–634), the father of Ayishah, Muhammad's favourite wife.[1]
2. *Umar* (Omar) (A.D. 634–644), the father of Hafsah, Muhammad's third wife. He was assassinated by a Persian slave.
3. *Usmān* (Othman) (A.D. 644–656), the secretary of Muhammad and also his son-in-law, having married two of the Prophet's daughters, Ruqaiyah and Umman Kulsum. He was murdered by the son of Abubakr and other conspirators.
4. *Ali* (A.D. 656–660), son-in-law and cousin of Muhammad, who was elected to the office in spite of the opposition of Ayishah, his implacable enemy. He was murdered in the mosque of Kufa by an assassin named Abd-ur-rahman.
5. *Al-Hasan* (A.D. 660), son of Ali and grandson of the Prophet. Reigned for about six months and then abdicated in favour of Muawiyah. He was subsequently (A.D. 668) poisoned by his wife Jadah at the instigation of Yazid, Muawiyah's son, who promised to marry her.
6. *Muawiyah* (A.D. 660–679) was the son of one of the leading companions of the Prophet. He made the Headship of Islam hereditary, and is regarded with great hatred by the Shiahs.
7. *Yazid* (A.D. 679–683), son of Muawiyah. It was in conflict with Yazid that al-Hasan was killed at the battle of Karbala.

[1] Ayishah is generally known as *the Virgin* and Abubakr as "the Father of the Virgin."

Now the Shiahs hold that the three Khalifahs who preceded Ali were mere usurpers, and that in reality Ali was the first Khalifah, al-Hasan the second, and al-Husain the third. They maintain that the Khalifate was a divine institution, that Ali was duly appointed by Muhammad to be his successor, and some Shiahs, going further than this, affirm that: "The Prophet declared that the Most High had created him and Ali and Fatimah, and Hasan and Husain before the creation of Adam, and when as yet there was neither heaven nor earth, nor darkness nor light, nor sun nor moon, nor paradise nor hell."[1]

In addition to the three above-named Khalifahs the Shiahs recognise only *nine* others, the last of these being Muhammad, son of al-Hasan al-Askari, known as the Imam al-Mahdi, who mysteriously disappeared long centuries ago, but nevertheless still lives and will reappear as the Mahdi or Director, before the end of the world, in accordance with the Prophet's prediction. And here I may remark, parenthetically, that this looking for some one yet to come in order to crown, as it were, the unfinished work of the prophets of the foretime, is a common feature of many, perhaps of all, the great existing religions, and is, doubtless, a pathetic admission of disappointment at the disparity between the alluring promises made by the prophets and the mean historical realities; coupled with a fond hope that things will yet be made right, and the long-suffering faithful receive their expected reward in full measure.

Of the nations who profess Islam, the Persians, hereditary opponents of the Arabs, are the most devoted to the Shiah beliefs and traditions. Amongst the Indian Mussulmans, it is said, that only about five or six millions belong to the Shiah sect.

The bloody events connected with the violent deaths of their first three *Khalifahs*, Ali, Hasan, and Husain, are annually recalled to mind by the Shiahs, in all Muhammadan countries where they happen to be in sufficient numbers to claim the licence of indulging their grief in public, the highest place in their sympathy being allotted to Husain.

[1] The author of *Hayātu'l-Qutlūb*, quoted by Mr. Hughes in his *Dictionary of Islam*, Art. "Shiah."

It seems that after Yazid had assumed the Khalifate, secret and perhaps perfidious overtures were made to Husain by certain citizens of the city of Kufa, urging him to put himself at the head of the fortunes of Islam, and promising him armed support.

Only sixty-one years had elapsed since the *Hijrah* or historic flight of Muhammad from Mecca, and already—such was the energy and enthusiasm of the early followers of the Prophet—the dominion of Islam extended over Arabia, Persia, Syria, and Egypt; so that the temporal power attached to the Khalifate was sufficient to excite the ambition even of a saint.

Against the prudent advice and affectionate entreaties of his relatives, Husain accepted the tempting invitation, and set out from Medina on his journey with a handful of attendants and the women and children of his family. But the conspiracy came to the knowledge of Yazid, and he forthwith took decisive measures to make rivalry on the part of al-Husain for ever impossible.

On reaching the boundaries of Babylonia, Husain was met, on the first day of the month of Muharram, by a party of horsemen under the command of an officer named Al Hur, who had been sent to seize and lead him captive into the presence of Ubaidullah, the Governor of Busra. Al Hur, with pious respect for the grandson of the Prophet, treated Husain with the greatest consideration, giving him the option of any road to Kufa which he might care to select, except one leading back to Mecca.

Husain chose his route and journeying by night, became sleepy in the saddle and nodded occasionally. This physical weakness he accepted, with Oriental fatalism, as prophetic of evil, remarking: "Men travel by night and the destinies travel toward them; this I know to be a message of death."

On the third day after Husain's meeting with Hur, another and larger body of the enemy, some 4000 strong, under the command of Umr Ibn Sa'd, came up with him and demanded an explanation as to what had brought him there. The leader would fain have dealt generously with the son of Fatima, but by command of Ubaidullah, the Governor of Busra, proceeded without delay to cut off

Husain and his little band from all access to the Euphrates, a strategical movement which placed the Prophet's grandson entirely at the mercy of his enemies.

Realising too late the futility of his adventure, Husain asked permission to return to Mecca, and Ibn Sa'd, influenced by Hur, communicated with the Governor of Busra on the point; but the latter peremptorily insisted upon Husain's unconditional surrender.

Six days, from the fourth to the ninth of Muharram, had been passed in these negotiations, while Husain's devoted little band of only seventy-two men and the comparatively considerable forces of the enemy lay encamped over against each other on an open plain named Karbala, by the banks of the historic Euphrates.

Suspecting Umar's loyalty, Ubaidullah had despatched to his camp a fanatical partisan of Yazid's family named Shamir, with peremptory orders to the commander of the forces to demand Husain's immediate and unconditional surrender, and in the event of a rejection of these terms to literally trample him and his followers under foot. Further, Shamir came secretly authorised to strike off Umar's head, and himself take command of the troops, should Umar exhibit any hesitation about dealing summarily with the Prophet's grandson, the dangerous claimant to the Headship of Islam.

On the 9th day of Muharram, Umar rode into Husain's camp and personally communicated to him the final decision of the Governor of Busra.

Husain pleaded for time till the next morning to consider his answer, and this request was apparently granted.

With noble generosity Husain urged his companions to return to their homes, as he alone was wanted at Kufa, but they one and all refused to desert him in his hour of need, remarking, "God forbid that we should ever see the day wherein we survive you!"

The steadfast band of heroes made ready to die like men; willing to exchange the troubles of this life for the peace of Paradise and the embraces of the dark-eyed Houris. During the night they protected their rear with a deep trench filled with lighted faggots, and awaited an attack at daybreak. In expectation of immediate battle, their leader, who had fought with credit against the Christians during the long but fruitless siege of Constantinople (A.D. 668–675), took up his position on horseback with the Koran before him, exclaiming as he faced his enemies: "O God, Thou art my confidence in every trouble and my hope in every adversity."

At this critical moment in al-Husain's fortunes occurred one of those rare incidents which, whether inspired by pure magnanimity, or by the hope of an eternal reward, undoubtedly ennoble humanity, and therefore should not be forgotten. It was this. A small party of thirty horsemen detached itself from the main body of the enemy and rapidly approached Husain's entrenched position. "The van of the attacking force!" thought Husain and his friends. No, it was Al Hur with a few followers, who had come over to the weaker side, resolved, with devoted courage to share inevitable death with the grandson of the Prophet and his faithful little band. As he left the army of Umar to cast in his lot with Husain, Hur (known to posterity as Hur-i-shahid, Hur the Martyr), fired with lofty disdain, turned round and shouted back to his former companions, "Alas! for you!" But there was no further defection from the enemy's forces. No other help for Husain was forthcoming.

Although naturally reluctant to destroy the son of Fatima, Ibn Sa'd's forces had to obey the orders of their commander. The fight began by the implacable and truculent Shamir shooting an arrow towards Husain's entrenchment. Thenceforward the conflict between the two very unequal forces was carried on in a desultory manner, with at least one truce for the performance of the prescribed midday prayers.

According to the Shiah traditions, at the commencement of the battle Ali Akbar, Husain's eldest son, animated by a burning zeal for vengeance and the martyr's crown, made no less than ten successful onslaughts on the enemy, killing at each charge at least two or three of his opponents; but in his eleventh attack, exhausted with fatigue and thirst, he was surrounded by his foes and cut to pieces. In

Husain's camp, amongst the members of his own family, there was the youthful Kasim, his brother Hasan's son. A solemn promise had been made to this youth's father that he should wed Husain's daughter, consequently, even with inevitable destruction before him, the Imam felt it his duty to unite them in wedlock, though the wailings for gallant Ali Akbar's untimely end were still in their ears. After the hasty wedding Kasim, a mere child, henceforth always remembered as "the bridegroom," went forth to combat the foes of his family, and fell an easy victim in the unequal strife.[1] Now Husain, attended by his brother, the standard-bearer Abbas, both having donned their cerements, sallied forth and made a furious attack on the troops of Ibn Sa'd, with the result that Abbas, fighting bravely for the martyr's reward, was mortally wounded.

In this desultory fashion, due, no doubt, to the feelings of respect entertained by the rank and file of the enemy's forces for the beloved grandson of their Prophet, the battle dragged on until Husain received a wound on the head. Faint from loss of blood, he dismounted and sat beside his tent with his little son Ali Ashgar or Abdallah in his lap. In his father's fond embrace the child was struck and killed by a random arrow.[2]

It was a bitter moment indeed, but al-Husain, placing his dead child upon the ground, exclaimed with pious resignation: "We come from God and we return to Him. O God, give me strength to bear these misfortunes."

Overcome with thirst, Husain now hurried towards the river, and as he drank of its refreshing stream, a flying arrow pierced his mouth. Raising both his bloodstained hands he lifted his troubled eyes to heaven and in sight of the opposing forces poured out his soul in prayer.

At last, encouraged and goaded on by the bloodthirsty Shimar, the troops closed upon Husain, who, facing the terrible odds against him, defended himself with undaunted bravery. In the heat of raging battle Husain's sister

[1] According to other accounts, Kasim was killed in his uncle's arms. Sir William Muir, *The Caliphate: Its Rise, Decline, and Fall*, p. 326.

[2] Sir William Muir includes Ali Ashgar amongst the survivors of Karbala. *The Caliphate*, p. 327.

Zainab threw herself recklessly amongst the excited combatants, pleading for the life of her brother: but her love availed not. Bleeding from many wounds, Husain was at length despatched by a spear-thrust through his body, and as he fell, Shimar rode a troop of horsemen over his prostrate corpse again and again, until the handsome form of the Prophet's grandson was mangled out of recognition under the hoofs of the horses. With cruel forethought, however, Husain's head was preserved to be carried aloft in triumph to Kufa, hanging from the point of a spear. Not a man of Husain's devoted band escaped with his life. The women and children of his household were captured and taken to Ubaidullah's palace at Kufa, having, according to Shiah traditions, been treated with the greatest indignity.

Husain's death occurred on the 9th October A.D. 680.

> "A thrill of horror," says Sir William Muir, "ran through the crowd when the gory head of the Prophet's grandson was cast at Ubeidallah's feet. Hard hearts were melted. As the Governor turned the head roughly over with his staff (though we must be slow to accept the tales of heartless insult multiplied by Shiya hate), an aged voice was heard to cry: 'Gently! It is the Prophet's grandson. By the Lord! I have seen those very lips kissed by the blessed mouth of Mahomet.'"[1]

There cannot be any doubt that the sufferings of Husain on the field of Karbala, where so many of his loved ones died fighting for him, and where he and his entire family with the women and tender babes endured the cruel agonies of thirst—cut off by their bitter enemies from the waters of the Euphrates—were indeed terrible and affecting in the extreme, and truly, as Gibbon writing of this event says, in his own stately way: "In a distant age and climate the tragic scene of the death of Husain will awaken the sympathy of the coldest reader."

[1] Sir William Muir, *The Caliphate*, p. 327.

THE MUHARRAM—*continued*

SECTION II.—The Passion Play of Hasan and Husain.

THE ceremonies of the Muharram celebrations fall into two classes :

The indoor performance, if such it can be called, of a long miracle play dealing in minute detail with a succession of painful events and tragedies which culminated at Karbala; and of public processions and open-air demonstrations. We may deal with these separately, taking the miracle play first.

Wealthy Shiah families set apart a special building, known as the *Imambara* for the annual performance of the play, and this sometimes serves also as a mausoleum for the proprietor and privileged members of the family.

Of the Imambaras I have visited, the one at Hugli in Bengal and the Husainabad at Lucknow are the largest. In each the principal feature is a spacious hall, hung with crystal chandeliers and decorated with mirrors and other glittering ornaments. It is usual in Imambaras to have on the side towards Mecca certain *tabuts* or *tazias* which are fanciful representations of the tombs of the martyrs. These are often handsome and costly structures on which the artistic skill of the East has been freely lavished. At night during the annual celebrations the hall or theatre is brilliantly lighted, and so is the *tabut* itself, the whole presenting a scene of rare and peculiar beauty.

The great Imambara at Lucknow, erected in A.D. 1784 by the Nawab Asaf-ul-Daulah, was not many years ago, and perhaps is even now, used by the British Government as an arsenal. It is a magnificent structure, with a hall 167 feet by 52 feet and 63 feet high.

Photo by William M. Spooner & Co.

THE MOSQUE OF THE GREAT IMAMBARA—LUCKNOW

The Passion Play.—Of the Passion Play as performed in Persia, the stronghold of Shiahism, we have an English rendering by Sir Lewis Pelly, which, revised and supplied with explanatory notes by Mr. A. N. Wollaston, makes a couple of substantial volumes, to which I am indebted for the quaint and significant details embodied in this section.

The play, as presented to us in Sir Lewis Pelly's work, has many peculiarities well worthy of attention.

In the first place, the action ranges over a period of time past and future extending from the days of Joseph and his brethren to the final resurrection of the dead. Anachronisms the most outrageous do not daunt the dramatist; exaggeration and hyperbole reign rampant. Beings of all orders come forward and *speak*, from the Almighty Himself with His angels and jinns,[1] down to men and women of all grades and characters. Disembodied spirits, as of Muhammad, Fatima, and Ali, appear and take a lively practical interest in the fate of their descendants, while even a talking lion is gravely introduced to enhance the honour and glory of Husain. Headless trunks speak rationally *from* the throat, and heads severed from their bodies hold long conversations. (Vol. ii. pp. 60, 61.)

Other wonders, too, find a place in the play, as when the whole of Ibn Sa'd's army fly terror-stricken before the great Imam Husain (ii. 44), and when Husain himself is spirited away from the battlefield of Karbala to distant India merely to rescue Sultan Ghiyas from the jaws of a lion. (Vol. ii. pp. 54–65.)

In the crisis of his difficulties, the martyr is, in the manner so familiar to the East, exposed to a great temptation. The angel Futrus comes with his legions to him and offers to utterly destroy his enemies; but Husain nobly replies that after the death of his beloved sons and kinsmen the possession of the throne of the entire world would yield him no pleasure, and that it were better to die than to outlive his children. (Vol. ii. pp. 49–52.)

Quite naturally, of course, some sensational *conversions of Christians to the Muhammadan faith* are brought into the play. (Scenes XXXI., XXXV., and XXXVI.)

[1] Genii, both good and evil.

A curious feature of the drama we are considering is the frequent protest made by the sufferers against the tyranny, injustice, and malignity of "the Heavens," or of "the Spheres." It may sound strange, this petulant accusation of the unfair and unfriendly Heavens; but it is intelligible enough. The endurance of unmerited calamities with absolute patience being an impossibility, the human soul in trouble must cry aloud, even if it be in impotent complaint. But against whom are its accusations to be directed? To lift one's voice in fretful murmuring against God, the *ordainer* of all things, would be too impious, too temerarious, and so the outraged feelings of the helpless are relieved by plaintive impeachments of an impersonal cruel *Fate*, or an equally malicious *Heaven*, or the silent treacherous *Stars* in their courses.

Writing for Westerns it seems to me that the prominence given throughout the play to the women of Husain's family, and the deep respect and unstinted affection with which they are, at all times, addressed or alluded to, is a feature of the play worth noting, in face of the unnecessary pity which European and American women usually express for the inmates of the harem.

Although the play is, of course, not history, yet the larger portion of it is devoted to a presentment of the main historical events which precede and follow the awful carnage with which the name of Karbala will for ever be associated.

After presenting in detail Shimar's bloody triumph over Husain, the play unfolds, to the accompaniment of heart-rending lamentations, the evil fortunes of the ill-starred women and children of his family; not, however, omitting to include in the plot, no doubt as a compliment to the native home of Shiahism, the happy escape of Shahrbanu, the wife of the murdered Husain, and sister of the Prince of Persia, and the later release of her daughter Fatima, "the bride," by the commander of the Syrian army, through the intervention of the same Persian prince.

Judged by the canons of Western dramaturgy, the play is really not dramatic or realistic. It is rather narrative in form, the different characters not so much acting as describing what they themselves had witnessed, performed, and experienced, and more particularly what they *felt.* With curious incongruity persons present in widely separated places are frequently made to speak one immediately after the other as if they were in the same spot.

The motive of the play is to work the feelings of the audience up to the highest pitch of sympathy with the martyrs of Karbala, especially Husain, the central figure of that memorable tragedy. Also to make it clear that the great martyrdom was purely voluntary and for the salvation of the faithful in the terrible day of Judgment.[1]

The first object is attained by the way in which the sufferings of the different martyrs are dwelt upon over and over again throughout the play, with a morbid iteration of all the harrowing details of the gory tragedy, followed by the brutal treatment to which the helpless women and children were subsequently exposed. Even before the event, prophetic vision conjures up all the sad scenes of suffering which the family of the Prophet would have to go through. Indeed, the way in which every one seems aware of the events which are about to come to pass, is surprising, and borders on the ridiculous. Thirst and its horrors being only too well known to the dwellers in the arid countries of Asia, the bitter cry for water haunts and heightens the tragedy of Karbala.

To keep before the minds of the audience the *voluntary* character of Husain's martyrdom it is insisted more than once that, possessed as he was of superhuman power, he could, if he had so desired, have easily produced water for his thirsty family and followers, or routed his armed assailants on that fatal 10th day of Muharram.

For attestation of the efficacy and the triumphant justification of the great sacrifice, we have the concluding scene of the Final Resurrection of the Dead, when the right of Husain, by virtue of his sufferings, to be the intercessor for the faithful is conceded by Allah himself.

To Muhammad the Angel Gabriel, the celestial messenger, says:

> "Peace be unto thee, O Muhammad, the elect, God hath sent thee a message, saying, 'None has suffered the

[1] The sacrifice (albeit predestined, vol. ii. p. 86) of Husain for the benefit of his people is explained at vol. i. pp. 210, 211.

pain and afflictions which Husain has undergone. None has, like him, been obedient to my service. As he has taken no steps save in sincerity in all that he has done, thou must put the Key of Paradise in his hand. The privilege of making intercession for sinners is exclusively his. Husain is, by My peculiar grace, the mediator for all.'"

In communicating this divine message to his grandson, Muhammad is made to say:

> "Good tidings, O Husain! Act thou according to thy will. Behold the fulfilment of God's promise. Permission has proceeded from the Judge, the gracious Creator, that I should give to thy hand this Key of intercession. Go thou and deliver from the flames every one who has in his lifetime shed but a single tear for thee, every one who has in any way helped thee, every one who has performed a pilgrimage to thy shrine, or mourned for thee, and every one who has written tragic verses for thee. Bear each and all with thee to Paradise."[1]

Thus it appears that the Persian Miracle Play of Hasan and Husain does more than merely describe the details of murders, slaughters, and wanton cruelties; it gives the doctrinal justification for the same in the Shiah scheme of salvation. Husain indeed expatiates upon the delight with which he had "for a great space of time" looked forward to the glorious martyrdom for the sake of the sinners amongst his people. He is even urged by a voice from the sepulchre of the Prophet Muhammed to end his miseries by getting soon to Karbala, and receives the advice with joy. (Vol. i. p. 212.) It would appear, then, that no futile mission, dictated by personal ambition to obtain the Khalifate, guided Husain's steps from Medina towards Kufa. Far from that, the details of the whole grim scene of thirst and slaughter to occur on the banks of the Euphrates were fully known to Imam Husain, and he went forward with complete pre-knowledge and delight to "drink the honey of martyrdom." Such, at any rate according to the Miracle Play, are the beliefs of the Shiahs, and though they might not be wholly endorsed by all members of the sect, yet it is evident that they must be familiar and acceptable to the Shiah public.

[1] *The Miracle Play of Hasan and Husain*, by Sir Lewis Pelly, vol. ii. pp. 346, 347.

It was apparently only for his own followers that the martyred Husain became a ransom, not for all Muhammadans,[1] and certainly for no individual outside the pale of Islam. At first sight this redemption appears narrow in spirit and restricted in application, but that is nothing new or peculiar. According to the accepted doctrines of the Christian Church the redemption purchased by the blood of Jesus, is, after all, only available for His own professed followers; its benefits do not extend to any others, whether they be virtuous or the reverse.

Religion, it is needless to insist, is not based on sober historical events, though such events, transformed and transfigured in the crucible of the believer's imagination, often serve to give a sort of actuality to the uncertain foundations upon which the composite superstructure of dogma and ritual has been reared by successive generations of subtle theologians and ambitious priests. Europe, in its long history, has witnessed with appreciation scores of Passion and Miracle Plays and Ecclesiastical Shows, both edifying and unedifying; based on apocryphal gospels, and dealing with the sacred mysteries of the Christian religion, such as the Miraculous Birth, the Crucifixion, and the Descent into Hell,[2] but it is not too much to say that the Passion Play of Hasan and Husain performed, or more properly declaimed, during the Muharram excites the fervid emotions of the hearers in a way no other miracle play, not even the decennial performance at Ober-Ammergau has ever done, eliciting touching demonstrations of unaffected, if hysterical, grief from large audiences. I have myself seen in an Imambara in Bengal a crowd of women energetically beating their almost bare bosoms and tossing their loose tresses forwards and backwards as they cried with pathetic emotion and with one voice, "Ya, Husain! Ya, Husain!" while the audience, melted to tears, sobbed aloud.

[1] According to Muslim belief, all Muhammadans will *eventually* be admitted to Paradise. The Shiah belief set forth above means a hastening of this blissful reception into heaven of believers in Imam Husain through the Saint's intercession.

[2] William Hone, *Ancient Mysteries described*, 1823.

THE MUHARRAM
—continued

Section III.—Open-air ceremonies.

HAVING explained the historical basis of the Muharram, the object kept in view in its celebration, and the characteristics of the Passion Play associated with it, I pass on to the more obtrusive and therefore better known open-air ceremonies of the great annual demonstration in honour of Imam Husain's martyrdom.

Shortly before the new moon of the Muharram the Shiahs enclose a space which they call the *tabut khana,* and in this the *tabut,* a portable structure representing the tomb of Husain or one of his martyred followers, is constructed. As soon as the new moon becomes visible, a spade is stuck into the ground before the enclosure, and here, later on, a pit is dug in which a fire is kept burning during the ten days of the Muharram celebrations, apparently in memory of the trench which had been dug for the protection of Husain and his followers at Karbala, and filled, as the reader will remember, with lighted faggots the evening previous to the final battle.

The ten days of the Muharram are, of course, days of lamentation, yet on the *seventh* day there is a procession to commemorate the marriage of Kasim and Fatima. On the *eighth* day a number of lances, each surmounted by an open hand, draped with green cloth—the standards in fact of

Husain—are paraded about the streets. On the *ninth* day the *tabuts* are brought out and carried, with much drumming and shouting, to some appointed centre, preferably one which is associated with the name of a well-known local Muslim saint, while the *concluding* day witnesses the interment of these *tabuts* at the local Karbala.

The following are brief accounts of these different phases of the Muharram celebrations as I have witnessed them.

1. The Marriage Procession on the Seventh Day.

Wending its way through the streets of a city in Northern India came the procession. At the head of it was a band of men beating their chests with their hands, or, in one or two cases, with short iron chains, and shouting, "Ya, Husain! Ya, Husain!" the whole party acting under the direction of a sort of manager or conductor. Then followed two led horses adorned with rich trappings and flowers. Both animals freely perfumed with rose-water till dripping wet, were doubtless representatives of the horses which centuries ago had the honour of carrying ill-starred Kasim and his luckless bride. Behind the horses were drummers beating their drums in a frantic way, meant, I presume, to be expressive of happy exultation. The rest of the procession, curving about like a mighty serpent through the narrow lanes of the city for at least a mile, was made up of camels bearing wedding presents, horses and elephants moving in single file, their riders carrying black or green banners in their hands. In its way the show was imposing, and as for spectators there was no lack of them, the streets being so crowded that pedestrians could hardly make headway. Eager onlookers crowded the windows, balconies, and roofs of the houses along the route. Here and there some poor attempts at decoration might be seen. A verandah or shop would perhaps be gay with hanging lamps and suspended spheres of variously coloured glass, while framed texts from the Koran were also displayed for the edification of the few who could read Arabic. At several places on the way raised booths were in evidence, adorned with leaves and plantain trees. At these places water sweetened with sugar was freely distributed, though the manner of serving it out to the thirsty souls who swarmed around was certainly open to improvement. At one spot I noticed that a woman had erected a booth of her own, where she presided in person, distributing the sherbet with her own fair hands. She was, I ascertained, a woman of the town, and had vowed to abstain for the entire ten days of the Muharram from plying her usual trade! Such is the power of religion!

Just outside the city, near the pleasant bank of a flowing canal, four men were chanting the memorable story of the great martyrdom to an attentive audience, who rewarded them with tokens of their appreciation in the shape of copper coins. I counted just twenty-four *pice* lying on the sheet that had been spread on the ground to receive these contributions. Two men stood at one end of the sheet and two at the other end, singing alternately in a very pleasing style, under the spreading branches of a large fig tree.

On the whole, the wedding procession of the unfortunate Kasim and Fatima was impressive enough, but necessarily bore not the slightest resemblance to the hurried nuptials of those young people on the fatal day of Karbala thirteen centuries ago; if, indeed, such nuptials ever did take place, seeing that Kasim was at the time, according to Sir William Muir, only ten years of age.

2. Tabuts or Tazias.

For the maintenance of order in the streets, the police, having ascertained the localities where the several *tazias* of the year have been built, prescribe the precise route which each one must follow in order to reach the appointed meeting-place. On these occasions the resources of the guardians of the public peace are, in the large cities, often taxed to the utmost, for the spirit of fanaticism is in the air, and the hostility of the rival sects of the Sunnis and Shiahs, inflamed to the highest degree, often leads to serious trouble. Muslims and Hindus also occasionally come into collision at Muharram time; and even between the different bands of Shiahs affrays sometimes take place owing to the eagerness of each party to be early at the meeting-place, as there is merit to be gained from precedence in this respect. I have myself witnessed much disorder in Calcutta during the Muharram.

Leaving generalities, however, I pass on to the details connected with a particular gathering of *tabuts* in Lahore at which I was present.

A few shops were lighted up as I walked down the street, at the end of which all the *tazias* were to be arranged. Near this appointed meeting-place a temporary bazaar had come into existence. One enterprising fellow had erected a canopy over his collection of tempting wares and curious toys, and had suspended from a bamboo frame a monster 80-candle-power German kerosine lamp to illuminate the little show.

At short intervals along both sides of the street itinerant vendors of sweets, each man provided with a flaring oil-lamp, were squatting near their baskets or flat trays, crying their wares in loud strident tones, and the passers-by were buying the pretty coloured sweet-stuffs which, dyed pink with cochineal, were no doubt very palatable to the Oriental taste.

One by one the *tazias* or *tabuts*, illuminated by flaring torches, accompanied by deafening tom-toms, and attended by their own proprietors and supporters, arrived from the different quarters of the town, escorted by constables, and were arranged under police supervision on the sides of the street. This marshalling of the *tazias* is a moment of intense feeling and keen rivalry. Whose *tazia* is the best, the biggest, the most elaborate, the most costly? these are the questions that occupy the minds of all the participators in the show, and each year the Muharram brings its triumphs and its disappointments to some or other of the *tazia* builders and their friends.

Amongst the specimens I saw there were many of considerable size, others quite diminutive; but all bright and glittering with tinsel, mica, and coloured paper; some were quaint, some pretty, and some decidedly grotesque. The underlying idea being that the *tazias* should, in one way or another, represent the tomb of Imam Husain, or of the other martyrs of Karbala, the designs were of course various; but an inspection of them made it clear that the designers had allowed their imaginations to run riot in a truly Indian fashion. One of these *tazias* might be merely a tower of four or five storeys built on a light bamboo framework. Another more elaborate and bizarre in form would have the appearance of a strange composite being, with a woman's face and the body of a peacock, bearing a house on its back. Some *tazias* were supported upon winged horses with long ostrich-like necks, surmounted with human faces of feminine type. One was borne on the head of a winged angel, who, by means of a simple contrivance manipulated from behind, was made to beat his breast in a rather ridiculous fashion. No doubt this huge mechanical toy brought forcibly, perhaps touchingly, to the minds of Shiah spectators that even the denizens of other worlds mourned the martyrdom of their Imam.

While the *tazias* stood in their appointed places on the roadside, devout women were fanning them with palm leaves and horse-hair *chauris* (fly-flappers), and even with their own *chaddars* (veils). Some were Hindu women, probably unfortunate mothers, who thus paid respect to these effigies of the martyrs' tombs, in the fond hope that Imam Husain would graciously extend his protection to their surviving children and grant them long life. As a rule, the women who thus dedicate themselves to the service of the *tazias* do not sit down at all from the time the *tazias* are brought out from the *tabut khanas* till they are finally disposed of at the local Karbala, a period which might well extend to twenty-four hours. In one instance I noticed a woman pinning on to a *tazias* with her own hands a paper on which her *arzi* (petition) to the martyr was written, and it need not be doubted that she did so in trembling hope of a favourable response. For the enjoyment of these special privileges the devotees have, in all probability, to make a contribution in money to the *tazia* building fund.

From time to time some persons, for the most part women with babies in their arms, approached the *tazias*, and made trifling offerings of flowers, sweetmeats, and money, which gifts were formally accepted by the attendants, and some trifling return, generally a garland of small flowers,

Photo by W. Bult

A TAZIA BELONGING TO A GUILD OF BUTCHERS

To face page 300

given in exchange by way of acknowledgment to the pious and now happy oblationer, who, beaming with satisfaction and hope, would place it without delay about her infant's neck.

Many children were to be seen in the crowd wearing peculiar caps, and with tiny bells suspended round their waists. These little ones had been dedicated as it were to the Imam Husain at birth, or at some critical period of sickness or danger.

So there before my eyes were exhibited in action those simple and touching sentiments which lie at the root of religion—solicitude for loved ones, and a trustful appeal for help to any unseen spiritual power that might possibly be won over by gifts or flattering attentions to hear and answer prayers. Woman's love, as always, was playing a leading part in the religious drama there unfolded, and, as always, man was reaping, in mundane currency and worldly goods, the harvest which sprang from the soil of her amiable and inexhaustible superstitions. My sympathies as a spectator were all with the dear women and their over-faith.

Not far from the spot where the *tazias* had been placed two or three toy shops attracted attention. I noticed amongst the articles displayed in them, pictures of Jesus and the Virgin, but I satisfied myself that no images of the Hindu gods were for sale on this occasion. I presume their presence might have led to trouble.

However, *tazias* or no *tazias*, the everyday life of the neighbourhood was by no means seriously interrupted. Near by, just on the roadside, but in his own verandah, a charcoal vendor, clad in a loin-cloth, was lying face downwards on a low *charpoy* (a string-bottomed bed), and another man, supporting himself with a long stick, was walking about upon his prostrate body. It was not a case for police interference—no brutal assault was being committed. The charcoal merchant was merely having himself massaged after his day's work—perhaps he was suffering from lumbago —and for all he cared the whole world might look on while his ailment was being attended to in this, no doubt, efficient if rather primitive fashion.

At a little distance, in the roadway, some pious persons

had erected a stall where *marsiyas* or elegies were being read in Urdu by a young man as I passed along. It was a small temporary structure made up of low wooden tables about a foot high, over which *daris* (cotton carpets) had been spread. The stall had no roof or covering, the sides were made of paper, and the chief feature of the façade was three moresque arches.

The stall was lighted with three kerosine lamps, and ornamented with two or three vases and a pot of artificial paper-flowers of the rudest possible manufacture. A few women stood and listened respectfully as the young minister intoned the *marsiyas*, but the words, though spoken in what is officially known in the Punjab as "the vernacular," were unintelligible to the country-folk, who, having no inducement to linger about, passed on and went their way.

As I was about to leave the bazaar, a band of *purbiyās* (men from the eastern districts of the United Provinces) arrived with a burst of tom-toming. Whirling rapidly with great skill long slender poles with lighted torches at their extremities, they traced curious and effective fire-figures in the air, while others showed off their skill in fencing, to the great admiration of the assembled crowds. This exhibition seemed to be the final event of the night's ceremonies, for almost immediately after their performance the streets began emptying rapidly.

3. The Duldul Procession.

Duldul is the name of the Prophet's mule which he gave to Ali, and the so-called Duldul procession takes place in the forenoon of the last day of the Muharram celebrations.

To see the procession I, in company with a friend, entered the city of Lahore by the Delhi gate, and passing by the mosque of Wazir Khan, near which a number of stalls had been set up by fruiterers and others, we took up the best position we could secure and waited, and while we did so the sun beat down upon us with uncomfortable warmth, although it was only about seven o'clock in the morning. As we stood in the sweltry sunshine, we had time to take note of our surroundings.

The street was crowded. At some distance to the right the minarets of the mosque of Wazir Khan made conspicuous objects against the sky. On the left the view was closed by the three gilded domes of the Sonari Masjid. Just opposite, with one side on the narrow lane through which we had found our way, was a picturesque dwelling-house three storeys high. On the first floor, from a very low and curiously carved window, three or four women were watching the street, one a particularly good-looking one, with a large gold nose ring, and many silver ornaments. On the floor above was a quaintly carved balcony, flanked on either side by windows surmounted by half domes of the familiar Hindu type. A long balcony projecting well over the street gave character to the third storey, and was full of people. The roof itself afforded good accommodation for many spectators. The houses along the side of the street were a repetition, with many variations, of the picturesque residence just opposite us, and led the eye along interesting specimens of Indian domestic architecture to end in the glittering domes of the golden mosque. Across the road, just in advance of the spot where we had taken our stand, some pious Muslims had stretched a canopy of carpets from one side to the other, spanning the entire width of the street, reaching from housetop to housetop, high enough to allow the loftiest flagpole to pass beneath without hindrance. The spectators were orderly, quiet, and sober. As we waited in expectation with umbrellas over our heads to protect us from the sun, a man came up and very politely asked if we would kindly put our umbrellas down as the *ráni* in the closed carriage behind us could not see what was going on, and would be grievously disappointed if she failed to witness the procession, as it was only on rare occasions that ladies of her rank ventured out. Of course my umbrella collapsed at once, and one look behind afforded me a glimpse of the presumably beautiful princess as she peered through the venetian blinds of her carriage (a *pálki gári*) to get a view of the throngs which filled the streets.

Amongst those waiting for the Duldul I noticed a woman in dainty white garments carrying above her head a parasol of silver paper smothered under a profusion of real flowers which hung in threads from the centre. She was so eager to meet the procession that she pressed forwards towards it, and a minute later I saw her a little way down the road sprinkling rose-water on the advancing mourners from an elegant spray bottle which she carried in her hand. This was doubtless an act of piety.

Heading the procession which had at last arrived, came a number of Muhammadan gentlemen of good position, some of whom were well known to me. After them came several urchins carrying little paper parasols ornamented with fringes composed of strings of flowers and of raisins, which latter, as might have been expected, attracted flies in their myriads. Next came a batch of small boys beating their chests and crying in plaintive tones, "Husain! Husain! Husain! Husain!" as a refrain to words chanted by adult voices. It was interesting to note the evident sincerity with which many of these little folk entered into the spirit of the occasion, and how they literally ill-treated themselves, while others again made a mere pretence of beating their breasts. Then came four or five men bearing poles surmounted by big flags of black and green, and in one case of red material. Behind these banners marched a troupe of big boys, some of whom were quite fanatical in the earnestness with which they thumped their breasts with their hands, and, in a couple of instances, with small iron chains laid on with right goodwill. Following these bigger boys came a party of stalwarts stripped to the waist, many of them as fine specimens of manhood as one could wish to see. These adults were without doubt all thoroughly in earnest, as in deep, quick, jerky tones they cried Hasan—Husain! Hasan—Husain! Hasan—Husain! and banged their bare chests with an energy that was positively distressing. The reader does not need to be reminded that the two brothers whose names were thus associated had both met violent deaths, though under quite dissimilar circumstances. The next place in the procession was taken by the chanters, followed by a led horse, which had not been ridden for the whole of the previous year, and would probably not be ever used again, its rich caparison disfigured with irregular red spots in imitation of blood, while many feathered arrows stuck in the trappings bore unmistakable witness to the terrible battle in which it had borne its gallant master. A profusion of flowers almost smothered the animal, and on one side (the left side) hung a fine large serviceable shield with brass bosses.

Immediately behind the horse came the police guard, forming a cordon about the animal and its attendants. There were women also in the procession slapping their breasts in lamentation for Husain's martyrdom, but I am not quite sure whether they came immediately before or after the horse. The latter I think.

Behind the force of constables, all of them on foot, rode the embodiment, for the nonce, of the British *raj*, a solitary Englishman with a resolute but bored expression on his face—the Assistant Superintendent of Police.

4. Karbala.

At four o'clock in the afternoon of the day of the Duldul procession, I visited the local Karbala, a large open space near green *juar* fields.

The afternoon was hot, but the sun was somewhat obscured by clouds, and a breeze was blowing which, at times, raised a great deal of dust. Many *tazias* were on the ground, amongst them a few elegant structures made of coloured paper and gold and silver tinsel, surmounted by Eastern domes and towers.

But amidst this collection of "tombs" I was surprised to come upon what was virtually a fair with the usual merry-go-rounds, bustling groups of people—mostly women and children—and itinerant vendors of sweetmeats. Under awnings the savory *Kabábs* were being cooked and sold to appreciative customers.

Occasionally there was a deal of rushing about amongst the men, as something that promised to lead to a fight occurred anywhere. The native police seemed to be having a lively time of it to keep the peace and ensure order. The women, I must say, took everything very placidly, and did not put themselves out. I wandered about waiting for the entombment of the *tazias*. At one end of the field, a number of huge graves were being dug, and in the furthermost one I saw a *tazia* laid out. It was, however, too long for the excavation, and had to be cut shorter. All the pieces were put in, and then the pretty but flimsy structure was ruthlessly smashed down by two or three boys who were standing in the excavation. *Bihishtis* (water-carriers) with full leather bags were in attendance, and I noticed that some women who came on the scene handed pice to them—a meritorious contribution, no doubt, towards the good work. The *bihishtis* emptied their *mashks* on the fragments of the pretty bamboo and paper *tazia* as it lay prostrate in the trench, after which the men with their spades began to cover the débris over with earth. Several women, with touching piety, busied themselves throwing handfuls of earth into the grave, assisting in this way the obsequies of that which an hour before had been the object of their pride and admiration.

Why the *tazias*, which are supposed to represent the tombs of the martyrs, should themselves be buried, seems, at first sight, rather strange; but I suppose it is simply to put them away decorously as having duly served their purpose; so that the new year might bring its own fresh supply to do honour to the great occasion. And, after all, most of them were very fragile and of trifling value. Such of them as were of a better sort received different treatment; for even in affairs of religion, economic considerations are rarely, if ever, forgotten. A close observer might easily notice here and there a substantial *tazia* of more solid and expensive construction being hastily covered up with white sheets and carried off quite unobtrusively without any noise or fuss. These better built and more costly *tazias* would be taken through quiet lanes back to the *tabut khana* whence they had been brought to Karbala, and would appear again in all their glory at the next and, may be, at many subsequent Muharrams.

THE MUHARRAM—*continued*

SECTION IV.—A tale of Muharram rivalries.

AS a pendant to the foregoing description of the celebration of the Muharram, I give the following characteristic story, which was told me by an old Muhammadan of the Suni sect, and which I now reproduce as if narrated in his own words:—

"Years ago I lived for some months in a large military cantonment occupied by both European and native troops—infantry, cavalry, and artillery. I had gone there on account of the wedding of my sister, and was easily induced to spend some time with her husband's family, as the *air and water* of the place were good, and the life in a military station was new and attractive to me.

"The General Sahib in this station was a great *bahadur* (swell), with lots of money, and he spent it freely. He was a really brave man too, and his breast was covered with medals. What with his bravery and his liberality, the sepoys all loved him as if he were their father.

"Now the general was as much devoted to love as to war, and had a number of wives, amongst others a *Mussulmani* of the *Shiah* persuasion. She was a pretty woman, and had great influence with the general, who humoured her in whatever she wanted. Jewels and clothes she had in abundance, but her great ambition was to bring out the largest and most magnificent *tazia* at the time of the Muharram. Of course, all well-instructed Mussulmans know that it is not proper to make *tazias*, and still worse to carry them about with drums and shouting at such a solemn time of mourning as the Muharram. But the foolish *Shiahs* spend their money in this improper fashion every year, and think they are performing a religious act when they are doing the very reverse. The general sahib's *begam* was one of these, and the chief butcher of the station, a very wealthy man, was another, and they were great rivals in the matter. People said that they had once been more than friends, hence their senseless rivalry; but, in truth, I knew nothing about this matter.

"Every year the general would have a magnificent *tazia* made for the *begam*, and as soon as one *tazia* had been left at Karbala, the work of constructing another, and a better one, for the next year's Muharram was taken in hand. Throughout the twelve months spies from either side were at work, trying to find out what the other party was about, and what the details of the form and dimensions of the new *tazias* might be. It was a grand piece of cunning, skill, and rich material, this annual *tazia* of the *begam's*, but there was invariably a worthy rival in the field, constructed at the expense of the chief butcher of the city.

"I have, as becomes a strict *Suni*, always abstained from taking any part in the objectionable processions of the *tazias*; but on this occasion, induced by the report of the rivalry of the *begam* and the butcher, I went out to see their *tazias*, not without a hope—for I was young and strong—that there might be some *marpīt* (fighting) between the rival parties, as does sometimes occur, notwithstanding the presence of the police.

"In the evening of the appointed day the *tazias* were brought out, with a tremendous shouting and the deafening beating of drums. I never heard a greater uproar in my life. The noise and the excitement of the crowd astonished me. The *begam's tazia*, headed and followed by policemen, was carried down one street, and the chief butcher's, similarly attended, was brought down another street. They gradually approached each other, and were finally deposited at a distance apart of about one hundred cubits in the main street of the Sudder Bazaar, not far from the *Dargáh* of one Sheikh Nanak Baksh.

"A great many other *tazias*, built by influential people in the town, were also brought to the bazaar. None of them, however, could be compared with those of the *begam* and the butcher. Multitudes of people came crowding about these two, admiring them and discussing their respective merits.

"Whatever might be the opinions of the spectators respecting the comparative beauty and costliness of these two principal structures, this at any rate was evident to all interested in the matter or not, that the *begam's tazia* towered some six or eight feet above its rival, and the *begam's* friends rejoiced accordingly. As the night went on, the low-caste people, who make a fair of this solemn occasion, came out in hundreds with their huge poles lighted at both ends, and wheeled them round about, and above their heads most skilfully, making great circles of fire in the air. In their competition amongst themselves, under the stimulus of strong drink, these low-caste fellows, *chūras* and others—got up many a disturbance, which was most disgraceful and annoying on an occasion which should have been observed with the strictest solemnity and mourning.

"The next morning all the *tazias* were drawn up in a great procession to proceed to Karbala. The *begam's* led the way, on the shoulders of not less than twenty-four selected men, the attendants in their pride throwing out, occasionally, various jeering allusions to the butcher's *tazia* just behind, which taunts were received in anything but an amiable spirit. When all had assembled at Karbala and the *tazias* had been placed once more on the ground, the astonishment of the onlookers knew no bounds on discovering, what was no difficult matter to do, for it was obvious enough, that the chief butcher's *tazia* was yards taller than the *begam's*!

"'Ya Husain! Ya Husain!' shouted the butcher's friends like men demented, beating their breasts frantically with their open palms till they resounded again.

"'Look at the miracle,' cried one man, and a great murmur went through the crowd. The *begam's* people were overawed and stood in mute wonderment at the miraculous victory of their rivals, who rent the air with their shouts. There was no one in that crowd who felt the defeat more keenly than did the architect of the *begam's tazia*, and, practical man that he was, he sneaked round and, unobserved, approached the now taller *tazia* quite closely. His quick eye detected that it had been built like a telescope, so that one portion fitted into another, and he concluded rightly that it had been *made to grow* on the way to Karbala. He returned to his party and told them what he had found out. Hundreds pressed forward, denouncing the trick, and determined to expose it. The consequence was a free fight, in which every one took part, and both the big *tazias* were torn to pieces. All over the ground quantities of silver paper and gold paper, coloured and shiny paper of all kinds, mica and glass, bamboos and canes, were strewn about, and many heads were broken.

"This was the chief butcher's first and last triumph over the *begam*, for within a few weeks of the event he died of fever. His son purchased a valuable piece of ground alongside a famous shrine for his interment. A great many mourners followed the remains of the deceased, who had been a wealthy man. The usual ceremonies were duly performed, and the body committed to the earth to rest there till the last Judgment. The burial party was about to return homewards, when, lo! to the surprise of every man, the grave cracked, a narrow fissure appeared, and a cloud of smoke commenced to issue from the ground.

"'Who is this that you have brought here?' asked the custodians of the neighbouring shrine. 'What man burdened with iniquities is this that the ground refuses to retain him, and the smoke of *jahannam*, the bottomless pit, issues from his grave?'

"His sins and iniquities, whatever they were, could not have been hidden from Allah, and would be revealed at the resurrection of the dead, but as far as we knew the chief butcher had been a good Muslim and a charitable man. The *Mulla*, however, said that it was clear that Allah was angry with him because of his sinful rivalry with the *begam*, and the unseemly trick he played with the *tazia* on the occasion of the recent Muharram, as such conduct was little short of an insult to Imam Husain, and not justifiable under any circumstances.

"This judgment ought to have satisfied the *begam*, but it would seem that, deprived of the excitement of the annual contest, which for years had been the chief object of her life, and bitterly chagrined at the butcher's final triumph, she became very ill and died before the next Muharram came round."

FAQUIRS OF SORTS

CHAPTER II

FAQUIRS

Legends and stories of Muslim saints and religious devotees, both ancient and modern.

IT is no part of my plan to attempt to describe the distinguishing characteristics of Muhammadan *faquirs* in their numerous orders, but Muslim ascetics are so conspicuous amongst the religious mendicants one meets in India, that the following sketches in which they figure will probably throw some light upon the views in respect to the ascetic life held by a large and very important section of the Indian people.

It is well known that throughout the Muslim world the saints of Islam are credited with extensive miraculous powers, *delegated to them by the Almighty as a proof of His favour, and a measure of their deserts.* To these favoured ones are attributed acts various in character and importance, such as, to mention only a few, the cure of ordinary diseases without the use of medicines, the raising of the dead to life, causing springs of water to flow in dry places, walking on the sea, flying through the air, becoming invisible, producing earthquakes, overturning mountains, being in two places at the same time, arresting the sun in his course, and punishing opponents by deadly pestilences and dreadful cataclysms.

India has been blessed with the last resting-places of so many Muslim saints of the first importance that volumes might be easily written about the great virtues and striking miracles of the faquirs, whose tombs, often beautiful and imposing structures, lie scattered over the land, objects of deep veneration to all pious Muhammadans.

Bearing the foregoing points in mind, the reader will not be moved to astonishment by any of the legends, or narratives of personal experiences, which I now record.

1. A Legend of Baba Farid.

I was conversing one day with a Mussulman regarding the fast of *Ramazan* just concluded, and remarking to him that in such excessively hot weather as we had been having, much hardship must have been experienced in observing the very strict rules of the fast. The Mussulman stated that after abstinence for a few days, the bodily system becomes habituated to the altered conditions of life, and does not feel the strain put upon it. In connection with this point I described to him Dr. Tanner's celebrated fast of forty days in America. The native listened without a word of comment, and then told me the following story about a famous Muhammadan saint named Baba Farid (A.D. 1173–1265), whose tomb was at Pak Patan on the road to Multan. The saint resolved to fast, not for a paltry *forty days*, but for no less than twelve years. He had a bit of wood shaped to resemble a piece of bread, and whenever he was hungry satisfied the cravings of his appetite by gnawing his wooden substitute for bread.[1] After twelve years of this, he returned home. As he seemed rather inclined to take credit for what he had done, his mother remarked that his penance could hardly be considered satisfactory, seeing that he had always kept the thought of bread before him, and even had a semblance of the real substance at hand to allay his wish for food. Taking these remarks to heart, Baba Farid left home again for the purpose of performing another penance. This time he abstained from all ordinary human food, but lived simply upon the leaves of trees. After the expiration of a dozen years he turned his steps homewards, and on his arrival was welcomed with joy by his mother. One day caressing him in maternal fashion she noticed a grey hair on his head and pulled it out. He winced; whereupon his mother expressed her surprise, and asked him how he, who shrank from having a single hair removed, found it in his conscience to strip the trees of their leaves during twelve long years, simply to sustain his own life. Struck by these reproachful remarks, the ascetic left home again, and for a third period of twelve years suspended himself head downwards in a well, without partaking of food of any kind, or even moistening his lips with a drop of water. As he hung in the well the birds fed upon the flesh of his body, while the only favour he asked was that his eyes might be spared. When this great penance, if such it can be called, was accomplished, Baba Farid heard heavenly voices assuring him that his devotion had been accepted by Allah.

At the tomb of this saint there is an annual fair on the fifth day of the Muharram, and Muhammadans in considerable numbers come there to pass through a narrow gateway known as the *Bihisti Darwáza*, or gate of Paradise, which leads to the Mausoleum, and is opened only once a year.

[1] "He (Baba Farid) was a thrifty saint, and for the last thirty years of his life he supported himself by holding to his stomach wooden cakes and fruits whenever he felt hungry."—W. Crooke, *Popular Religion and Folk-lore of Northern India*, vol. i. p. 216.

2. Baba Jungu Shah, a Punjabi Saint.

This Muslim saint, as I learned from one of his fellow-countrymen, was in his younger days a very strong, active fellow, and a daring robber. In fact, all his family lived by plundering their neighbours. They went about the country armed, for it was in the time of the Sikh *raj* that they flourished by high-handed depredations. On one of their *business* visits to the town of Gujrat where they had reaped a good harvest, Jungu was appointed to remain behind as rear guard, to settle accounts with any one who might venture to pursue the party engaged in carrying off the spoil. As he lingered skulking near the wall of the house where the robbery had been committed, he observed some one looking over the wall, and unhesitatingly struck at him with his trusty sword. The blow, well delivered, seemed to sever the head from the body, and Jungu crouched down to await events. Again a head peered stealthily over the wall. "Surely," thought Jungu, "that is the very same man whom I decapitated only a minute ago." But it was no time for considerations of this sort, prompt action was needed; so swinging his sharp blade with unerring skill and immense force, he struck the head off at a blow. With something akin to fear he looked up again, and to his horrified astonishment saw the same face looking at him sternly as before. Overcome with terror, the thief prostrated himself before the apparition, for such he deemed it, and joining his palms together, humbly placed himself at its disposal.

"Go," said the apparition, "to the *syad*[1] who lives at —— (naming a village not far off), and ask him what you are to do."

Jungu, obedient to the command, went off at once and narrated to the *syad* the startling events that had taken place.

"It was Hazrat Ali, the son-in-law of our Prophet, who appeared to you," said the saintly man at the conclusion of Jungu's story, "and you are to stay here in order to learn and ever repeat a *mantra* (spell) which I shall teach you."

[1] Syad, a lineal descendant of the Prophet Muhammad.

Jungu waited on the faquir as his humble disciple for some time, acquiring and practising the *mantra* which was duly communicated to him. His violence of temper did not, however, leave him, and one day, in a fit of rage, he killed his own mother and threw her body into a well. He escaped punishment for his shocking deed, as it was committed in Sikh times when all sorts of lawlessness prevailed.

But Jungu, struck with remorse, now embraced an ascetic life. He gave up his evil courses, and with them all worldly concerns. He sat idle all day covered with ashes, and hardly deigned to notice any one.

For years and years he sat in the same place rubbed over with ashes, and with time his fame grew wonderfully. From all the countryside folks came to consult him about their ailments, or to invoke his assistance in times of domestic or public trouble. A pill made from the mud upon which he sat, if given with his own saintly hand, would cure almost any disease, and his help in other matters, too, was most efficacious; for example, men often came and pestered him for assistance in some business or other pending in a law court. In such cases the *Baba* would sometimes wax wroth and chastise his too importunate visitor with a heavy stick for tormenting him. The beating would be taken in all humility, and then the saint, relenting, would probably say, "Go, brother, it is all right," and all right it assuredly was; for, whatever the facts of the case might be, the Court was sure to decide in favour of the man whom the *Baba* had sent away with cheering words.

On the spot where Baba Jungu Shah was buried, a tomb has been erected, and is an object of veneration to the people near and far.

The tombs of Muslim saints or men of consequence are commonly covered over with a cloth, which might, according to circumstances, be of any material, from an ordinary white cotton sheet to a valuable gold-embroidered coverlet.

A devotee of Baba Jungu once brought a sheet worth four or five rupees and laid it over the grave. At night a thief came and removed it. The custodian when he missed it remarked, "Oh, Baba! do you allow your property to be removed by thieves?" A faint voice came from the grave,

"I have no need of coverings, but the sheet shall be his to whom it rightfully belongs."

In three days' time a half-starved man came to the shrine and restored the sheet. He was the thief who had stolen it, but he could not keep it. Do what he would, as long as he had the sheet about him he could not find his way home. Everything before him seemed dark and confused, but the moment he set his face towards the shrine, his way was clear. His attempts to carry it away being thus frustrated, he had brought the sheet back to its rightful owner.

3. The Khazanah-wallah Faquir.

There came to the beautiful Himalayan station, Murree, while I was enjoying a holiday there, a pious Kashmiri *faquir*, who took up his abode near a small mosque in the bazaar. He made a stir in the place, and after he went away I learned from a Muhammadan who professed to have been much interested in his doings, the following particulars, which, whether accurate or not, are at least quite in keeping with the peculiarities of Indian life and Indian modes of thought, and therefore worth recording here.

When people came to the good man, as they did daily, he would often, in the case of the very poor, return them silver coins for the copper ones they had presented to him, drawing the former from below the *dari* (carpet) on which he used to sit. Naturally his fame went abroad, and the holiness of Pir-ji, or the *Khazanah-wallah faquir* (the wealthy ascetic) as he came to be called, was common talk in the town and the neighbouring villages. When he had been established in Murree for a short time a blind beggar came inquiring for him, saying he had travelled all the way from the Kashmir Valley in quest of the *Khazanah-wallah faquir*. He asked this one and that one to lead him to Pir-ji, and at last a good-natured person undertook to present him to the saint on the next Friday, after the hour of prayer, as Pir-ji, absorbed in his devotions, was not always accessible. On Friday the blind man was duly conducted to the mosque and taken up to the faquir. When he reached the good man he fell prostrate at his feet, saying, "Hazrat, I have sought you long. I have followed you, stone-blind though I am, from Kashmir along a difficult and dangerous road. Many troubles have I endured to gain your honoured presence. Have pity upon me; have pity and restore your slave's sight. My children are starving because I am blind. Take pity upon us, for the sake of Allah the most merciful!" Thus pleaded the blind man, but the saint heeded him not. The poor sufferer renewed his plaintive entreaties again and again, and, at length, touched by his faith and perhaps harassed by his importunity, the *pir* ordered some water to be brought. An attendant hastened to fulfil his command. While the wondering crowd looked on in hushed reverence, he poured a little of the water into the hollow of his palm, he blew upon it, uttered a prayer to Almighty God, and then dashed the handful of water against the closed lids of the blind man. Several times he repeated this, while the patient trembled visibly from the emotion which possessed him.

The increasing crowd pressed closer and closer about Pir-ji and the sightless beggar. Requesting the assembly to pray earnestly for the restoration of the poor man's vision, the ascetic applied his fingers to the beggar's closed eyelids, and gradually but firmly forced them open. Upon this the blind man recovered his visual powers so far that he could dimly discern objects about him. Gradually, under the healer's touch, the eyes regained their lost efficiency. The form of his benefactor became distinct to the patient, the presence of the wondering crowd of men and women was no longer only felt; the lovely hills, the blue sky, and the glorious sun once more entered into the life of the man, thus strangely cured of his terrible affliction.

In a transport of gratitude, the beggar declared that he would never, never leave Pir-ji. He vowed he would be his humble and devoted attendant, and *slave*, as long as he lived.

And remain he did. To remind him of his starving wife and children was useless; for in an ecstasy of pious confidence he would say that the hand which had restored him to sight would never let his children die for want of bread.

Of course Khazanah-wallah Pir's fame increased mightily after his miracle. Crowds flocked to him, and in very self-defence from the pertinacious attentions of his admirers, he had to seek strict seclusion. He hid himself in a house in some out-of-the-way place, and the quondam blind beggar constituted himself doorkeeper. The *pir's* hiding-place was soon discovered, but only deserving people got access to him, namely, such as were able to satisfy the doorkeeper of their sincerity, their urgent need of spiritual or other help and—*their ability to pay up.*

All went on pretty well for a time, till a certain Friday when Pir-ji emerged from his seclusion to go to the mosque for worship. There were several men and women waiting to interview him, but not paying any attention to them, the saint began to sniff about in a peculiar way.

"There is a very unpleasant odour here," he said. "A very disagreeable smell, the smell of ill-gotten money," and looking very seriously at his self-constituted doorkeeper, cried angrily, "Begone for ever, under fear of the displeasure of God!"

Every one felt and admitted the justice of the sentence, because many had suffered from the doorkeeper's exactions, which had indeed been no secret.

Pir-ji got still more honour from this act of his; both on account of the spiritual insight which enabled him to detect the evil-doings of his unworthy servant and the summary justice which he had meted out to him.

Applications for his help and favour increased in number, and amongst others, there came a man hobbling along with soiled rags about his feet and hands, dirtily clad and most likely a leper—an object of mingled pity and disgust. Pir-ji, having compassion on this miserable being, took him into his room and give him a bath with his own holy hands, and whatever his previous condition may have been, the unclean mendicant emerged whole and sound.

The man thus wonderfully healed was installed as doorkeeper to Pir-ji, but, such is the weakness of human nature in face of the temptation of money, that notwithstanding daily intercourse with the saint, and full knowledge of the unhappy, if deserved, fate of his predecessor, the new doorkeeper could not refrain from drifting into similar objectionable courses. With unerring sagacity Pir-ji literally *smelt* out his unlawful cupidity, and angrily sent him about his business.

After this the good man was a martyr to the assiduities of his numerous and devoted admirers, who, though they gave him no rest, never came to him quite empty-handed. Daily a little pile of presents would accumulate before him, for it would have been indecorous for any one to approach him without a gift, yet it was well understood that the saint cared for none of these things, and that from his own mysterious treasury, he could, if so minded, produce as much gold and silver as he wished.

However, one night Pir-ji himself disappeared, leaving no trace behind. He had gone, doubtless, because he wished to separate himself more effectually from the distractions and disappointments of a wicked world, but the unregenerate, with the perversity which characterises the class all the world over, began to suspect that the three Kashmiris were confederates who had been driven out of the Happy Valley by the famine prevailing there, and had found in the pious credulity of their co-religionists a means of escaping hard times, and of replenishing their empty purses.

4. Adventures of a Pseudo-Faquir.

A Mussulman named Amir belonging to a family of *professional* beggars, whose members, even should they happen to be rich, may not marry till they have solicited alms, for at least one day, did not care to confine his mendicancy to such a very limited time. Both amusement and profit might, he thought, be got out of an extensive begging tour, so he started on his travels with hopeful anticipations.

In the course of his wanderings he reached a certain native State in the Bombay Presidency, and there, far away from his native Punjab, set up for a great saint. To give plausibility to his pretensions, he let it be understood that he lived without food, and consequently was in no danger of being starved to death; of course, his fame spread abroad, and crowds came to visit this holy man from a far land, and to ask his help towards the attainment of their various desires. He began waxing quite rich from the offerings of the people, and excited the jealousy of the local *sadhus* and Brahmans, who represented to the Rajah that the man was a mere impostor and a wholesale robber of the people. Now the Rajah himself had at least one longstanding desire which the local clergy and professional *sadhus* had not been able to gratify. It was the desire, so common and so imperious in India, to have a son born to him. So, he went in person to the faquir and solicited his good offices towards this end. Amir promised him a son within the year, and in his heart resolved to put hundreds of miles between himself and the Rajah long before the twelve months should have run their course. The chief, elated by the ascetic's solemn promise, showered presents upon him; but the astute local Brahmans were still influential enough to induce their Rajah to forcibly detain the Punjabi saint till the fulfilment of the prophecy, and they did not conceal from the faquir their private determination that if he proved to be a mere impostor he should lose his life for having imposed upon and robbed the people.

Our seer, though honourably treated, was now, day and night, under police surveillance; flight was impossible, and his only hope of saving his life lay apparently in the fulfilment of his prediction. Through the infinite kindness of Allah, his lucky star prevailed. Within the year a son was born to the Rajah, who, in his joy and gratitude, loaded the successful prophet with gifts of value. Having vindicated his power and good faith in the eyes of men, the wonder-working saint, now homesick, expressed a wish to take his departure, having, as he pretended, vowed a pilgrimage to the holy city of Amritsar. Thither he was permitted to go at the Rajah's expense, attended by an official escort worthy of his greatness and the important service he had rendered to the Prince.

When he reached Amritsar he was quite near home, and his anxiety to escape public notice and possible recognition became very great; so, bidding farewell to his escort, upon whom he bestowed his saintly benediction, he quickly sneaked back to his native city, Lahore, *with his booty.*

On his way home from the railway station he was met and recognised by an intimate Muslim friend, who learned from his own lips the above story of his adventures and narrow escape, and the same day related the whole affair to me.

5. The Influence of Faquirs in Secular Affairs.

At the gate of my compound I observed a group of three persons, a mendicant *faquir* seated, a *baniya* saluting him with joined palms raised to his forehead, and a Muhammadan standing near by in a very deferential attitude. This somewhat heterogeneous group at my gateway, backed as it was by the picturesque tomb of a Muslim *pir*, on the other side of the road, interested me, and when the Muhammadan referred to came in to pay his respects, I learned from him that the *baniya* was passing the *faquir-sahib*, and in the act of so doing made him a low *salaam*, saying, "Sir, I am going to my business, be pleased to extend your favour to me." The *faquir* took not the slightest notice of the Hindu's salutation. Such conduct, of course, proved his importance, so the Muhammadan stopped to take special notice of him, and at once discovered that he was a well-known ascetic who was in the habit of spending his time near the Lahori and Shahalmi gates of the city. He was much sought after by persons who were in trouble or longed for the gratification of some special desire.

My informant said: Many seek the good man, but he is very inaccessible, they follow him about but he seems always to be eluding them. Sometimes to escape the importunities of his votaries, he hides himself in the houses of quite low or even disreputable people, publicans and sinners in fact, but his credit is so high that men come from distant places to gain his favour. As I expressed a wish for more particulars about this remarkable personage, I was told the following story:—

It is well known to the native public that an important official in a native State incurred the unjust displeasure of his master, and was summarily removed from his high position. In his great trouble he came to *faquir-sahib* for help, but the man of God would not condescend to notice the fallen statesman. Discouraged but not despairing, the discarded minister followed the saint about persistently day after day, showing him the greatest respect and attention. Weeks went by without the faquir deigning to so much as notice his petitioner. One day, however, irritated by the untiring importunities of the ex-official, he flew into a rage, and gave him a good beating with a stick, till he drew blood from him. Later on, mollified by the patient, uncomplaining humility of the fallen man, *faquir-sahib* said to him, "Go away, why do you persecute me? Your wish is already accomplished, you waste your time in following me." Never doubting the words of the man of God, the humiliated courtier hurried off rejoicing towards his home, and on the way thither was met by a trooper who, respectfully dismounting from his horse, handed him a letter, which was actually a summons from his august master, with a promise of reinstatement in his old position.

After he had been reinstalled in his office he came and gratefully presented the faquir with a bag of rupees and a silk *choga*, for he felt certain that it was his devotion to the saint that had caused justice to be done to him.

There and then the saint flung the rupees amongst the crowd. The silk *choga* he presented to a passing *dervish*.

Of the faquir's past history I learned some further curious details. He was a Kashmiri, and in his younger days followed the very ordinary calling of a common porter. The ease with which he carried the heaviest loads on his head attracted the attention of his fellows, and close observation satisfied them that the burdens did not actually rest upon his head, but seemed to be floating in the air, as if carried by unseen hands. This uncanny circumstance went against him with his brother-porters, who objected to his being in their fraternity, and effectually "boycotted" him. There was nothing left for him but to become a religious mendicant.

If this austere saint has a weakness it is to have himself attended to by the barber, and all the barbers who know him are only too glad to serve him, not only with an eye to prospective spiritual advantages, but for the immediate pecuniary benefit they derive from their professional ministration, for it invariably comes to pass that while *faquir-sahib* is being attended to in the open air, probably under a tree by the roadside, some inquisitive person or other loiters about to see what is going on. Taking advantage of this, the faquir, as soon as the barber has done his work, simply but authoritatively directs the idle onlooker to pay the man eight annas or a rupee, just as the fancy takes him. The bystander, without demur, does what he is ordered to do, and the barber goes away rejoicing at such handsome remuneration.

6. A Syad's Fire-Bath.

Information reached me that a wonderful *syad* was in Lahore who would miraculously *bathe in fire* in the presence of all who cared to see him do it. Admission to his performance could be gained only by duly paid-for tickets.

Having purchased the needful passports, I went at the appointed hour to see him execute the advertised feat.

Through a tall arched gateway I was admitted into the ample quadrangle of an Indian *serai*, having on each of the four sides an arcaded verandah running along the front of a range of little rooms provided for the temporary accommodation of passing travellers. In the centre of the court a considerable place had been rudely railed off with bamboos, and round it were ranged chairs and benches for the use of the spectators. The night was intensely dark; the lighting of the place, if of quite primitive character, was suitable and effective enough. On the top of posts set up at irregular intervals about the enclosed area, large earthenware saucers containing oil-seed flared away restlessly in the night breeze, producing smoke as well as light. At one extremity of the railed-off space, a bed of glowing charcoal about twelve feet long and four feet wide was a conspicuous object, and round it, like gnomes or ghouls, two or three almost naked men were flitting about, now raking up the fire, now fanning it into a fierce glow, now beating it down to a level surface.

All the chairs and benches were soon occupied by eager

spectators, and a large number of men stood crowding up behind those who had secured seats, at rates varying from two to eight annas each. In the front row of chairs were a few Europeans of the lower ranks, subordinate railway employees, and suchlike. Respectability was, of course, contemptuously absent from such a place as this! No women, whether European or native, were present. A band of drummers and cymbalists placed near the *field of fire* treated us to such music as they could produce out of their instruments, in the way of rhythmic throbs and clangs and jingles, enlivened occasionally by strange demoniac cries from the musicians themselves.

After considerable delay, during which the audience behaved in the most orderly manner, the *syad* made his appearance in the arena with many attendants. He was a spare-built young man, a trifle above the average height. His attire consisted of a dark blue *loongee* or sheet tied round his waist, and a shirt of the same colour hanging over it and terminating about three inches above the knees. On his head he wore a crimson *fez.* As soon as the *syad* appeared, he commenced jumping about the place, shouting Husain! Husain!! Husain!!! in crescendo tones, till many Muslims present caught up and echoed back the cry with fervent enthusiasm. When he had shouted for a few minutes in this way, and worked up the feelings of his audience, the *syad* commenced a long harangue proclaiming in well-turned sentences his own unworthiness and his utter insignificance in the sight of God. He then protested that his miraculous fire-bath, as performed by him in many places in the presence of thousands of spectators, was possible only through the help of Imam Husain, a statement received with appreciative applause by many followers of the Prophet, who had mustered in force on this occasion. But the *syad* went on to tell us that there might be sceptics and cavillers who would say that he protected his person by some chemical substance or other from the effects of the fire, and so, in order to disabuse our minds of any such erroneous notion, he would, as a preliminary step, give himself a water-bath in our presence. Off went the red *fez* and also the blue shirt, and the *syad*, seated on a chair, called for *bihishtis* (water-carriers). A score or more were present with their goat-skins full of water in readiness for this event. The *syad*, who had taken up a position quite close to where I sat, now enjoyed an elaborate cold water bath, soaping himself freely and having a deluge of water poured over him, which caused the ground for many yards around to become a puddle and nothing else. When his ablutions were over, he resumed his red *fez* and blue shirt. More haranguing now followed, more deafening shouts of "Husain! Husain!! Husain!!!" responded to again and again by the excited Muslims. By this time clouds of inky blackness were gathering fast overhead, angry flashes of vivid lightning and low muttering thunder warned us that a storm was brewing and would soon be upon us. The assembly becoming impatient of mere harangues and shoutings, made noisy demands for the promised exhibition, and at length, after at least two hours of fooling, the business of the evening was reached. Our *syad*, waving a bamboo with a flag at the end of it, capered wildly about the place, and then with loud cries of "Husain! Husain!" ran rapidly over the bed of almost white-hot charcoal from end to end. He was certainly barefooted when he did this; but as he often ran over the spot which the *bihishtis* had deluged with water, the soles of his feet could not have been otherwise than moist, and most probably coated with damp mud.

Enthusiasm amongst the Muslims now waxed stronger and stronger, and volunteers came forward to essay the perilous run over the coals, avowing their firm trust in Imam Husain and complete confidence in the *syad's* help. With the rest came a young Hindu, who offered to run over the live coals without any help at all; but he was rudely hustled to the rear, protesting with emphasis against the unfair treatment he was receiving. Two or three men now crossed rapidly over the coals one at a time, while the *syad* himself ran along the ground beside the adventurous hero of the moment, holding him by the hand encouragingly. How they all fared, I could not tell; but one man certainly complained aloud that he had been cruelly burned. He demanded of the *syad* to ease his pain, and bewailed his own sufferings as only an Oriental can do. But the *syad* could not help one who was obviously enduring the just penalty of his own want of faith. So the moaning and groaning went on.

"The fire-bath! the fire-bath!" cried the impatient people, and after some more talk and some more shouting of "Husain! Husain!" the *syad*, with clothes and cap on, and sitting quite low, allowed a follower to pour over his head a pan of live charcoal. There were so many of his followers clustered round him, and the dying light from the cressets was so uncertain, that I could not see very well what occurred; but there was a good deal of commotion and tremendous shouting over the event, though the risk to the performer seemed ridiculously small. Following the master, a disciple came forward and underwent a similar ordeal. I stood up to see what was going on. Scarcely had the live charcoal reached his head when he sprang to his feet and leaped about. The glowing pieces fell on all sides as they would naturally do; the attendants and the followers of the Prophet shouted "Ya! Husain" in exultation.

As ill-luck would have it, however, one bit of red-hot charcoal had effected a lodgment in a fold of the cap of the performing Muhammadan, and it began to smoke visibly. When his attention was drawn to what was going on, he removed his cap with ludicrous haste, and smothered the fire between his hands, to the great amusement of the unbelievers present.

By this time the big rain drops began to hiss upon the bed of lighted charcoal, a downpour of rain was imminent, and the assembly broke up hurriedly.

Exaggerated and incorrect accounts of the night's doings found their way into both English and native local newspapers, and probably the *syad* is already numbered amongst the miracle-workers of this generation.

The performance as such was not nearly as satisfactory as some of a similar kind described by writers who have witnessed them elsewhere in India, and also in Polynesia, Japan, and other places; but some interest attaches to the instance I have brought before the reader because of the fact that the performers were Muslims, the leader professing to act under the protection of Imam Husain, the Prophet's grandson.[1]

Europeans have seen and described instances of fire-walking performed by natives of India, not only in their own country—as at Benares in 1898—but in Mauritius and Trinidad also. However, Indians do not enjoy a monopoly or this art, for the practice of fire-walking is known in Fiji, the Society Islands, the Straits Settlements, Japan, Bulgaria, and no doubt in other places also. Some Europeans, for example Colonel Judgson at Raratonga, have, it is stated, actually gone with the performers barefooted over red-hot stones, and escaped scathless.

Some modernised Hindu *sadhus*, who gave such exhibitions, modestly aver that the ability to perform the miracle is a manifestation of Divine grace,[2] while others claim that it is by their incantations and ceremonies that they are able to subdue the fierce heat of the fire.[3]

The Shinto priests of Japan affirm that their God, propitiated by acceptable religious ceremonies, casts out the soul of the fire, and thus makes manifest his power to his faithful followers.[4] The Polynesian hereditary fire-walkers, who do not always have recourse to incantations

[1] An interesting description of a wonderful display of rival fire-walking by a wicked magician and a saintly "Friend of God," will be found in the story of Sidi Ikhlef (A.D. 1552), narrated by Colonel Trumelet in his *Les Saints de l'Islam*, Paris, 1881. In this story the magician walked scathless over a bed of burning wood, performing his perilous journey barefooted and without haste. The saint of course outdid his rival, for he actually halted in the midst of the flames, which bent down to lick his feet, and there rested himself in the furnace, surrounded by tongues of fire.

[2] "*Fire-walking Miracle.*—The residents of Benares were afforded one more opportunity of witnessing the 'fire-walking miracle.' Maharajah Bahadur Sir Jotindra Mohun Tagore, who is now at Benares, invited the Civil and Military Officers at the station, as well as the native nobility and leading gentry of the place, to witness an exhibition of this 'miracle,' which was to take place on the 6th instant. Jangam Baba, the *sadhu* who performs this miracle, claims his performance as a manifestation of Divine grace, and challenges scientific men to account for it in any other way."—*The Tribune*, (Lahore).

[3] "Les Dompteurs du Feu," by Dr. Th. Pascal (*Annales de Sciences Psychiques*, July–August 1899).

[4] "The Shinto Fire-Walkers of Tokio," by Miss Ozaki (a Japanese lady), in the *Wide World Magazine* for December 1899.

or religious ceremonies of any kind, declare that they possess *power* over the heat and the destructive energy of fire. An Indian domestic to whom I mentioned this matter, assured me that it was a well-known fact that many persons possessed the *mantra* or spell for "*tying up fire.*" He was acquainted with some cooks who when they coveted a particular situation would "tie up" their rival's fire, so that with ever so big a blaze under the pot, there would be no cooking done. Of course, the rival cook, deprived of the heat necessary for preparing food for the table, would get into trouble with his employer and be dismissed; and the possessor of the *mantra*, if he played his cards well, would be installed in his place.

It cannot be denied that there is ample testimony to prove that certain persons, in various parts of the East, are able to walk barefooted for a few yards over a bed of white-hot charcoal or stones, and suffer no injury thereby; but unfortunately no explanation that adequately accounts for the various phenomena in this connection described by professed eye-witnesses has, as far as I know, been yet put forward.[1]

7. The Faquir of Manasbal.

On the banks of pretty lake Manasbal in the valley of Kashmir, there used to live some years ago—perhaps he lives there still—an old *faquir* who had acquired a sort of reputation from the fact that he had with his own hands constructed the grave in which he was eventually to lie. There could be no doubt, after five minutes with the old man, that he was proud of his work, of the attention it received from visitors, and the consideration it seemed to bring to himself.

On one of my visits to Manasbal he conducted me very ceremoniously, but with ill-concealed pleasure, to see the

[1] Readers who care for more particulars on this subject are referred to Mr. Andrew Lang's *Modern Mythology*, chapter xii. and his article "The Fire-Walk" in the *Proceedings of the Society of Psychical Research*, February 1900. An excellent summary may also be read in the *English Mechanic*, 9th and 16th March 1900.

Photo by Fred. H. Andrews

THE FAQUIR OF MANASBAL

grave which he had prepared for himself at the further end of a tunnel some fifty or sixty feet long, which had been excavated in the hillside entirely by his own hands.

Although the "rock" through which he had worked was not hard, still his labour had not been inconsiderable, for the tunnel he had excavated was over six feet high, and wide enough to allow two persons to walk abreast in it. At the end of it was a chamber containing the gaping sepulchre. As became a pious recluse, the proud owner of the grave discoursed in the usual way about the uncertainty of life, and the fleeting, illusive enjoyments of this world, while drawing my attention to the neatness and cleanliness of his future and last abode. For the present the good man lived alone, in a very neat cottage, cultivated a small patch of ground adjoining, and grew upon it the most delicious peaches. Of some of these really excellent fruits of his labour he made me a formal present, and, hermit though he was, did not disdain a return in the shape of current silver coin, for which I fancy he could find many good uses. Strange stories, not always to his credit, were told about the Manasbal faquir by his Kashmiri countrymen; but as far as I could learn his greatest claim to the consideration he expected and certainly received, was the strange grave he had made ready by his own toil for the reception of his body after death.

The devotee and his grave have for a generation been well known to travellers in Kashmir, and have been mentioned in books relating to that country.

Opposite this page is a photograph of the hermit, for which he posed willingly enough, not having quite extinguished in his breast the insidious vice of vanity, which, by a strange irony, was encouraged and kept alive by his open grave, which was intended no doubt in the first instance as a symbol of his detachment from this world of sorrow, and as an indication of his desire for an early release.

8. The Name of God.

Four or five *faquirs* who had in the usual way been roaming about the country, like mediæval wandering scholars, happened to meet casually at Lahore, and, as is the wont amongst such persons, fell to discussing various abstruse matters connected with theology and metaphysics, airing the ideas they had formed or picked up in their intercourse with thoughtful men in many cities.

A Muhammadan with whom I was in constant touch, and who had an especial weakness for the society of *faquirs*, being himself in diligent quest of a competent alchemist and transmuter of metals, found himself in their company and listening to their discourse, was struck by the subtlety they displayed, and charmed by the manner of their speech. "While they talked," he said, "it was as if roses fluttered about from mouth to mouth." One anecdote or story which was related by one of the faquirs especially took the Muslim listener's fancy, and was retailed for my information. As an illustration of the kind of talk indulged in by some of these wandering devotees, it seems worth reproducing here.

There once lived a faquir who, it came to be known, would not utter the name of God. Pious people were surprised and scandalised at such behaviour on the part of a professedly religious man, while the wicked and light-minded would annoy the man when they met him by calling upon him to utter the word "Allah." His invariable answer was "*lahoul*," the initial word of an Arabic text used as an invocation against evil spirits. Such very unseemly behaviour became a subject of comment, and he was at length summoned to appear in person before the Great Mogul Emperor Akbar, when the following dialogue took place:—

"What conduct is this of yours, *faquir-sahib*?" inquired the Emperor. "It is reported that you, a professedly religious man, object to utter the name of God! Surely this is the conduct of a *Kafir* (infidel), and should be punished with death. What have you to say for yourself?"

"Am I already condemned, Great King, or is your Majesty willing to hear me?" asked the faquir.

"Speak!" said the Emperor sternly; "I listen!"

"Is there amongst your Majesty's courtiers any men who have the good fortune to be regarded by their master as heroic and noble personages?"

"Yes, many," replied the Emperor, "but amongst my generals there are four who, I believe, are quite unmatched in heroism throughout the wide world."

"And amongst these four, is there one whom your Majesty considers especially deserving of honour and esteem, and standing in the very first rank of men?"

"Yes, there is one pre-eminent even amongst the band of heroes I am proud to have about me."

"May I, Great King, speak to this hero aside, and has he your gracious permission to do as I ask him to do?"

"Yes, I freely afford him my permission to do anything proper and reasonable."

The accused led away the great noble to a retired corner of the Durbar and requested him to go up to the Emperor on his throne, and say to him these words and these words *only*, "Akbar, the faquir has desired me to stand before you."

The great noble refused to carry out this request; but after a little while returned to his place near the Emperor.

"Ask the great nobleman, sire," said the accused man, "if he has done what I, with your Majesty's permission, bid him do?"

Interrogated on this point, the courtier had to admit that he had not carried out the faquir's wishes. "They were," he said, "too outrageous. The man actually wanted me to come forward in open Durbar and address our lord, the Emperor, familiarly by his name."

The ceremonial propriety of the courtiers was shocked at the indecorous suggestion; but the faquir addressing the Emperor said: "Now, Great King, if a courtier next to yourself in rank will not venture to accost your Majesty—who, after all, are only an earthly sovereign—by your august name, do you wonder at my hesitating to pronounce the name of the Divine King of Kings, the Almighty Ruler of the Universe?"

The few examples I have given of *faquirs* and their doings, and of the stories current about celebrated Muslim saints, will be sufficient to indicate a very marked contrast between the standpoint of the Muhammadan in relation to Allah, and that of the Hindu towards his gods. The Hindu *sadhu* or saint acquires supernatural power over himself, his fellow-men, and nature generally by virtue of ascetic practices, even in spite of the lesser deities of his Olympus; whereas the Muslim saint derives his prepotency only through the favour of the one God. This striking dissimilarity is of course due to the uncompromising monotheism of Islam on the one hand, and the polytheism lost in pantheism of the Brahmans on the other; and though it may be admitted that the Indian Muslim legends are often tinged with Hindu feeling to a considerable degree; that the mystic doctrines of the Sufis were probably derived from Hindu philosophy and that the Brahmanical caste system has, to some slight extent, influenced the social arrangements of certain Indian Muhammadans, nevertheless there is no possibility of any effectual bridging of the abysmal gulf which separates the two great religions of India, Hinduism and Islam.

INDEX

INDEX

C

D

E

INDEX

INDEX

INDEX

INDEX

INDEX

Photo by Col. Constable

BRAHMAN AT PRAYER

Frontispiece